French Labor

From Popular Front to Liberation

French Labor

From Popular Front to Liberation

HENRY W. EHRMANN

NEW YORK / RUSSELL & RUSSELL

STUDIES OF THE INSTITUTE OF WORLD AFFAIRS

TO JULIEN COFFINET

FRIEND OF DAYS IN FRANCE

AND TO MY STUDENTS AT

FORT KEARNEY, FORT WETHERILL,

FORT GETTY AND FORT EUSTIS

Preface

PREVIOUS publications of the Institute of World Affairs, particularly Arnold Brecht's *Federalism and Regionalism in Germany* and Joseph B. Schechtman's *European Population Transfers, 1939-1945*, deal with aspects of the political and social transformation that the last decades have brought upon the countries of central and eastern Europe. Less spectacular, but in long-term implications hardly less important, are the changes that the Second World War has imposed on the social structure of western Europe. In this region it is, above all, France, and within France organized labor and the intelligentsia allied with it, that hold a key position. Their social orientation will largely determine the course to be taken by domestic reconstruction. In addition, it is to them that the fateful role of intermediary between East and West, once held by the progressive groups in Germany, seems to have fallen. Thus the part played by labor in the recent history of France commands attention that goes far beyond the interest customarily attaching to studies of particular social groups in a particular nation.

In this book Dr. Ehrmann reviews the development of the French trade-union movement during the decade from 1934 to 1944, from the rise of the Popular Front to the time of liberation. The study is in some respects a sequel to the works of David Saposs and R. Clark, which deal with earlier stages of the labor movement in France. It is built on original sources, and constitutes an essential segment of the pre-history and history of the last war.

The original draft of the study was drawn up in connection with a research project conducted by the Graduate Faculty of the New School for Social Research. The revised and much enlarged version here published belongs to a series of investigations dealing with problems of European reconstruction, in which the Institute of World Affairs has been engaged since 1943. As is the case with all publications of the Institute, the author alone bears the responsibility for his findings.

ADOLPH LOWE

DIRECTOR OF RESEARCH,
INSTITUTE OF WORLD AFFAIRS

Acknowledgments

I AM particularly indebted to the Institute of World Affairs, under which the original draft of this study was much enlarged for publication. The unflagging and active interest shown by the Research Director of the Institute, Professor Adolph Lowe, was a continuous source of encouragement.

I am also grateful to the Social Science Research Council, which at an earlier moment awarded me a generous grant in aid for the completion of the book. The *Journal of Politics* kindly permitted the reprint of material first published there and now contained in Chapter x. The helpfulness of the librarians of the United States Department of Labor, the Library of Congress, the New York Public Library, the Columbia University Library, and the Baker Library of Harvard University enabled me to reconstitute a documentation which was first collected in Paris and which, because of the course of events, was subsequently lost to the last note.

I wish to express my gratitude to several persons who were kind enough to read the manuscript at various stages, and made many helpful suggestions for improvement and clarification: to Richard Eldridge, Louis Franck, Leo Gershoy, Ernest Hamburger, Franz Neumann, David Saposs, Walter Sharp, Paul Vignaux, and Frieda Wunderlich.

Able research-assistance and advice were provided by Mr. Alfred Griot, himself a participant in the activities of the French labor movement of an earlier period. Mrs. Nancy McGranahan rendered invaluable help in the preparation of Part III. I owe a very special debt of gratitude to Miss Elizabeth Todd, whose thorough and careful editing of the entire manuscript represented a Sisyphean effort from which, it is hoped, the reader will profit as much as did the author.

The major part of this book was written and rewritten during off-duty hours while I was in federal service. It would never have been finished without the patient and enduring courage of my wife.

HENRY W. EHRMANN

Fort Eustis, Virginia
10 *March* 1946

Contents

... le vrai dieu de l'histoire le travail.

JEAN JAURÈS

PART I. PREWAR

1934-1939

I

Roots of the Popular Front

EARLY in the spring of 1936 Léon Jouhaux, secretary-general of the Confédération Générale du Travail, concluded the trade-union convention which had taken place in Toulouse with an emotional speech. The convention had sanctioned the re-unification of the French labor movement, which for fourteen years had been divided into a communist and a reformist wing; the delegates had approved the guiding principles for the new organization of the French wage earners. Carried away by a somewhat rhetorical enthusiasm, Jouhaux exclaimed: 'A new dawn rises. It shines with a brilliancy that begins to drive off the darkness. In its light we shall achieve our emancipation and will liberate the world.' [1]

At about the hour Jouhaux was speaking, Hitler's troops were occupying the Rhineland. The headlines of the very same *Le Peuple* (the daily paper of the French trade-union movement) which recorded Jouhaux's speech announced the violation of the Locarno pact and the threat to the frontier across which French soil had been invaded twice in seventy years.

It has been said that the real shackles on the freedom of the Popular Front were riveted on the day of Hitler's coup against the Rhineland, for from that day France was no longer free to decide her own destiny.[2] In our times, however, no country is free to direct its course without consideration of the happenings outside its frontiers. The truth is that the international situation was to give to the Popular Front experiment a new significance that was not quite realized by either its protagonists or its enemies. It also cast its shadow on every phase of French trade-

3

union history between 1936 and 1940. All too often the principal actors in France's social drama were unaware of this fact, and as a result their actions and discussions were sometimes enveloped with a haze of unreality which was to be dispelled only by the catastrophe of the new invasion.

From the very origins of the Popular Front, at the time of the *émeute* staged by the right-wing organizations against the Parliament in February 1934, its solid backbone had been the organized labor movement, then still divided into the Confédération Générale du Travail (CGT) and the Confédération Générale du Travail Unitaire (CGTU). When labor held its Extraordinary Congress of Unification in Toulouse, the great electoral success which the Popular Front was to obtain in the elections of 1936 was still to come. But in its final declaration the Congress confirmed by a unanimous vote 'the adherence given by the representatives of the trade-union movement to the program drawn by the Popular Front Committee, whose aim it is to mobilize the popular masses of France for the improvement of their living conditions and for the defense and the triumph of liberty and peace.'[3]

Thus the reunited union movement solemnly renewed the dramatic oath taken on Bastille Day in 1935 by all the organizations which constituted the Popular Front: 'to defend the democratic liberties acquired by the French people, to give bread to the workers, work to the youth, and great human peace to the world.' The new political grouping was looked upon by many as the harbinger of a new social democracy, a Fourth French Republic. 'This great idealist movement,' a prominent trade-union leader declared later, when the Popular Front had already been officially buried, 'had the confused but magnificent and exalted ambition to regenerate France through social justice and through the development of progress in all its forms.'[4]

The movement to be known as the Popular Front was based on a twofold rapprochement which began in 1934: that between the proletariat and the rural and urban middle classes; and that between the two workers' organizations, the CGT and the CGTU. The rapprochement between the factions of organized labor seemed to be completed by the organizational amalgamation effected at the Congress of Toulouse. It was hoped that the course of action to be taken by the government as an outcome of the 1936 elections would seal the alliance of proletariat and middle classes.

This twofold rapprochement, representing a unity of wage earners, farmers, and an important part of the urban middle classes, proved to be only ephemeral. When the new cleavage appeared among the components of the Popular Front, the Third Republic did not long survive. But while the rapprochement endured it accomplished what was possible in the effort to rescue French democratic institutions from the grave crisis into which the country found itself precipitated. It was the particular nature of that crisis which made possible such a unity of diverse social elements, a unity which had so completely failed in the German republic.

I

The importance of the rural population in the social and political structure of France has often been stressed.[5] It is true that after World War I the majority of the French population no longer lived in rural communities: between 1911 and 1936 the rural population fell from 56 to 48 per cent of the total, a development which corresponds almost exactly to that which took place between 1910 and 1930 in the United States. But this result was due very largely to an increase of population in a few city centers, and the general character of the country was not greatly affected. Thus of the 90 departments into which France was divided, there were still 68 in which the majority of the population was rural. Only 3 departments, outside the 3 eastern ones that France acquired by the Treaty of Versailles, shifted from a predominantly rural to a predominantly urban structure between 1911 and 1936. In the latter year only 17 cities had more than 100,000 inhabitants, and 4 of these had fewer inhabitants in 1936 than in 1911. Paris with its suburbs had 5 million inhabitants, but less than 4 million of a total population of nearly 42 million lived in other cities of more than 100,000 persons. This situation had all the more important implications for political life as the French electoral system, especially the one devised for senatorial elections, greatly favored the population of rural districts.[6]

In regard to the proportion of the population engaged in farming, the situation in France was altogether different from that in the United States. The number of persons in agricultural occupations in the United States had fallen, by 1930, to 21 per cent of the total number gainfully employed, but in France at the time of the 1931 census 35 per cent of the 21.6 million working population was still engaged in agricultural pursuits. This was a large proportion, even though it had been still higher—around 45 per cent—before World War I. To a lesser extent than in other countries was this diminution due to migration from the countryside to the cities. One important reason for it was the fact that no other section of the French population contributed so much to the hecatomb of the war as the French peasantry. The feeling that the country owed a special debt to the tillers of its soil was continuously kindled by the war memorials erected in every village. For years there was resentment of the workers, who during the war had made 'big money' in defense plants while the farmers were dying in the trenches. At the outbreak of the war in 1939 such feelings flared up again.

In the 'thirties the social composition of the rural group among the French population had not changed considerably since the beginning of the century. Over two-thirds of the persons actively engaged in agriculture owned the land or cultivated it at their own expense. Little more than 2 per cent of the agricultural properties were larger than 125 acres (50 hectares), but these properties comprised more than 30 per cent of the total cultivated area; among them were the great landed estates, which had by no means disappeared in France, as is commonly supposed. At the other end of the social scale were those who had very small holdings; 25 per cent of agricultural properties were smaller than 2½ acres, and 47 per cent were between 2½ and 25 acres. The great variety of conditions prevailing in different regions and for different crops makes it impossible to gauge the economic status of the French farmers solely on the basis of the size of their property, but conservative estimates indicate that for the whole of France more than one-fourth of the cultivated soil was broken up into acreage too small to be economically useful. In the eastern part of the country 50 per cent of the land was so minutely divided that its owners fell into the class of the rural proletariat.

Until the economic crisis made itself felt in France, agricultural prices, while they did not rise so fast as those of industrial products, were sufficiently high to make the situation of the French farmer tolerable. In spite of her falling rural population France had become to a considerable extent self-sufficient in regard to agricultural produce, partly as a result of her high tariffs. At the same time, however, there was a widespread neglect of improvement in techniques. Some increase occurred, of course, in mechanization and in the use of chemical fertilizers, but it was insufficient, and this development lagged considerably behind that in other countries. The minuscule size of the majority of the holdings and the traditional individualism of the French farmer, who in many regions was opposed to any cooperative scheme, were to a large extent responsible for this situation. But an important role was played also by the dearth of credit for the small farmers and by the fact that no extensive or effective educational program was offered by the authorities, continuously handicapped, as they were, by their strictly limited budget.

Hence when French agriculture finally had to bear the brunt of the world crisis, prices began to dwindle in dangerous proportions, while costs did not diminish. The prices for wheat and wine, for example (average for 1932-6), fell below their prewar average by 14 and 25 per cent, respectively; at the same time the wages of agricultural labor were slightly higher than in prewar times, and prices of machinery were considerably higher. To lower production costs by improved methods seemed impossible. Definite help could be hoped for only from action by the state.

As a buyer of agricultural machinery or of fertilizers, and also as a seller of his products, the farmer was confronted with cartels and trusts which had attained a high degree of concentration and seemed to impose their conditions everywhere. Sugar refineries and the distribution of dairy products were almost as much centralized as milling, where a single trust dominated the market. When in need of credit, the farmer, especially the small one, saw himself denied the necessary sums by the offices of the big banks or of the Bank of France, which had succeeded in eliminating the local banks of prewar days.

In spite of these conditions all attempts to organize the farming interests behind powerful pressure groups had been in vain. 'Every union of postal employees fills the ears of the government with more noise than the entire French agriculture.'[7] One factor in this failure of right-wing groups was, again, the individualism of the rural masses of France, making for a distrust of collective action. In addition, some of the endeavors showed too clearly the hand of the wealthy landowners not to arouse suspicion on the part of the small holders. Others failed because of their anti-parliamentary slant, which did not seem to the French farmer to offer a way out of his plight. In the eyes of the farmer the anonymous power of capital had become a greater threat to his existence than the alleged inefficiency of parliamentary institutions.

Thus in 1933, when a rural fascist organization, the Peasant Front of Henri Dorgères, started to clamor for 'direct action,' that is, for open resistance to the payment of taxes and the foreclosure of mortgages, it obtained an important following only in Brittany; elsewhere it met with the old distrust. This movement called for resistance against the state, the very power from which the farmers hoped to obtain relief; and it did not become particularly vocal about the forces with which the agricultural producer was directly faced and which, to an increasing extent, he made responsible for his difficulties.

While Dorgères's rural fascist organization struggled with difficulties in its offices in Paris, the teachers in the 60,000 rural classes of France explained to children and their parents the reasons for their economic distress. The large majority of these educators were members of the teachers federation, a national union affiliated with the CGT. The latter had all but ceased any propaganda against the farmer as an 'exploiter of rural labor'; in 1935 it recruited, at most, 12,000 adherents from the 2.2 million agricultural workers. On the other hand the CGT and the teachers federation were well aware of the excellent opportunities afforded by the fact that year after year the teachers in rural classes could provide plenty of examples to illustrate to pupils and their parents the exploitation of the farmers by the great concerns and by the power of the big banks in Paris.[8] At the same time the teachers could talk about the horrors of wars engineered by the international 'merchants of death.' The anti-capitalist and anti-militarist traditions of the French labor movement left a lasting imprint on that generation of French farmers which in 1939 was to be called into another war.

During the early 'thirties still other factors made the French peasantry swing rather to the left than to the right. In 1933 a radical-socialist government fixed minimum prices for wheat, but when the inefficiency of this regulation became apparent a right-wing cabinet was once more in power. Hesitating to intervene too drastically in the market mechanism, the National Union cabinets did not offer to buy the wheat of the 1934 and 1935 harvests at the minimum price established by law. Thus, though the price of bread rose in the cities, the farmer was faced with the alternative of keeping his unsold stocks or selling his wheat (and the situation was substantially the same for wine)

at an illegal price. When he was forced to do the latter, he had
no recourse but to denounce once more the grain merchant and
the milling trust for the gap between legal and actual prices. But
where the right-wing cabinets had failed, the program of the
socialist party and a new plan for economic recovery elaborated
by the CGT offered at least the possibility of hope: they promised the establishment of a National Wheat Office which would
buy the harvest from the farmers and hence detract from the
power of trusts and banks. If this was socialist propaganda, it
was definitely a socialism of the middle classes.

II

During the same period resentment of the 'curse of bigness'
was invading also the middle classes engaged in business and industry. To all appearances France was still the typical country
of small-size enterprise. In 1931 about 64 per cent of the 1.6
million registered industrial enterprises had no paid employees;
an additional 34 per cent employed fewer than 10 persons, and
only 0.5 per cent belonged in the category of big plants, employing 100 or more. The organizations of handicraftsmen estimated that there were still 2 million shops operating on an
artisan level, two-fifths of them in rural communities; the figure
is significant, even though it is probably exaggerated (unlike
the official statistics, it includes the non-registered establishments). Among the commercial enterprises the percentage of
smallest shops had changed very little since the beginning of the
century—largely because of the fact that by the outbreak of
World War II only 400 towns in France numbered more than
10,000 inhabitants; no less than 98 per cent of the commercial
enterprises fell within the category of fewer than 10 employees,
or no employees at all.

These data are significant as an indication that the middle
classes had a relatively greater importance in the economic structure of France than in other industrial countries. Also, they

partly explain the lack of modernization and rationalization from which a large sector of production suffered in the period between the two world wars. But such figures would be altogether misleading if they were taken as an indication that France had remained aloof from the development of capitalist concentration. More revealing, though still not adequate as a picture of the power behind the few large enterprises, is the fact that in 1926 about 43 per cent of the roughly 6.5 million wage earners employed in industry worked in establishments that had more than 100 employees; this was an increase of about 80 per cent when compared with 1906.

Immediately after the armistice in 1918 the labor movement, as will be discussed later on, had based its line of action on the assumption that the capitalist system was sufficiently weakened by war and destruction to succumb to the well-directed strokes of a socialization program. Actually capitalist enterprise emerged considerably strengthened, and French management was soon in a position to retract most of the concessions made to organized labor during the war emergency. The devastated regions of the north had to be rebuilt so entirely that a new start on a high technical level was possible. The incorporation into France of the highly industrialized regions of Alsace and Lorraine, with their rich iron, bauxite, and potash deposits, gave an impulse to the expansion of old and the development of new industries.

With a decreasing population, an insufficiently developed colonial empire, and only slowly changing living habits, the internal market was altogether too small to absorb the increased industrial production. In order to see exports facilitated and the domestic market protected against foreign competition, French industry had to turn to the state. But tariffs and import quotas alone were no longer sufficient. Thus it became a frequent practice, in order to make possible the absorption of French production, to enter into joint selling agreements concluded by international combinations, after the pattern set by the French-German steel agreement.

For the effective defense of its interests, both before the state and on the international scene, French industry acted on the assumption that a unification of forces was indispensable. Thus the interrelationships that already existed among different companies and different branches óf industry were supplemented by an amalgamation of the various management bodies. In 1919 about 1500 organizations representing management, among them the powerful Comité des Forges (the organization of the steel and armament industry) and the Comité Central des Houillères (representing the coal-mining interests) united to form the Confédération Générale de la Production Française (CGPF), the counterpart of the CGT. In the words of one of its spokesmen:

The CGPF intends to intervene as often as it is necessary, with individual members of Parliament and with the great committees of the Chamber and of the Senate, in order to make sure that all resolutions or bills which disregard economic realities will be usefully amended in the interest of general prosperity. Moreover, the CGPF purposes to ask the government to safeguard internally and externally the interests of French industry and commerce, soliciting from the government, on the points it will bring to its attention, the necessary administrative regulations.[9]

Although the CGPF made rapid progress in its organizational drive and obtained the adherence of another odd thousand employer organizations, it was looked upon with suspicion by the mass of small entrepreneurs. Until 1936 no important function within the organization was reserved to them. The majority of small businessmen, afraid that their interests would be altogether sacrificed to the demands of the bigger concerns, refused to join.[10]

Not only was the economic concentration of French business hidden by the numerical prevalence of small and medium-size enterprises, but also there existed to a higher degree than elsewhere a tradition of concealing the degree of concentration in industry and banking. Partly responsible for this was the French law against restraint of trade, Article 419 of Napoleon's Penal

Code. In its original form this provision penalized those who had agreed 'not to sell, or to sell only at a certain fixed price,' and in its revised form of 1926 it provided for the punishment of those who exercised 'any influence on the market for the purpose of acquiring profit other than that derived from the natural operation of the law of supply and demand.'

This law against restraint of trade was ill-adapted to solve the competitive problems of a modern society. Its only achievement was to encourage evasion of the penalties by the concealment of cartel and other price-fixing agreements; it was altogether unable to control or even to bring to light the high degree of actual concentration and domination of the market. The complete breakdown of enforcement of the law was precipitated by the lack of any administrative machinery and by the insufficient backing of public opinion. The consumers felt impotent in the face of organized economic power; also, they were often actuated by the hope that the arbitrary fixing of prices might further the dreamt-of security—be it even at the price of freedom.[11]

When the economic crisis of the early 'thirties revealed that this hope had been vain, wide circles of the public began to take a passionate interest in a campaign denouncing the activities of what was decried as the 'economic oligarchies' and 'financial feudalism.' It was shown how 'two hundred families,' through common stockholding, interlocking relationships, and similar devices, kept the posts of command of French economy firmly in hand, and publicity was given to the fact that fewer than 150 persons, most of them connected by marriage and family ties, held more than 1900 seats in the administration of the most important corporations in the fields of coal, power, steel, oil, chemicals, railroads, banking, and insurance. How disastrous such a state of affairs was deemed to be for consumers and middle-size enterprises alike was demonstrated by comparisons between the profits of the smaller concerns, which during the crisis had diminished by 66 per cent, and those of the public utilities, entirely in private hands and subject to but little regulation on the part of the authorities, which had realized benefits about 29 per cent higher than in 1929.

The facts described here were used by the trade unions and the socialist party, between 1933 and 1936, in order to invite the support of the middle classes for the cause of labor.[12] The almost complete obscurity in which the integration of French economy had taken place made people inclined to believe that free competition had altogether ceased, and that wherever it seemed to exist the parties were merely staging a sham fight in order to cover up a general 'conspiracy.'

Public attention was particularly attracted to the anomaly of the Bank of France, which was ruled by regents coming from great banking and business families. The increasing importance which the Bank was assuming in the economic life of the nation made the unbroken and often hereditary predominance of the important railway, shipping, banking, and industrial interests in the Council of Regents subject to especially violent criticism. The paucity of credit facilities for small and medium-size enterprises was easily attributed to the Bank's strict conditions for re-discounting—conditions that could be met only by the more important concerns.

Thus in the polemics of those days the Bank was thought of as 'another Bastille to be taken' if the French people were to live in freedom. The slogan, to be sure, may have belonged at least partly to the category of 'those historical parallels so stimulating to oratory, so crippling to thought.'[13] But it was directly instrumental in mobilizing behind the striving for a new economic deal those generally inert masses whose traditionalism included faithfulness to the memories of the Great Revolution. The symbolic value of the claims against the Bank was enhanced by the fact that the Council of Regents of the Bank of France, as well as the administration of other important banks and industrial concerns, included names with a century-old tradition for economic rule. Some of the families had been installed in the Bank by Napoleon I and had remained there ever since.

The universal knowledge of the extent to which the Bank of France determined the financial policy of the government gave to the struggle against the 'two hundred families' the halo of a fight for an emancipation of republican institutions from enchainment by the mammoth concerns. The Governor of the Bank, it is true, was appointed by the government. But since the statutes provided that only those persons were eligible who possessed a certain number of shares, the appointee was bound to belong to the circles from which the Regents came, or had to be sufficiently *persona grata* with them to obtain from them temporarily the necessary amount of stock. Both a left-wing and a right-wing cabinet, the Herriot and the Flandin ministries, had been obliged by the threat of financial catastrophe to resign when faced with the Regents' determination not to permit anything but the most conservative policy of deflation and the reduction of expenses by cutting salaries and war pensions.

The deflationary measures of the National Union cabinets served to bring another numerically important category of the middle classes into closer rapprochement with the workers. The civil servants, who in other European countries often tended toward the right, took a leading part in the founding of the Popular Front, after having constituted for years the very core of the CGT.

Between 1906 and 1931 the number of persons with civil-service status (exclusive of the military administration) had risen from 549,000 to 787,000, an increase of 43 per cent. In 1931 over 6 per cent of the wage and salary earners were civil servants, and the figure rises to nearly 10 per cent if persons with civil-service status in the armed services are included. On the top this situation created a caste of high civil bureaucracy, severed from the life of the nation.[14] But the hundreds of thousands of new civil servants who flocked into the offices came from worker and peasant families. For a long time officials were denied the right to organize—a right granted only in 1924—and their striving for recognition brought them even closer to the aims of organized labor.

On the eve of the unification of the CGT and the CGTU the two organizations together claimed a membership of approximately 335,000 among those having civil-service status in a civilian occupation. Thus 42 per cent of the persons belonging in this category of public employees were organized in a trade union. All these *fonctionnaires* were as much interested in the maintenance of republican institutions as they were in a reversal of the policy of deflation. Since they had had to sustain repeated curtailment of their income by governments which tried in vain to achieve an equilibrium in the public budget, the civil servants were no longer looked upon as a privileged group by farmers and workers.

The economic crisis hit France later than other industrial countries, and the slump in production persisted longer than elsewhere. In 1935, when the indices of other countries were again on the upswing, the index of French industrial production reached a new low—72.5 per cent of the 1929 average, as against 105.6 per cent for Great Britain and 94 per cent for Germany.[15] At the height of the crisis, in March 1935, the number of totally unemployed was approximately 850,000, or more than 8 per cent of all wage earners in private industry, commerce, and agriculture.[16] This figure, which was considerably lower than that of other countries at the height of the crisis, must be viewed, however, in conjunction with the rather widespread partial unemployment. At that time about 45 per cent of all those employed were working less than the legal 48-hour week.[17] Exact figures for industry as a whole are not available, but for enterprises of more than 100 employees the labor inspectors, taking into account both total and partial unemployment, calculated that employment was reduced by 39 per cent in comparison with the corresponding month of 1930.[18]

As to wages and salaries, there was a notable difference between the average earnings of the entire working class and the money or real wages of certain particular groups of employees. Between 1930 and 1935 the average diminution of hourly earnings amounted to only 7 per cent, that of normal daily earnings to 12 per cent. During the same period the cost of living index fell by 22 per cent (for Paris only 13 per cent), and therefore certain categories of workers experienced a notable increase in real wages. But these overall figures conceal the fact that in certain regions and for certain categories of workers (such as those in the dressmaking industry and in department stores) wages, which had been very low even during prosperity, were cut far beyond the decrease of the costs of living. Even more significant is the fact that in October 1934, as a result of the increase in total and partial unemployment, the total sum of wages and salaries was over one-third less than it had been in 1930. No total figures are available for 1935, but from data for single industries, such as mining, it can be gathered that a further diminution of 3 to 5 per cent must have taken place in that year.[19]

This economic situation had important repercussions on the attitudes of the working class throughout the period during which the Popular Front movement was forming and at the moment of social explosion in 1936. The relatively small number of totally unemployed, many of them foreign immigrant labor, prevented the growth of that mass army of jobless workers, despairing of ever finding employment, which had precipitated the ascent of Nazism in Germany. Many categories of skilled workers, important in numerous branches of mass production, acquired a feeling of strength from the fact that they had been able to maintain their earnings at a relatively high level. But the great mass of the workers had less work than formerly, and therefore less pay. They were inclined to follow the lead of those who contended that only a complete reversal of the policies of deflation, indeed a general overhauling of the economic structure of the country, would be able to improve the situation substantially and permanently.

Such was the economic and social milieu in which the French middle classes and working class effected their rapprochement, which eventually led to the constitution of the Popular Front. To find the common denominator in the aspirations of rural and urban masses was less difficult than it would have been in other circumstances. Political and economic liberties seemed interwoven as perhaps never before since the establishment of the Third Republic. The constant political crises of the government, evidenced by the much complained-of ministerial instability, seemed to be due to a constant defiance of the intentions of the electorate. Every election year a majority oriented toward the left was sent by the voters to the Parliament, but before long the *féodalités économiques* had a right-wing government creeping back into power, where it maintained itself, albeit with difficulty and artifice.

The rioting staged by the right-wing organizations in Paris in January and February 1934 only precipitated the concentration of the left which it could not prevent. The badly led antiparliamentary organizations lacked unity of action and of purpose. They had not secured the support of the army, which until the defeat of 1940 stuck to the attitude of 'the great mute,' adopted after the Dreyfus Affair. The high bureaucracy, while sordidly hostile to every democratization of traditional institutions, could not be relied upon to swing the machinery of the state in favor of rioters. The fascist leagues themselves had failed to enlist substantial masses outside of Paris. Only in the capital had the crisis produced a large enough number of uprooted among the middle classes and intellectuals. If these groups believed that parliamentary institutions were sufficiently discredited to be overthrown with ease, they overlooked the fact that their side had made practically no concrete proposal on how to overcome the crisis which suffocated society.

On the other hand, when the CGT appealed to the population of the whole of France to join, on 12 February 1934, in a general strike of protest against the agitations of the foes of the republic, it touched strings designed to sound in the ears of all the discontented.[20] The CGT carefully avoided any defense of discredited institutions. It only showed that the scandals preceding the rioting were but a pretext for forces which had for a long time determined to assault democratic governments and individual liberties.[21] To maintain the 'fundamental liberties . . . without which life is not worth living,' the youth, the farmers, the intellectuals, and technicians were invoked to join cause with the workers 'against the present disorder.' For the first time organized labor in France directly addressed groups outside the working classes.

The strike was called for 'as a warning and as a manifestation of strength and decision.' As such it was an undeniable success. In Paris and its suburbs alone more than a million struck. Work was stopped in most of the public services—in schools, the postal service, and the transportation system—and also in many private enterprises. Outside of Paris the movement was in many places even more general.[22]

But perhaps the most notable event was that the strike order was followed by both the reformist and the communist trade unions, which had never joined forces since they had split in 1921. The *émeute* of the fascist organizations was among the factors contributing to that second rapprochement which was completed two years later at Toulouse: the amalgamation of the CGT and the CGTU.

II

Labor's Split and Reunification

1

THE schism in the French trade-union movement, which became complete during the winter of 1921-2, began with a cleavage that appeared during World War I and was deepened by the turbulence of the postwar period.[1] During the war the leadership and the majority of the CGT had shifted from revolutionary internationalism to patriotism, but a minority remained opposed to such a change. After the armistice Jouhaux, secretary-general of the CGT, and his friends wanted to turn the French labor movement away from prewar syndicalism to active participation in the reorganization of French postwar economy; the opposition, however, wished to follow the lead of Russia, who had rid herself altogether of a bourgeois economic system. After the formation of the communist party, which set out to enlist the support of trade-union members for active opposition to the reformist leadership, it became evident that open conflict was unavoidable. Internal dissension and a series of ill-co-ordinated strikes, which culminated in 1920 in the disastrous failure of a general strike, brought about a near collapse of the trade-union movement.

At the beginning of 1920 the membership of the CGT had risen to more than 1.8 million, a figure at least treble the prewar level.[2] At the end of the year, however, there were no more than 750,000 members—and probably not even that many—affiliated with the organization. This rapid increase and decline of trade-union strength was to repeat itself after 1936. Such a development is an expression of the general reluctance of the French worker to organize, a reluctance that is especially difficult to overcome as long as the exaltation which in moments of emotional and social tension pushes workers toward class organizations is marred by internal dissensions within the union movement.

In the heated discussions of 1920 and 1921 both sides invoked the authority of a document which had been adopted by a CGT Congress in Amiens in 1906 and which until the dissolution of the CGT by Pétain in 1940 was to be considered the 'fundamental law of French trade unionism.'[3] In 1906, when the socialist party was making an effort to get hold of the trade-union movement and certain elements of that party were tempted to take part in ministerial responsibility, the so-called Charter of Amiens answered the challenge of a particular political situation by expounding the two main principles of revolutionary syndicalism to which French organized labor adhered: first, recognition of the class war, 'which in the realm of industry unites the working class against all forms of exploitation and oppression, material as well as moral, practiced by capitalism at the expense of labor'; and second, the non-partisan character of the union movement. Although 'all members shall be free, individually and outside the trade unions, to take part in such activities as their political or philosophical beliefs may require,' they were asked to 'refrain from bringing to the trade unions the opinions which they profess outside.'[4]

In the disputes after World War I the elements that were to form the CGTU denounced the economic program of the CGT leadership as a betrayal of the revolutionary spirit of this Charter. And in turn their demand that the CGT adhere to the newly formed 'Red International of Labor Unions' in Moscow was stigmatized as an attempt to subordinate the union movement to political communism, equally incompatible with the Charter of Amiens.

When the CGT and the CGTU parted, the unions affiliated with the latter confederation had a membership of approximately 500,000, leaving the CGT with barely 250,000 members. That the radical wing of the labor movement exercised a far greater force of attraction on the masses was due to several factors: the high hopes of a coming revolution, inspired in the French workers by the aftermath of the war; the deep impression made by the events in Russia; and a genuine distrust of the old leadership of the CGT, which by its wartime collaboration with a 'bourgeois' government had offended the basically anarchist feelings of numerous elements among the vanguard of French organized labor.

But though the CGTU started out with relatively strong support from the working class in industrial centers, its force of attraction was soon diminished by its lack of internal unity. At its outset the CGTU was composed not only of communists but also of anarchists and syndicalists. Divergent views on developments in Soviet Russia and on the character of the relations with the Red International of Labor Unions led to new feuds and new scissions, and by 1924, after the exclusion of all nonconformist elements, the CGTU was completely in the hands of the communists. From then on it not only abandoned any attempt to elaborate an original trade-union doctrine, but also, little by little, instituted a close-knit interpenetration of party and trade-union functions: the secretaries of the CGTU belonged to the party's Executive Committee, and a non-communist was hardly ever elected to the post of even a minor union organizer.

Frequent strikes—often launched for political purposes at the orders of communist organizations, without consideration of the situation, and most of them ending in debacle—caused the CGTU to lose its hold on the masses. 'If the two great proletarian organizations,' remarked a communist writer, referring to the communist party and the CGTU, 'have a political line which corresponds to the workers' interests, they apply it badly. In too loose a contact with the masses, they launch watchwords which are far too abstract to mobilize the masses.' [5] Thus in 1935, when the CGTU sought readmission to the CGT, its membership, according to its own claims, was only 230,000, and actually it may well have been far lower. Only a fraction of the workers who deserted the CGTU rejoined the CGT; some of them aligned themselves with insignificant anarchist or syndicalist sects, but the majority stayed outside any trade union.

The CGT, left in 1922 with but a skeleton organization, engaged in a slow internal reorganization, confining its activities merely to the defense of social legislation enacted at the end of the war and to lobbying in favor of new laws favorable to the working class. The social insurance law of 1930, covering sickness, premature infirmity, old age, death, maternity, and in part unemployment, invited the collaboration of labor organizations for the establishment of insurance funds. Between the enactment of the law and the reunification of the trade-union movement one of the principal activities of the CGT consisted in establishing and administering within the framework of the law these autonomously administered insurance funds.

The collaboration of the CGT with the state extended to a number of other fields. Since the end of the war the CGT had asked that the Parliament be supplemented by a functional representation of labor, industry, and consumers; and when a National Economic Council was established in 1925, under a radical-socialist cabinet, the CGT took an active part in its work. The Council's function was to advise the cabinet on all government and private bills of an economic nature, and the cabinet, in turn, often consulted the Council concerning the administrative measures for the application of such laws. A similar participation of labor in the fields of legislation and administration was established in numerous other boards.

Quite apart from other reasons, the composition of the CGT was in itself a conclusive factor in the confederation's failure to indulge to any considerable extent in what was considered in prewar days the normal function of the labor movement: 'direct action' against capitalism and its exponents. To a large extent the organization had lost its character as a representative of the industrial proletariat. In 1929 the civil servants federation joined the CGT, after long negotiations. It included, even at that time, close to 300,000 members, affiliated with almost 100 national unions, corresponding to the various departments of the government. Since the CGT in general organized workers by industry and not according to the employer for whom they worked, it would have been in order to dissolve the civil servants federation and to affiliate each national union separately. But that body refused to destroy a form of organization which had proved its strength, and hence a compromise was reached whereby some of the national unions were affiliated directly with the CGT, and the others remained united in the civil servants federation.[6] The numerical importance of this organization, and of other unions of employees who had the state as employer, enhanced the transformation of the CGT. More and more it devoted itself to lobbying activities and to bargaining with political parties and state authorities.

Also the age composition of the organizations affiliated with the CGT favored a more reserved attitude. The union movement of that period was unable to attract young workers. In order to escape the job atmosphere the younger generation joined political or cultural and sport organizations rather than trade unions.[7]

By its slow effort of reorganization the CGT had so increased its membership that at the moment of reunification it could claim organizations totaling 775,000 members. Thus at the Congress of Unification in Toulouse the joint membership of the CGT and the CGTU amounted to roughly a million.[8] But of this number almost 350,000 were civil servants or other public employees. In view of the fact that a further 165,000 belonged to the unions of railwaymen, whose working conditions were regulated by a special statute very similar to that of public employees, a statement made by the civil servants federation is certainly true: that at the time of the Congress of Toulouse the large majority of the reunited CGT membership 'were more or less public employees.'[9]

Even if one counts the railwaymen among the workers of private industry, the combined CGT and CGTU—the former after a patient activity of reconstruction, the latter after vain efforts to revolutionize the masses—counted no more than 650,-000 members among the wage earners in industry, commerce, and agriculture, a figure substantially the same as that recorded for the prewar period and for the latter part of 1920. Hence, with the exception of short periods of sudden growth in membership, the trade-union movement had not succeeded in making serious inroads among the masses of privately employed. Between 1911 and 1931 the number of wage earners in private trades had increased by 1.6 million, and thus in relative terms the membership in organized unions had substantially declined. At the time of the Toulouse Congress only 6.3 per cent of those employed in private enterprises belonged to the union movement. This weakness was in some localities even greater, for the proportion of union members varied considerably in the different regions of France. While a relatively important number among the working population of Paris and its suburbs was organized, and the number of union members was not too insignificant in the northern regions and in Alsace-Lorraine, the labor movement was extremely weak in the industrial regions of the west, the center, and the south of the country.

II

This state of affairs explains why the situation of the French working class, while it improved and worsened with the general changes in economic conditions, was little influenced, during the years of the schism within the labor movement, by the action of the trade unions.[10]

After France entered the world economic crisis in 1930, the number of labor conflicts remained very low indeed. In the five years from 1931 to 1935, respectively, only 35,200, 53,700, 83,-900, 59,900, and 88,300 workers went on strike. An average of one-third of all the strikes called between 1931 and 1934 ended in complete failure; not until 1935 did the proportion of strike failures decline.[11] This apparent calmness of industrial relations was not due, however, to an equilibrium of forces or to an active collaboration between labor and management. It resulted simply from the strong predominance of management over labor.[12]

In the immediate postwar period the law of 25 March 1919 [13] had provided a statutory framework for collective bargaining. French legal theory, in its discussion and interpretation of the institution, had furnished what was considered in the whole of Europe an essential contribution to the clarification of the legal nature of collective trade agreements. But the actual importance of collective bargaining in France declined steadily after 1921. During the years 1930-35 the yearly average of newly concluded collective agreements was 22 for the whole of France. In 1933 only 7.5 per cent of all wage earners in industry and commerce had their working conditions regulated by collective agreements. Since these figures include the mining industry and the maritime trades, where collective agreements had become a permanent feature (57 and 64 per cent, respectively, of all labor contracts), it is evident that in most trades collective bargaining played no practical role at all. Of the 1.3 million persons employed in the metal industry only 1.4 per cent had their working conditions regulated by a collective agreement; in the textile industry the figure was 2 per cent.[14]

That this situation was to a large extent due to the hostility of employers and their organizations toward collective bargaining was not denied. In 1934 the spokesmen of the CGPF declared that they were opposed to collective trade agreements because these agreements constituted for the enterprises a 'limitation of their freedom contrary to their normal functioning.' French management expressed concern that an extension of collective bargaining would lead to periodical and generalized conflicts and hence would invite an increasing intervention of the state in industrial relations. A memorandum prepared by the CGPF went so far as to make collective bargaining, which had been widely adhered to in the German republic, responsible for the advent of Hitlerism.

This opposition of French big business to collective trade agreements explains why the number of such agreements dwindled practically to nothing as soon as the economic crisis made itself felt. A further factor that was not favorable to the extension of collective bargaining was the great number of pygmy enterprises in France.

As for the unions themselves, the CGTU was at its inception opposed on principle to any systematic method of collective bargaining. After a few years, however, the CGTU unions entered into trade agreements wherever they found employers willing to conclude them. The CGT regarded collective bargaining as a vital means of promoting the immediate interests of the workers; its officials' only complaint was that French management refused to enter into agreements.[15] In general, organized labor not only was unable, because of its weakness and its division, to induce the employers to conclude agreements, but also was frequently incapable, because of the high percentage of unorganized workers, of enforcing the clauses of existing agreements—a weakness which in turn led to the further decline of the institution.

Thus the years of crisis, if they did not bring actual misery to the households of French workers, deepened the feeling of complete helplessness in the face of employers, and increased the desire to overcome what appeared to be one of the main reasons for this impotence: the schism between the two labor organizations. Throughout the years of the scission there had always been within the membership a clamor for the re-establishment of unity. At each of the six conventions which the CGT held between 1923 and 1933 the problem of unity was discussed and resolutions in favor of reunification were passed.[16] There was no real basis of understanding, however, the less so since the communist line after 1924, with one short interruption, swung steadily further to the left, with such slogans as 'united front from below' or 'fight against the social fascists' (reformist leaders), and did so with insurrectionary gestures.[17] Hence the attempts to reconcile basically different views, undertaken by both the CGT and the CGTU leadership, led only to more violent recriminations.

During the days of rioting in February 1934, which started one week before the workers of the CGT and the CGTU joined hands in the general strike of 12 February, the French communists in both the political and the trade-union press performed a 'revolutionary somersault.' At first, when the anti-parliamentarian leagues began to gather before the Chamber of Deputies, the communists called upon the masses to join in a protest against 'social democracy which by its division of the working class tries to weaken it so as to open the way to dictatorship.' As then viewed by the communists, the demonstrations of 6 February, which had been organized by the fascist leagues, were a powerful protest by the masses 'against fascism and against democracy in the process of fascization.' An appeal signed by both the communist party and the CGTU concluded with a plea to 'take the offensive against the treacherous maneuvers of the socialist party and the CGT.'

Two days later, however, the communist organizations, although already committed to a demonstration of their own called for the 9th, declared their desire to join in the general strike of the CGT. The attacks against the CGT leaders had not ceased altogether. Before 12 February, Jouhaux, who had called the general strike, was accused of sabotaging it. And while the appeals of the CGT in the days preceding the strike endeavored to gain the sympathy of the middle classes in the cities and in the countryside, the communist appeals still seethed with 'class against class' tactics. Finally, after the event there was boasting that only the CGTU and the communist party had imparted 'true revolutionary character' to the striking masses, and that they alone had been 'prepared for the success of the day.' [18] Nevertheless it was obvious that in the course of a few days a fundamental change had taken place in the policy of the CGTU. The factors that brought about this change cannot yet be entirely determined. There can hardly be a doubt that the joining of hands with an organization so violently denounced shortly before was authorized by Moscow. But it is quite possible that this authorization was given under pressure which emanated from French communist militants and sympathizers. There is evidence that since Hitler's advent in Germany it had been difficult to keep communist party and union officials in line. The policy of the German communist party in regard to the problems of a united front had been outspokenly criticized. There had been some proclamations of loyalty to the democratic regime of France in the event of an attack by fascism. Doubts about the usefulness of a continued fight against the Versailles treaty had been voiced, on the grounds that the communist slogan, 'Down with Versailles,' was playing into Hitler's hands. The confusion among party and union organizers had been enhanced by the rumors of an impending Franco-Soviet alliance: some wanted an official denial of these rumors from Moscow, others seemed to welcome the development as a means of opposing Hitler. It is true that in December 1933 these manifestations of independence of thought on the part of French communists, however contradictory, had been denounced by Maurice Thorez, at a Plenary Session of the Executive Committee of the Communist International, as 'vacillations and mistakes.' But after the events of February another leader of the French communist party criticized the party and the CGTU for having 'displayed a certain tardiness' in mobilizing the masses against the fascist threat.[19]

On the whole it can be considered probable that the communist directives inaugurated the change at this critical moment because there was actual danger that to do otherwise would mean to lose whatever influence with the masses the communist party and the CGTU had retained. Such a development was evidently considered especially undesirable at the precise moment when efforts for an encirclement of Germany by a Franco-Soviet treaty seemed to be making headway, and when, therefore, a new orientation of the Soviet Union not only needed the support of the French masses but also had new and better prospects for gaining it.

III

Whatever the motives of the communists, the workers of France regarded the twelfth of February as a victory obtained through unity. And at that time, when the names of Laval and Pétain made their first appearance together in a ministry of France, the membership of both the CGT and the CGTU brought more defined pressure on their leadership to make unity permanent. For months after the events of February 1934, the attacks in the communist press against the reformist leaders continued: Jouhaux and Belin, assistant secretary of the CGT, were accused of a desire 'to make the CGT into a fascist organization immediately.' Communist leaders were excluded from the party as 'right opportunists' because they had attempted during the events of February to replace the tactics of the 'united front from below' by a policy of a 'bloc' with reformism.[20] But such recriminations were merely a variation of the often-made denial that a change of line had occurred.

After the conclusion of a united-front agreement between the socialist and communist parties, on 27 July 1934, the movement for unity gained momentum. At that time the spontaneous desire of the masses for unity (as Léon Blum, the socialist leader, wrote later,[21] 'anyone who resisted the plea for unity would have witnessed the disaffection of the masses') was in harmony with the desire of the Soviet Union to see united and strengthened whatever force would actively oppose Nazi Germany. In August 1935 the Seventh World Congress of the Third International formally legitimated the change in communist tactics; a month later Litvinov, in his first speech at the League of Nations Assembly, concluded with the assertion that the Soviet Union 'will be second to none in the loyal discharge of assumed international obligations, more especially in the noble task of securing to all nations the blessing of peace.'

For some months the CGTU tried to induce the organizations of the CGT to enter into an agreement of united front similar to that concluded between the political parties. The CGT refused and frustrated every attempt in that direction because such an agreement would have singularly facilitated the communist tactics of 'boring from within.' When the CGT declined to accept unity under other than its own conditions, the CGTU chose to make one concession after another. In view of this willingness of the CGTU to grant every demand, and under the persistent pressure that was exerted from below, the CGT had no choice but to advance on the path of unification, despite the reluctance of its leadership.

Remarkably enough, the communist party was far more adamant during this period in its negotiations with the socialist party, which wished to see the united front of the two parties succeeded by their unification. The explanation of this difference in attitude is to be found in the fact that the communist party still had possibilities of development, while the membership of the CGTU had been declining for more than twelve years. Moreover, the communists were much less interested in joining forces with the French socialist party, which was largely composed of middle-class producers and civil servants, ill-disposed toward communist ideology, than they were in holding a firm grasp on a working-class movement, such as the CGT was or could become. Finally, the communists may have reckoned that a preservation of party and front organizations would prove helpful in controlling large sections of the union movement; later developments showed that this would not have been a miscalculation.

In 1935 the CGT succeeded in imposing the procedure of unification it had proposed from the very beginning. The amalgamation started with the *syndicats*, the union locals, a procedure desired by the CGT because at this level the disparity in membership, unfavorable to the CGTU, would become apparent.

From there the amalgamation was carried to the *unions départe-mentales*, regional organizations in which the unions of an entire French department were represented. And finally it extended to the *fédérations*, which in general grouped the wage earners according to industries, not on craft lines.

The amalgamation 'without victors or vanquished,' as it was officially styled, did not always proceed without difficulties. Mutual accusations that unity was being sabotaged were recurrent. But the communists, determined as they were to obtain unity at all costs, finally insisted on nothing else than the 'largest possible application of internal trade-union democracy.' [22] The leadership of the old CGT could not well refuse this; some of them, it is true, declared later that they had never had any illusions about the possibilities which this formula provided in the hands of a well-organized faction.

In the Congress of Unification at Toulouse, which laid down the statutes of the newly constituted CGT, the discussions revealed that on most important problems there was dissension between the followers of the two organizations. By its final voting the Congress accepted the statutes in the form advocated by the old CGT. In spite of the fact that every question had already been threshed out in discussions preceding the Congress, the communists insisted that on every point of disagreement a vote be taken, and they actually made a better showing than could have been expected. On the eve of the reunification the numerical strength of the CGT was 3.3 times higher than that of the CGTU, but the ballots at Toulouse gave only 2.2 times as many votes to the point of view of the CGT as to that of the communists.[23]

It was decided that the CGT remain affiliated with the International Federation of Trade Unions (IFTU). The communists would have preferred to see the CGT outside of any international organization until the IFTU and the Red International of Labor Unions had reached the unity that was desired in Moscow. In 1936 the influence of the British labor movement was predominant in the IFTU, and therefore the communists, who had scant sympathy with the British movement, were little inclined to increase the strength of this international organization by a possibly powerful CGT. Although the communists' wishes were overruled by the vote, the CGT pledged itself to use every influence and effort for the early achievement of international trade-union unity.

Of more immediate importance were the votes on the structure of the new organization. The communists advocated 'democratic centralization.' They wished the Administrative Committee, endowed with great powers over the regional unions and the federations, to be elected directly by the biennial Congress of the CGT; the members of the Central Office were to be designated by the Administrative Committee but approved by the Congress. The opposite solution, which eventually prevailed, was 'federalist' in character. Under this scheme the administration of the organization remained in the hands of a National Council, convened at least twice every year. The Council was composed of one delegate (usually the permanent secretary) for each federation and each regional union (two for Paris), without regard for the numerical importance of affiliated locals or members; thus the barbers federation, with its 3000 members, had as much weight in voting as the railwaymen, with 165,000 members, and a regional union of an agricultural district in the west had as much as the workers of the strongly unionized Nord department. The Administrative Committee was designated by this National Council, and was intended to be merely its permanent organ. Also the secretaries of the CGT—who formed the Central Office (*Bureau*) of the organization—were nominated by the National Council. The Congress of the CGT, which convened every other year, had far more limited powers than those of the National Council.

It may appear very doubtful whether this extreme federalism, carried over from the beginning of the century when the CGT had only co-ordinating and discussing but no directing functions, still corresponded to the needs of a modern labor organization. Actually, however, both before and after 1936 the Central Office and the Administrative Committee had much more importance than the statutes would indicate.

When the statutes were discussed at Toulouse, the real controversies did not center around the principle of centralism versus federalism. The communists hoped that after having obtained a grasp on the union locals they could gain ascendancy in the CGT Congress, which would install an Administrative Committee amenable to influences from the trade-union members in mass production industries. Their opponents wanted to counteract such hopes. The old CGT had an overwhelming majority in the National Council because the amalgamation, as a result of the weakness of the CGTU, had left in office most of the old-time secretaries of federations and regional unions. For the future the federal structure seemed a guarantee that even if the communists became influential in certain trades, this would not necessarily affect the composition of the central organisms of the CGT.

In accordance with the new statutes the National Council at Toulouse appointed the new secretaries of the CGT. As agreed to previously, the two sides were represented on the basis of their membership figures. Consequently the new Central Office was composed of six former CGT and two former CGTU officials.

A quid pro quo similar to that which arose over the question of the organizational structure prevailed in the discussion on the so-called 'incompatibilities': the prohibition of the holding of political and CGT offices at the same time. Since the officials of the CGTU and of the communist party had very often been identical, the communists tried to resist a ban which might have prevented active communist members from holding a leading trade-union position. In the end only the combination of a political post with that of a secretary of the CGT was forbidden, each federation remaining free to decide the matter for itself.

Thus the question of incompatibilities was given importance in the discussions mainly in regard to the general problem of relations between political parties and the trade-union movement. And once more the Charter of Amiens was invoked by both sides in the dispute. The statutes as finally accepted incorporated in their preamble and their first article provisions almost identical with those that had attempted, thirty years earlier, to guarantee the 'independence' of the trade-union movement. This independence, however, was no longer interpreted in the same way as in the days of Amiens. The preamble to the statutes stated that the CGT was no longer politically indifferent, and that against dangers which might threaten democratic liberties or social reforms, collaboration with political parties was considered desirable (the text is presented in Appendix 1, below).

What was hidden behind the discussions was the desire to keep one political party, the communists, from again forming a faction inside the union movement. It is true that the statutes explicitly forbade the activities of such factions. There was nothing in the statutes, however, to prevent their formation. In the debates at Toulouse as well as in subsequent discussions, the masking of the real issues behind an apparent emphasis on trade-union independence proved to be a 'paralyzing abstraction.' It spread confusion among the trade-union members and it seriously hampered the adaptation of the newly constituted CGT to the situation that arose with the victory of the Popular Front at the 1936 elections.

III

Labor Legislation of the Popular Front

THE extent of the success which the Popular Front obtained in the elections of 1936 came as a surprise even to the organizations affiliated with the new formation of the French left. Moreover, the voters had, to an unexpected extent, expressed their confidence in socialists and communists rather than in the moderate radical-socialists. As soon as it became clear that the main governmental responsibility would be incumbent upon the socialist party, its leader, Léon Blum, without awaiting his official installation as Prime Minister, offered a place in the future government to the most important working-class organization, the CGT. But the Administrative Committee and the National Council of the CGT, after consultation, declined the offer politely but firmly. A direct collaboration between organized labor and the government could be established, declared the CGT, only through such agencies as the National Economic Council, the International Labour Office, and the tripartite boards which the CGT hoped to see established for the regulation of economic life but which actually never materialized.[1]

It was not difficult for the directing bodies of the CGT to reach a unanimous vote on this refusal. To the representatives of the old-time CGT a direct assumption of ministerial responsibilities was still a contradiction of their general philosophy. However far the CGT, since the outbreak of World War I and the reconstruction period following it, had gone toward classical trade unionism, the French trade-union movement was still far from even conceiving the idea of a labor party. In spite of the fact that the activities of the CGT, like those of the labor movement in other European countries, could no longer be disassociated from political action, the heritage of syndicalist beliefs was still strong enough to condemn any mingling with politics as an infringement on the 'independence' of the labor movement.[2] The great influence that Proudhon had exercised on the official philosophy of the CGT leadership had been reaffirmed explicitly by Jouhaux.[3] Proudhon's famous remark about 'the workshop which will take the place of the government' had not lost its attraction, notwithstanding the gap existing between such utopian-anarchist dreams and the practice of the French trade-union movement. To enter into a government, even one headed by a socialist, was thus considered impossible by the majority of the new CGT.

The communist minority reached the same decision, though from different motives. The communists had always denounced as 'old anarcho-syndicalist prejudices' the stress that was laid on the independence of the labor movement. During the debates at Toulouse one of the communist spokesmen had indulged, much to the displeasure of his new colleagues, in a lengthy refutation of Proudhon's doctrines. But neither the communist union leaders nor the communist party was willing to forego, by sharing government responsibilities, the liberty of criticizing a government led by a man whom many communist trade-union members viewed with distrust as a 'bourgeois' or 'just another Kerenski.'

I

The immediate accomplishments that the CGT expected from the new government were most moderate. After the election results became known, the demands of the trade-union movement centered around a comprehensive public works program, intended to absorb unemployment and to be financed by a National Reassurance Fund. It was expected that in due course there would be legislation which would shorten the work week and reform collective trade agreements, but the immediate approach to these goals was believed to lie only in public works and work under government contracts.[4]

The wave of mass strikes [5] that swept France in May and June 1936 fundamentally altered, however, the plans of both the CGT and the new government.

In April 1936 only 32 strikes occurred in the whole of France, but in June the number of strikers amounted to almost 1.9 million, or nearly one-fourth the total number of wage earners in industry and commerce.[6] Nearly three-fourths of all the strikes in June were sit-down strikes, a form which the labor organizations and their press had never sanctioned or even discussed.

There is no doubt that these strikes were a spontaneous mass movement altogether unforeseen; they certainly were not initiated by the CGT or any political party. When the first sit-down strike broke out in northern France, five days after the elections, the event passed altogether unnoticed in the labor press. After other sit-down strikes in the provinces (Le Havre and Toulouse) were imitated in the industrial suburbs of Paris, the labor press, it is true, mentioned that the working-class population had assisted the strikers who occupied the plants by providing them with food. But the National Council of the CGT, which met while these strikes were occurring and had already been partially successful, did not discuss the strike movement at all—a clear indication that the strikes had not been planned or even foreseen by the CGT. It is also impossible to attribute the strikes to the efforts of extremist plotters, such as the anarchists and the Trotskyites, for these elements, while they most thoroughly rejoiced in the manifestations of mass spontaneity, had no influence whatever with the masses.[7]

The success at the polls had added to the self-confidence which the workers had regained by the unification of the labor movement. It is significant that the strikes increased considerably after the traditional yearly manifestation in honor of the Communards of 1871—not that the revolutionary example inspired the workers to similar deeds, but the orderly demonstrations, which were particularly successful in 1936, offered an opportunity for the establishment of contacts, for the exchange of experiences, and for mutual encouragement. When the CGT formulated its modest demands, between election and strikes, it did so in the name of the people, who wanted the new cabinet to 'govern against misery.' By their strikes the workers spontaneously sought a way to strengthen the government's intention of abolishing misery and forcibly-imposed humbleness.

In most of the preliminary movements as well as in the broad mass strikes that flared up after 26 May, it was characteristic that the claims for a raise of wage rates played a definitely minor role. As is understandable from what has been said in the preceding chapters, most of the conflicts were based on demands for a recognition of the right to organize and to conclude collective trade agreements and on protests against the dismissal of individual workers. In the metal and automobile industry of Paris the sit-down strikes took on unprecedented and almost symbolic character. There the workers who occupied the premises were observed shining and polishing the idle machines, and they joined with the population in celebrations of their certain victory. It was in this same industry that the employers and their organizations, since the beginning of the year, had steadfastly refused to conclude the collective agreement sought by the unions.

In view of the numerical weakness of the union movement among the workers in private enterprises, it was altogether impossible for the union officials to lead the strikers. The main effort of the CGT during the weeks of May and June was aimed at regulating and co-ordinating the strike movement and thereby avoiding for the strikers the 'mortal danger of popular hostility.' [8] Even after measures of broad social legislation had been initiated by the government, and after the CGT had concluded an agreement with the CGPF which was tantamount to a complete victory of the working class, the workers were slow in calling off the strikes, fearful of being driven into a disadvantageous position once they resumed work.

In order to bring the workers back to the plants, the communist party threw into the balance the considerable influence it had with the workers of Paris. The communists seem to have done everything in their power to avert the outbreak of the strikes, in order that their attempt to establish a broad anti-Hitlerian front with the French middle classes would not be endangered. Finally their leader, Maurice Thorez, warned that 'not everything is possible' and that 'one should know how to terminate a strike, as soon as the essential requests are granted.' [9] Not so much because of this appeal as because the new social legislation brought immediate results, the effervescence died down after July. In November 1936 the number of strikers was even lower than in April.

Meanwhile, at the end of May, when the strike movement had already grown considerably, the managements of some of the large enterprises, especially in the metal industry in Paris, agreed to the principle of negotiating with the trade unions. As a precondition for negotiation, however, the employers and their organizations demanded that the workers cease their occupation of the premises. While this request was favorably viewed by the CGT, the union movement was simply not in a position to comply with it. The government, which was then still headed by the radical-socialist Sarraut, was unwilling to terminate its interim activities by the forcible evacuation of the plants. And the new Prime Minister, Léon Blum, declared before the Chamber, after he assumed power on 5 June, that while the sit-down strikes constituted a violation of French civil law it would nevertheless be futile to expect the Popular Front government to expel the strikers from the plants. After the Chamber of Deputies, by an overwhelming majority, expressed its confidence in the government, Blum succeeded, however, in bringing together the two central organizations of management and labor, the CGPF and the CGT, and presided over the conclusion of the so-called

Matignon Agreement, on the night of 7 June (the text is presented in Appendix II, below).

During the preceding days negotiations between representatives of employers and workers had been initiated in several trades, in spite of the continuing occupation of the premises. While some of the negotiations were broken off because of conflicting claims concerning who was entitled to speak in the name of management, others led to agreements wholly or partially satisfactory to labor. The fact that the attempts to organize French management in the CGPF had never been wholly successful, and that the entire organization was based on a loose scheme of federation, resulted, in those critical days, in a lack of co-ordinated action on the part of the employers. Previously the organizations of French management had refused to take official notice of the existence of an organized labor movement. In the Matignon Palace the delegation of the CGPF saw itself forced to conclude an agreement with a delegation of the CGT (among which were two avowed communists), under the manifold pressure of nearly two million workers occupying the enterprises, of a government friendly to the cause of labor, and of public opinion overwhelmingly in favor of the strikers. (It may be noted that on the very same day the Cardinal of Paris made an appeal that industrial relations be established on a new basis.) The pressure to give in was increased by the substantial number of agreements already concluded in several trades and regions.[10]

French management regarded it as a capitulation to have concluded an agreement under such conditions. To hide under the cloak of a contractual accord what in reality amounted to a complete and unilateral abandonment of long-established privileges and principles was considered to be a shameful surrender to the 'class enemy.' Such feelings were intensified by the expressions of contempt with which the employers found themselves addressed. On the day preceding Matignon a right-wing deputy, Fernand-Laurent, criticized in the Chamber the various individual agreements which had already been concluded as an inexcusable expression of 'imbecile cowardice of a management which capitulated in the face of threats.' [11] When a French minister, Anatole de Monzie, later discovered in the files how 'lightheartedly' the French employers had acceded in all points to the workers' 'threats,' their attitude appeared to him as a justification of Sorel's prediction that because of its cowardice the bourgeoisie was condemned to disappear.

Until the end of the Third Republic, and often beyond, industrial relations in France were impaired by the psychological reactions to the June days of 1936. In the streets and plants the working class celebrated a bloodless and barricadeless victory with the songs of the Great Revolution. French management, its pride hurt, was left with no other consolation than its hopes for the day of 'revenge for Matignon.'

II

The night of Matignon has been compared to the night of 4 August 1789—but not quite rightly, for in 1789 the French Third Estate had been the vanguard of the bourgeois revolution in a feudal continental Europe. In 1936 the French working class obtained social legislation whose main features had been realized in other countries for twenty years or more—indeed, had already been lost again in two of France's totalitarian neighbor countries.

Matignon transformed the institution of the collective trade agreement from a dead letter into a living reality. It blazed the path to a definite recognition of the trade-union movement and to full recognition of the freedom to organize. The parties agreed to the appointment of shop stewards and to an immediate raise in wages of from 7 to 15 per cent, which was later to be completed by an additional increase in abnormally low wages.[12] In legislation that was promptly passed by both houses of Parliament the fundamental principles laid down in the Matignon Agreement were recognized; and they were supplemented by the further requirement of holidays with pay and by a reduction of the work week to 40 hours without a reduction in weekly earnings.[13]

These reforms of the summer of 1936 were hailed by labor as the harbingers of a new era. But it was only a few weeks before the new era began to reveal its inheritance of many of the old problems.

Among the new measures none was more important than the regulation of collective bargaining by the law of 24 June. The Matignon Agreement, by making the inclusion of certain provisions compulsory in every collective labor contract, eliminated a weakness that had rendered the previous legislation on collective bargaining ineffective. The new law, on the one hand, facilitated the conclusion of new agreements in spite of the possible reluctance of one of the parties; and, on the other, it made it possible for the Minister of Labor, under certain conditions, to extend the agreements originally concluded between private organizations into a public regulation for the whole of the industry in a defined region.

In case of refusal to conclude a collective agreement, a joint committee was to be charged with mediation between the parties concerned. This committee was to include 'delegates of the most representative trade associations of employers and workers in the branch of industry or commerce in the district concerned or in the whole country, as the case may be.' While the joint committee had no power to compel the parties to conclude an agreement, it was ruled that an employer who refused systematically to conclude a collective agreement with the most representative group of his workers committed an *abus de pouvoir* which might entail suit for damages against him.[14]

The extension of a collective agreement, whereby the essential provisions of the agreement would be made binding on all employers and employees in the trade and district, was to be ordered at the joint request of the most representative groups of management and labor in the industry and district concerned.

Before taking such a decision the Minister of Labor had to consult the competent sections of the National Economic Council, whose management and labor members were also delegated by the most representative trade associations.

Thus from all sides the 'most representative organizations' became the cornerstone of the institution of collective bargaining. French public law theorists had formerly contended that collective bargaining could play its full role only if and when the trade organizations acquired sufficient strength to be regarded as representing the quasi-totality of management and labor, respectively.[15] The legislation of 1936 invested with rule-making power organizations which had not necessarily acquired the degree of absolute strength envisaged by the theorists, but which were relatively speaking *most* representative. By giving such powers into their hands, however, this legislation so strengthened the respective trade organizations as to transform them into actual representatives of the quasi-totality of employers and employees.

A circular of the Minister of Labor defined the 'most representative organizations' by reference to an interpretation of Article 389 of the Treaty of Versailles, made by the Permanent Court of International Justice at The Hague, on 31 July 1922; as a result, the trade unions (union locals, regional unions or federations) that were affiliated with the CGT were almost everywhere to be considered, for labor, the 'most representative organization.'[16] In a given industry or region the most representative body was the one that had the largest number of members, regardless of whether this majority was maintained in every particular enterprise or category of employees. These directives, which were later supplemented by an arbitration award,[17] sanctioned industrial unionism. To be sure, they did not establish any *de jure* monopoly for the CGT, and they stated that more than one organization of the employees could be regarded as 'most representative.' But in 1936, except in the Alsace region and in some white-collar workers' organizations where the Catholic unions were sometimes more numerous, it was always the CGT and its affiliated organizations which signed collective agreements and requested their extension. Under such conditions attempts to establish company unions that would benefit from employers' support were almost hopeless. If the CGPF wanted to break the *de facto* monopoly of the CGT it had to proceed in other ways.

Under the influence of the new legislation, coming after a desuetude of almost twenty years, the practice of collective bargaining spread rapidly to all trades and districts, in spite of the aversion to the institution which the employers had voiced as late as 1934. By the end of 1936 no less than 2336 collective trade agreements were registered; the number of agreements whose extension to the whole trade or district had been requested amounted to 256. By 1939 the total number of collective agreements had reached 5620.[18] As regards the extension of collective agreements in that period it should be noted that between the request for an extension and the decree actually ordering it, a delay of at least one year, and often considerably longer, was customary. In 1939, for example, the extension had been granted in only 329 cases, but hundreds of requests were pending.[19] Such delays, which resulted from a serious understaffing of the Ministry of Labor, considerably diminished the usefulness of the new institution.

In remarkable contrast to other countries, in France the parties to a collective agreement were bound to their contract beyond the period they had originally fixed for its validity. The reason for this was a situation which again was different from that prevailing in other countries: almost all collective agreements were concluded at approximately the same time, and most of them for the same period—one year—and therefore industrial strife involving millions of workers was to be feared when the agreements expired, which would occur more or less simultaneously. Hence the government repeatedly prolonged the legal duration of collective agreements by legislative action.[20]

This situation could not fail to have an important bearing on the nature of industrial relations and on the attitude of the organizations involved. By action of the state the two partners were prevented from seeking in continuously renewed negotiations the compromise solution which is the goal of every bargaining process. If both parties acceded, however reluctantly, to the repeated prolongations, they did so because they had little confidence that such a compromise could actually be reached by their own negotiations. But the more remote the conclusion of the original agreement became, the more the stipulations assumed the character of state-imposed regulations. Moreover, the changes which occurred in the actual situation over a period of years very often made the original agreements obsolete and inadequate.

Since the annulment of contracts even at their expiration was not desired, it was necessary to create a machinery of mediation and arbitration for the peaceful adjustment of controversies arising out of existing collective agreements. At first it was hoped that such procedures could be worked out by the parties themselves in their bargaining contracts. But when the Popular Front government was forced to devaluate the franc in September 1936, and a rise in prices, followed by the workers' demand for a rise in wages, was foreseen, it became clear that more general measures were needed.

The proposal of the government and of the Chamber of Deputies to link by a sliding scale every change in the cost of living with a corresponding variation in wages was defeated by the Senate.[21] The French Senate which in June and July, under the pressure of the mass strikes, had endorsed the bulk of the social legislation with uncustomary zeal, had quickly returned to its role of conservative moderator. Half a century earlier Gambetta had ridiculed the Senate because of its peculiar status as a body 'elected by 75,000 bourgeois.' Before World War I Clemenceau had denounced the electoral colleges which chose the senators as 'most absurd and disparate.' Now two-thirds of the senators who judged the actions of the Popular Front government had been elected three to six years before the swing of the country to the left had asserted itself. And in the debate over the possible consequences of devaluation, the Senate, confronted with the anticipated rise in prices, refused to consider automatic wage adjustments and agreed only to authorize the government to establish machinery for the arbitration of the labor conflicts that might arise.[22]

An attempt was made to have the CGPF and the CGT agree upon the modalities of such procedures, for it was rightly believed that a voluntary agreement would considerably ease the smooth functioning of the arbitration machinery. After more than two months, however, the negotiations were admittedly broken off by the CGPF. The revival of some sit-down strikes was a sufficient reason for the employers' organization to declare that it did not wish to enter into further contractual agreements with the CGT.[23] By thus shifting to the government the responsibility for establishing arbitration procedures the CGPF avoided giving the CGT, by another central agreement, another opportunity to act in the name of all of French labor. The fact that it was not possible to introduce arbitration of industrial disputes by agreement left its mark on the subsequent legislation to which the government had to resort.

A law of 31 December 1936 included in Article 1 the statement that 'all collective labor disputes must be submitted to processes of conciliation and arbitration before any strike or lockout.'[24] But the continued resistance of the Senate to measures of broad reform, and the groping empiricism with which the government and the interested parties alike faced the novel institution, led to frequent changes and reforms intended to fill existing loopholes in the law. The procedure as originally envisaged proved exceedingly slow and burdensome for both parties involved. Even the arbiters of last resort rendered varying and often contradictory decisions on similar points. It was clear that unless drastic changes in the law were made, the arbiters would be unable to enforce their decisions. As Léon Blum said, sanctions were limited to the moral pressure of public opinion;[25] and a pressure of public opinion in matters of arbitration, such as exists in Anglo-Saxon countries, was almost unknown in France and certainly did not exist in the field of labor relations. Moreover, in spite of the designation 'compulsory' arbitration, the right to strike was never abolished. Strikes that broke out without awaiting the decision of the arbiter could at best be penalized through a judgment for damages.in the ordinary courts.

Little by little reforms straightened out the most criticized defects of the law. A Superior Court of Arbitration was instituted, consisting of three members of the Council of State, two high civil servants, and, whenever other than purely legal questions were involved, two representatives of workers and employers, chosen by the most representative organization.

In the course of the changes the essential features of the original law were thoroughly transformed. The legislators had at first been careful to leave the arbitration procedure as much as possible in the hands of arbiters chosen by the disputing parties. Thereby it was hoped to avoid the political dangers that were bound to arise from a continuous resort to government action for the settling of labor conditions. Since the law provided that the arbiters of first instance were to be designated by the most representative organization, the trade unions affiliated with the CGT were supposed to hold a firm grasp on the institution of arbitration. But because of the antagonism between management and labor, the interested parties were increasingly unable to agree, and hence were only too glad to be deprived of their responsibility by a third person, the 'super-arbiter,' who represented the state and was practically always nominated by the state authorities.[26] Statistics show that more and more of the cases submitted to arbitration were decided by the super-arbiter and not by arbiters chosen by the parties (of 2471 awards rendered from March 1938 to February 1939, all but 4 per cent). Super-arbiters were designated in no less than 3000 cases, and the Superior Court of Arbitration, in the nine months of its existence during 1938, had more than 1800 cases referred to its decision.[27]

It should not be denied that the system of conciliation and arbitration, from its inception in 1937 to the outbreak of the war, when it was suddenly abolished, yielded important results in the settling of industrial disputes. Minor conflicts, especially, often found a quick solution and did not have to go farther than the stage of conciliation; the statistics reveal that 60 per cent of all collective disputes of which the authorities were notified were settled in the first stage of mediation. But these figures are not truly indicative, since almost all of such conflicts were of little importance. On the whole the system weakened rather than strengthened the active participation of business and labor in the normalization of industrial relations.

The legislation of 1936 contained no explicit provisions regarding shop stewards, except the requirement that they be provided for in the collective agreements. From the outset the trade unions arranged that a link be established between the shop stewards and the unions, in order to avoid the dualism which had prevailed during the war, when the institution had first been tried out. Actually the first elections—which took place in all shops with more than 10 employees where collective trade agreements had been concluded—brought active union members to the post of delegates almost everywhere.

The results of the shop stewards' activities were disappointing, however, to the labor movement. Entitled to present the individual grievances of their fellow workers, the shop stewards either were alienated from their own unions or were identified by the employer as the representative of the union interests and hence, because of generally unsettled conditions, met with an unwillingness to collaborate. Since no special sanctions were provided, as in other countries,[28] against employers who dismissed shop stewards, and since the courts were moving only hesitantly toward regarding the firing of a shop steward as a collective dispute and hence a matter of arbitration, there developed, even in the second elections, a situation in which many workers hesitated to be a candidate.[29] Daladier, after he became Prime Minister in 1938, found it necessary, on the occasion of the Radical-Socialist Party Congress, to launch a vigorous attack on the shop stewards, among whom there were 'too many foreigners and court-arraigned.' Actually both categories were barred from becoming delegates by the wording of the Matignon Agreement.

The introduction of the 40-hour work week in most industries was probably the most controversial and most highly publicized aspect of the labor legislation of 1936. Indeed, this question assumed a symbolic significance which was completely out of proportion to its economic importance. For employers and employees alike the length of the work week developed into a myth which was for the most part discussed by both sides without consideration of the actual legal and economic situation. These dissensions captured attention to such an extent, even outside the country, that after the defeat of France her downfall was still discussed in terms of the 40-hour week.[30]

Before the enactment of the wage-hour legislation in 1936 the workers had believed that most of their social and economic problems could easily be solved by a mere shortening of the work week: unemployment and economic crisis would be overcome, dignity, leisure, indeed the further emancipation of the working class, would be assured. These inflated hopes concerning the results of the 40-hour week failed to materialize. But the story of their collapse is reserved for another chapter, as its primary significance lies in its connection with the problem of war production.

III

Meanwhile the new labor legislation of the Popular Front was not only changing the conditions of life of French wage earners but also leaving a distinct imprint on the organizations of both labor and management.

It is certainly safe to say that when the Matignon Agreement was concluded, only a minority of the strikers belonged to a trade union, though the representatives of the CGT acted in the name not only of all organized labor but of the entire working class. In 1936-7, however, the CGT experienced an increase in membership which in suddenness and extent had not been equaled by the union movement of any other country. From about 1 million, the number of members supposedly climbed to 5.3 million.[31] More than 41 per cent of all French wage and salary earners were thus organized in the CGT. In quite a number of industries the 1937 figures were ten to twenty times the levels of a year before—in some even much more (see Appendix III, below). The most impressive growth was in mass-production industries and among certain skills that were previously almost unorganized, like white-collar workers and technicians.

In the chemical industry 80 per cent of the employees became unionized, in mining 75 per cent, among the railroad employees 60 per cent, in the food industry 55 per cent, and in the metal industry 48 per cent.[32] The French workers generally poured into the unions with little or no pressure brought upon them to join. The close connection which existed, as events had demonstrated, between the mass strikes, their successful conclusion, and the Matignon Agreement reached by the CGT, provoked an enthusiasm which overcame the natural reluctance of the French worker to organize. Organization seemed the best means to safeguard the improvements already won and to obtain new advantages. The workers' profound aversion to polemics and controversial discussion was overcome by a confidence that the achieved unification of the union movement had eliminated the causes of disagreement. From an organization whose main function had been lobbying on behalf of minor civil servants and employees of similar status, the CGT grew almost overnight into the legitimate representative of the French working class.

But this massive influx of members placed almost all unions and federations affiliated with the CGT before organizational tasks not easy to solve. As a rule the offices of unions and federations were seriously understaffed, because trade-union bureaucracy was traditionally much less developed in France than in other countries. (It was not without importance for future development that in general the CGTU was better off in this respect than the CGT.) A handful of extremely low-paid secretaries had to cope with the avalanche of new problems that arose out of the flood of new members and the Matignon legislation.

In these circumstances there remained little if any room for propaganda or education among the newcomers. Although the necessity of acquainting the rank and file more deeply with the aims and philosophy of trade unionism was recognized as early as July 1936,[33] very often the mere payment of union fees remained for months the only contact between the millions of new members and their organizations.

As early as 1931 the CGT had organized a beginning of working-class education. There existed in Paris a Workers' Institute of Higher Education, with which a number of labor colleges in the principal industrial towns were connected. But in 1936, when the CGT became a mass organization, the Institute had very little influence. At a time when the regional union of the Paris area counted a membership of 1,250,000, the number of registered students amounted to 2,000, or less than 0.2 per cent of the total membership.[34]

The reason for this lack of success lay partly in the method and approach of the teaching staff. The teachers were almost without exception rather doctrinaire intellectuals, devoted to a definite philosophy, the so-called 'planism' (to be discussed in the following chapter). The educational organization had become a training place for a definitely oriented kind of union organizer, but not a center for a form of propaganda that would have been capable of reaching the masses of the new membership. The efforts of the educational center were equally hampered by the more or less outspoken hostility of the communists, who were opposed to the personalities and ideologies of its promoters. Finally, the meager success was due also to the fact that the

majority of new members did not want to become familiarized
with the ideas or ultimate goals of unionism. They had joined
in order to obtain immediate advantages, and in delight over the
achievement of unity. They were bound to quit as soon as advantages and unity were again endangered.

At Matignon the president of the CGPF and his associates had
acted on behalf of French management as a whole, just as Jouhaux and his co-signers had served as representatives of all labor.
In the eyes of the employer groups the framework of the new
labor legislation and the increased strength of the trade-union
movement called for a continuation of such unified representation of management. Failure to achieve it would have forced the
employers permanently into the defensive and to further concessions.

A complete shake-up of the employers' organization was the
first step taken.[35] As early as August 1936 the association's name
was significantly changed from a reference to 'production' to a
reference to 'employers'—from Confédération Générale de la
Production Française to Confédération Générale du Patronat
Français. A new president was elected, as his predecessor, René
Duchemin, had been criticized for having steered too conciliatory
a course in matters of industrial relations, and for having given
in too easily during the days of June. The new president, C. J.
Gignoux, who was not an industrialist himself, represented the
new activist type of pressure-group official who had not been
customary in France. Before he was made leader of the CGPF
he had been the editor of a newspaper sponsored by French
heavy industry. He now addressed an urgent plea to management: 'Employers, be employers . . . rally around your professional syndicate . . . there must be no more isolation.' He
added that the individualism of French management, while it
had had its days of grandeur, was now impossibly outdated.[36]

The new statutes of the association drew the lessons of the
past and incorporated three principles for a new orientation of
the CGPF. First, the previous federalist structure of the organ-

ization, which was deemed responsible for the lack of unity of action, was abandoned in favor of the power of the central administration over member groups. Second, in order to obtain the adherence of the mass of small businessmen, hitherto inimical toward organization, big business was asked 'to withdraw from the control of the direction of the great professional organizations and to leave a predominant influence to the owners of small and medium-size enterprises, to whom big business will continue to provide advice and wholehearted collaboration.'[37] Third, a new post of Deputy General for Industrial Relations was created; whereas other activities of the CGPF were to reckon with conflicting interests of various business groups, the department of the new deputy was to represent the common interests of management in confronting the claims of organized labor.

A new and extremely active public relations committee, the Comité de Prévoyance et d'Action Sociale, placed outside of the CGPF proper, further emphasized the new direction.[38] The rich literature with which it swept the country combined an ostensible defense of small business interests with steady attacks against 'totalitarian' practices of the CGT.

It is impossible to ascertain the degree of success obtained in the drive of French management for a complete organization of all business circles. There are indications that even then a not unimportant number of enterprises remained averse to organization. But the economic importance of these outsiders was practically nil. The new CGPF and its auxiliaries, especially when the heyday of the Popular Front was over, did remarkably well in realigning public opinion, which had to such a large extent backed the workers during the June strikes.

Thus it was in almost complete unity that French management was facing the 5 million workers organized in the CGT. At the Matignon Palace Léon Blum had called together the CGPF and the CGT for the purpose of collaboration, and their co-operation was supposed to form the basis of the new labor legislation that followed. But it was not for co-operation that the employer organizations strengthened their ranks and perfected their defenses.

IV

In August 1937, only fourteen months after the conclusion of the Matignon Agreement, the National Council of the CGT, in a message to the Prime Minister—no longer Blum but the radical-socialist Chautemps—complained about what it called the attempts of management to sap the foundations of the labor legislation of 1936. The control of jobs, which the CGT had obtained for a moment and hoped to conserve, seemed to be slipping away.

In a country where industrial relations appeared to be much less business relations than relations of classes, the class antagonists were considered free to organize or not. Since trade unionism was not a business proposition, it was regarded as contrary to the *liberté syndicale*, supreme principle of the French labor movement, to make employment dependent on union membership. Thus any check-off or similar system was altogether unknown, and closed-shop practices were very rare. They were so contrary to traditions that Jouhaux issued a strong warning against communist attempts to have employment refused to non-union members.[39] On the other hand, when organized labor spoke about 'workers control,' *contrôle ouvrier*, the request for a control over jobs merged into the demand for a change in ownership.[40]

This had a twofold consequence on the development of industrial relations between 1936 and 1939. Many employers, encouraged by their trade associations, attempted to break the position of the CGT unions as 'most representative organizations' by ridding the plants of at least the most active union members. On the other hand, when French management wanted to elude further negotiations sought by government and CGT for the betterment of industrial relations, it was able to point to the alleged intentions of the labor movement to offset existing property relations.

In its message to the Prime Minister in August 1937,[41] the CGT called for certain legislative reforms to insure the conservation of the labor legislation and the maintenance of the favored position granted by it to the CGT. Both the problem of hiring and firing and that of the shop stewards had developed into irksome matters of controversy which frequently led to disputes and protracted strikes. And these matters, among numerous others, were included in the CGT proposals. New legislation was sought concerning the shop stewards, in the hope that labor-management relations in the plants might thereby become more normal. As for the problem of hiring and dismissing, it was requested that this be solved by compulsory use of the public employment offices. Here again the union movement sought, with the aid of state institutions, to obtain what it was unable—or in the interest of social peace, unwilling—to secure by its own action. Although in France, as in most other European countries, public employment exchanges existed, the employers ignored them wherever possible. They saw in them yet another instrument of state interference, and feared that the influence of the trade unions on the employment offices, which functioned as tripartite boards with representatives of labor and management, would become preponderant.[42]

The government welcomed the suggestions of the CGT for reformatory steps in various fields of labor legislation. It sought again and again to secure an agreement of the two central organizations representing management and labor, for it understood that more essential than single reforms was a transformation of the mores and the spirit prevailing in industrial relations. Thus a new agreement, without the stigmata which the Matignon accord bore in the eyes of management, seemed desirable. But the spokesmen of the CGPF steadfastly refused, now openly declaring that they would not enter into any negotiations as long as the CGT was the sole representative of labor.[43]

There remained no other course for the government but to resort again to legislation. Bills were introduced to prepare a comprehensive modern labor code, embracing all aspects of industrial relations and laying down, among others, rules for a 'democratization' of strikes by a preceding vote of the employees. But in view of the attitude of the Senate and of the general decay in the process of regular legislation during the last years of the French republic,[44] it was impossible to hope for the passing of such statutes. The so-called Reynaud decree laws which were finally enacted in November 1938 were certainly no solution. They initiated a new reform of the arbitration procedures, but otherwise their only contribution toward meeting the CGT proposals was a legal definition of the functions of the shop stewards, limiting their activities and thereby sanctioning a situation that already prevailed.[45] In the meantime the job control held by the CGT unions had been further whittled down. As will be discussed in a later chapter, the CGT called a general strike in protest against the Reynaud decrees, and the failure of that demonstration not only provoked a rapid decline in union membership but also threw the CGT out of the position in national life to which it had been promoted by the labor legislation of 1936.

And that position, despite the ephemeral nature of its circumstances, had been of undeniable importance. Outside of their participation in collective bargaining and arbitration, representatives of the CGT sat on some thirty-odd official national boards, councils, and committees, not to mention the even greater number of departmental bodies. Through these activities the CGT, which continued to act at least tacitly in the name of the nearly 13 million wage earners of France, took a part not only in the adjustment of labor relations but also in manifold regulatory activities pertaining to a wide range of social and economic questions. As has been pointed out, such practices had been followed by the CGT since World War I. With the Popular Front legislation, however, the partial integration of the trade-union movement into state institutions and its sharing of official responsibilities became so generalized that actually the character of French labor was considerably transformed. The development was not unexpected. Indeed, it was only to be anticipated that French trade unionists would 'tread the same path as their European comrades'[46] once modern labor legislation was introduced and the CGT succeeded in organizing an important part of the industrial proletariat.

It is remarkable, however, how little this transformation was reflected in the philosophy of the trade-union movement. In spite of the fact that the CGT, for reasons that have been discussed, relied even more heavily on the support of the government than did the labor movement of other countries, there was almost no discussion whatever about the relation between organized labor and the state. When the secretary-general of the CGT, at the height of trade-union development, wanted to make the functions and objectives of the labor organization better known to the general public,[47] he gave a penetrating analysis of the economics of capitalism and a detailed description of the system by which the CGT proposed to overcome capitalism, but there was hardly any mention of the role that the CGT actually played in the framework of the existing legislation, and no discussion at all of the extent to which its activities determined the political objectives of the labor movement.

To accept without reservation an institution like compulsory arbitration amounted to an almost complete abandonment of labor's principle of 'direct action,' still advocated in 1936 in the debates of the Congress of Toulouse. Yet almost the entire CGT, including the communists, accepted the principle of compulsory arbitration without recognizing the implications of what it was doing.[48]

There were a few exceptions. René Belin, assistant secretary of the CGT, attempted to draw certain decisive lessons from the new situation when he wrote: 'French trade unionism is no longer in opposition, or an outlaw; it accepts the idea of a labor law. Social reforms no longer seem unclean to it. It submits to arbitration. It seeks to conclude collective agreements. It places itself under the power of the law, which gives protection but which also demands subjection.' [49]

A step further was made by officials of the civil servants federation. Belin, who belonged to the group of those trade unionists who fervently defended the 'independence' of the labor movement, spoke only about the 'law' without admitting that the 'protection' it offered to labor was bound to vanish when the government was no longer determined to uphold the law. But Lacoste and Laurent from the civil servants federation warned that those who considered the June strikes of 1936 a justification for 'mere trade-unionist' activity overlooked the large extent to which political factors had contributed to the success of the Popular Front and to its labor legislation. They emphasized that the new place which French labor occupied in the framework of existing state institutions implied that it also assume political responsibilities. [50]

On the whole, such warnings remained unheeded. The practical participation of union officials in the administration of the new legislation gave excellent results—as long as the new legislation was allowed to function normally. But since the CGT went through the new experience almost unwittingly, the failure of the Popular Front added to the confusion of the leadership and precipitated the reflux of membership.

IV

The Shoals of Economic Reform

THIS study, concerned as it is with organized labor rather than with the vicissitudes of government, will not discuss the reasons for the failure of the Popular Front, the conditions under which it would have been permitted to succeed, and the relationship, if any, of the Blum experiment to the downfall of France in 1940.[1] By its own decision the CGT bore no governmental responsibility in the French 'New Deal.' It played an important part in rousing the masses toward the formation of the Popular Front, but it did not determine the fate of what had become an alliance of political parties. One of the issues that shadowed the existence of the Popular Front from its very inception cannot, however, be neglected: the problem of economic reform. This was fundamental in the dissensions that harried France between the wars, and it was the focus of an important divergence of opinion between the Popular Front and organized labor, even though organized labor was not itself of one mind on the matter. Hence the following pages, without attempting a full picture of the government's economic policies, will outline the views of the CGT regarding economic reform, and the consequences that the economic actions of the Popular Front had on the trade-union movement.

I

At the Toulouse Congress of Unification the CGT had unanimously approved the adherence of the trade-union movement to the Popular Front. But even then fundamental differences had

60

appeared over the question whether the CGT should maintain its own program of economic action or adopt the Popular Front program drafted in January 1936. The communists favored the second solution; the majority of the newly constituted CGT emphatically advocated the rallying of the working class and of democratic forces behind the 'plan' which the CGT had accepted before the reunification. What was later called 'planism' had originated in the very last period of the free German labor movement. At a time when political reaction and the rise of Nazism had already suffocated the German republic, a group of intellectuals, active both in the trade unions and in the social democratic party, outlined as a new program a 'plan' which advocated the establishment, under the leadership of the labor movement, of a system of mixed economy.

The Belgian, Henri de Man, then professor in Frankfurt am Main, had a strong influence on this last-minute attempt at reorientation. De Man, his thinking determined to a large extent by developments he had witnessed in the German labor movement, traced back the bureaucratic conservatism of party and trade unions to a passive determinism buried in Marxist doctrines.[2] The inability shown by traditional reformism as well as by communism to deal adequately with the economic crisis and with the growing danger of fascism convinced de Man that only a wholly new form of action could save the labor movement. The crisis could be overcome by nothing short of a reform of the very structure of the capitalist system. Fascism could be successfully opposed only if the labor movement, by a revision of its tactics and its psychological approach, gained the support of the middle classes.

On his return to Belgium after Hitler's advent to power, de Man, with undeniable success, promoted planist ideas in his mother country. At least for a certain time he created for these ideas an almost mystical enthusiasm among the most miserable of the Belgian workers, the miners of the Borinage. From Bel-

gium the movement quickly spread to the French CGT. Marxism
had never deeply penetrated the French trade-union movement,
and there had always been great distrust of the German labor
movement. Thus a doctrine which criticized both found a pro-
pitious soil.' De Man was greatly admired, especially by that
group within the trade-union movement which monopolized the
educational activities of the CGT.³

Shortly after World War I the so-called 'Minimum Program'
and subsequent proposals submitted by the CGT had already
presented a fairly coherent plan for postwar reconstruction,
based on a thorough economic reorganization of society. In two
respects this program had been a departure from previous syndicalist beliefs. First, it no longer spoke in the interest of the
laboring classes alone, but endeavored to promote the interests
of the whole nation, and hence abandoned any mere pressure-
group outlook. And second, instead of clinging to the old socialist conception of nationalizing all means of production and trade,
it asked for the socialization only of mines, transportation, and
power energies. The proprietors of the enterprises to be nationalized were to be at least partly compensated. Industries and
trades that were not, or not yet, regarded as suitable for socialization were to be co-ordinated, rationalized, and fitted into the
framework of a planned economy.⁴

It cannot be ascertained what would have been the fate of this
program if its promoter, the labor movement, had been able to
maintain the strength it reached for a short time after the war.
As it was, the CGT, torn by internal dissensions, unable to cope
with the aggressiveness of a strengthened French capitalism, and
dismayed by the failure of the general strike in 1920, was brought
near to collapse, and its program of reconstruction fell into almost complete oblivion.

In the following decade the economic crisis, the threat of
fascism, and de Man's propagandistic success in Belgium drew
attention anew to the objectives of democratic planning. Especially in a country where the general resentment of trusts and

monopolies was rising, and where the middle classes occupied an important social and a not negligible economic position, the objectives of planism seemed to invite wide support.

Conscious of the fact that a purely negative resistance to fascism could not attain definite results, the CGT started the movement for a plan immediately after the events of February 1934. The elaboration of the plan was in itself an achievement of collaboration between the labor movement and intellectuals, for a great number of outstanding economists and lawyers participated in it. The final draft of the plan gave a thorough analysis of the French economic and political crisis and proposed broad structural reforms.[5]

The plan started off by recommending, for a speedy economic recovery, a series of emergency measures, some of which the Blum government put into practice two years later. Among the measures it called for were a 40-hour week, extensive public works and paid vacations for the resorption of unemployment, a National Wheat Office and a general revaluation of farm products for the alleviation of the agricultural crisis. The plan went on to declare, however, that 'these immediate measures, intended to fight the economic crisis, presuppose, in order to be efficient, a transformation of the structure' of the country. It was considered necessary, if social reforms were to be maintained, to transfer a sector of economy to public ownership and to nationalize the credit system.

Since the inadequate organization of public and private credit was considered one of the worst handicaps of French economic life, a thorough overhauling of the entire banking apparatus was advocated. A public credit system that would strengthen the co-operative banks (Banques Populaires) and establish a government deposit bank was to be supplemented by a strict public control of private banking institutions. The Bank of France, transferred to public ownership, was to become a central organ for the regulation of a planned economy. As in the program of 1919-20, the so-called 'key industries,' now defined as consisting of the entire armament industry, mining, power plants, and transportation, were to be socialized and be administered by councils composed of representatives of producers, consumers, and the public interest. In other sectors of the economy, private ownership would not be abolished, but all enterprises would be subject to directives of a Superior Economic Council. To this Council much broader powers were to be assigned than to the existing National Economic Council. In explicit condemnation of any corporative scheme, however, the supremacy of the parliament was upheld. Indeed, it was hoped that parliamentary institutions would be strengthened by reforms relieving them from the pressure of interest groups.

The promoters of the plan hoped that it could become a new 'myth,' similar in force to the myth of the general strike during an earlier period of the labor movement. But the first attempts to propagandize the new program were not too encouraging. In 1934, when the CGT called for a mass meeting in favor of the plan, the streets of Paris were covered with posters in which the communists exhorted the workers to demonstrate against the 'fascist plan' of the CGT, and the meeting finally had to be called off.[6] When the economic program of the Popular Front was under discussion in 1935, the representatives of the CGT vainly attempted to have the plan accepted by all member organizations. The Popular Front program, as finally decided upon, was merely a catalogue of electoral promises which did not, except in vague terms, consider how popular aspirations could be fulfilled in the face of the well-known weakness of France's economic structure.[7] Both the communist and the radical-socialist parties opposed the inclusion of more fundamental reforms. Nationalization was requested only for war industries, typically enough not for economic reasons but under the slogan 'Defense of the Peace.' In regard to the Bank of France, the controversial question of credit control was evaded by a sweeping generality: the Banque de France should become the Banque de la France.

At the Congress of Toulouse the situation was similar. The

former CGTU members opposed the CGT plan and recommended its abandonment in favor of the economic program of the Popular Front. The Popular Front movement, they said, had already been able to mobilize the masses, while the CGT plan had developed enthusiasm nowhere. The most modest accomplishments would give strength to the workers and eventually open the path toward revolution, whereas the reformist illusions of the plan endeavored to perpetuate capitalism.

Into this criticism of the plan entered various, not to say contradictory, motives which were not all revealed in the debates at Toulouse. There was the old rather genuine communist distrust of all methods short of outright revolutionary action. There was also a prejudice against any attempt at establishing a planned economy outside the Soviet Union. It was feared that the 'myth' of the Russian Five-Year plans would suffer if it were admitted that any planning was possible without being preceded by a revolution under the leadership of the communist party. In the communist polemics the CGT plan was often compared with the American New Deal of the first period, and equally censured.

But the foremost reason for the communists' opposition to the plan was the fact that by that time their primary concern was the strengthening of France's material and moral war potential. In 1935 Laval had obtained Stalin's much publicized approval of the French rearmament effort. And there could be no doubt that the far-reaching reform proposals of the CGT plan were bound to antagonize big business and lead to unwelcome disturbances. It may well be that the communists, at least for a time, believed, though erroneously, that opposition to any radical request, such as the plan's plea for nationalization, would serve to eradicate former distrust and to establish the *union sacrée* of the vast majority of the French nation. The communist attitude during the June strikes of 1936 showed sufficiently and clearly that Soviet Russia at that period feared any upheaval which could endanger national unity and defense production.

Since the communists represented only a minority it was de-

cided at Toulouse, in spite of their opposition, to regard the plan
as the programmatic platform of the reunified trade-union movement. No real synthesis was established, however, between foes
and friends of planism. Only the speakers for the civil servants
federation, especially Robert Lacoste, one of its secretaries, and
André Delmas, secretary-general of the teachers federation, revealed the real dilemma. Making predictions that were to prove
all too precise, both declared that the program of the Popular
Front was totally insufficient. Without fundamental reforms a
mere increase in purchasing power would not be sufficient to
overcome the economic slump. A devaluation would be unavoidable, even though the Popular Front parties had waged their electoral campaigns under the imprudent slogan, 'Neither devaluation
nor deflation.' Reactionary circles would eagerly look out for
errors and final failure, both inescapable, if the program was
allowed to be muffled by the pressures of economic and financial
distress. After the hopes which the people had fastened on the
Popular Front were disappointed, the way would be opened for
French fascism.

But these speakers who so strongly criticized the Popular
Front program did not deny that even a technically irreproach-
able 'plan' would leave unanswered questions of primary importance. How would it be possible to mobilize sufficient strength
behind the proposals for structural reforms? Who would bring
pressure to bear for their realization, since the future goven-
ment was bound only by the Popular Front program and since
the organized forces in the country either were not strong
enough or were unwilling to throw their weight into a struggle
for the plan? In the socialist party there was a generally friendly
disposition toward the objectives of the plan, but the debates at
the Congress of Toulouse showed clearly that the communist
party could not be counted upon to exercise its influence in the
direction of basic reforms. Therefore no unanimous or vigorous
action in favor of the plan could be expected from the new
CGT, with its strong communist minority. During the changing

fortunes of the Popular Front period, promoters and opponents of the plan clung to their positions in endless and sterile controversies.

II

When Léon Blum declared before the Chamber that the aim of his government was not to transform the social system but to carry out the program of the Popular Front, and when he declared before the Senate that the objective of the experiment bearing his name was to 'attain a certain amount of social progress and human equality within the legal framework of the republican regime and within the system of society and property which is the present system of France,' [8] he disclaimed any intention of instituting such fundamental economic changes as were proposed in the plan of the CGT. The economic reforms initiated by the Popular Front government, while not altogether negligible, cannot be compared in importance with the social legislation. In its measures extending the hold of the state on French economy the government merely amplified trends that had also been present under the reactionary governments of Flandin or Tardieu.[9]

The reform of the Bank of France ended the rule of the former regents. Jouhaux, as secretary-general of the CGT, became one of the new members of the Bank's Council. But the government's attempt to nationalize the Bank or to turn its reform into a reform of the French credit and currency system was frustrated by the combined resistance of the Senate and the communists, the latter declaring that this was no time for a 'Marxist expropriation.' [10] At the very first meeting of the new General Council of the Bank it became clear that the new Governor, just as his predecessor had been, was empowered and determined to act as a brake on the government's financial policy.

When the government had to devaluate the franc, in the fall of 1936, its action was approved by the majority of the CGT, which for a long time had recognized the necessity of an operation postponed only too long for fear of unfavorable political reactions. But the fact that currency manipulation always met with popular distrust, especially after the inflation and subsequent devaluation of the 1920's, was reason enough for the communist trade unionists to denounce the measure as being in contradiction with the Popular Front program.[11]

Because of its tardiness, certain technical ineptitudes in its operation, and the general problems which hung over France, the devaluation brought about only an ephemeral and, in comparison with the results in other countries, altogether disappointing improvement of the economic situation. Since budgetary deficits persisted, and since such deficits were regarded by wide circles in France as an immediate peril to the currency, the flight of French capital—which had started long before the Blum government—ceased only for a short time after the devaluation. It was soon considered likely that under these conditions a further devaluation of the franc could not be avoided. The Popular Front program contained a provision which would have permitted exchange restrictions and penalties for exporters of capital. But the first Blum government hesitated to take measures which an adroit propaganda had denounced in every corner of the country as leading inevitably to a totalitarian control of economy and Gestapo-like restrictions on individual liberties. Vacillating between the desire to practice deficit spending and the hope of inspiring capital with 'confidence,' the government almost passively looked on while the country was drained of funds by the flight of capital. Most of the remaining credit was absorbed by the growing needs of the public treasury, which had to turn to the private banks every month to meet its deficits.

Under such conditions the government saw no other way than to call for a 'pause' in the striving for new social gains. This, which it did in February 1937, actually meant an attempt to return to a more orthodox financial policy. A reduction of the deficit was sought by abandoning the public works program, which had never been as extensive as the CGT had proposed. By placing at the head of currency and credit manipulation three eminent 'technicians' fundamentally opposed to the principles of the French New Deal, it was hoped to soothe the fears of capital.[12] When these technicians resigned their posts, four months later, their action was the signal for the banks and the Senate to force the resignation of the Blum government.

A few days before Blum announced the 'pause,' Jouhaux, speaking at a vast public meeting, not only warned that the hour of revenge was dawning for the French reactionaries, but also declared that the CGT considered the realization of its plan the only way to turn the initial successes of the Popular Front into permanent gains. Nevertheless, certain trade-union leaders did not hesitate to approve of Blum's decision to call the pause. To them the fact that such a decision had become necessary was only proof that no substantial reforms could be obtained before the very structure of French economy had been transformed. Thus exchange control was more and more openly requested by those who spoke in the name of the trade-union movement.

After Blum had fallen and Georges Bonnet had taken over the Ministry of Finance, the CGT, on a decision of its Administrative Committee, approached the Steering Committee of the Popular Front and asked that the main points of the plan be included in the Popular Front program, since the first Popular Front government was 'driven into failure by the financial powers and the industrial trusts.' [13] But it was hopeless to obtain a favorable decision from the Popular Front Committee, which had refused a broader program of reform at an earlier moment when the dynamism of the movement was still unbroken. And the radical-socialist party, to which the new Minister of Finance and an important number of senators belonged, could not be expected to identify itself with a plea for credit control and for socialization of industries. It even disassociated itself from its partners whenever the Steering Committee of the Popular Front took a position which could be regarded as favoring exchange control.

The communists inside and outside the trade-union movement

constantly stiffened in their resistance to any structural reform. Why should one enter into a discussion of a broader program, they asked, as long as important parts of the Popular Front program were not yet realized? They were altogether deaf to the objection that more far-reaching reforms were needed in order to realize the objectives of the Popular Front in their totality. To the 'impracticable' claims of the plan the communists opposed seemingly practical but purely demagogic slogans, such as 'Let the rich pay.' There can be no doubt that the income-tax reform which the communists proposed under this formula would not have yielded results quickly enough to relieve the pressure on the financial situation of France.[14] It is even certain that in a country where large-scale income-tax evasion was prevalent, and hence where the tax system was based mainly on indirect taxation, thorough reforms would have had to cover more than the tax laws if a change of income-tax rates were to be rendered effective. But these further reforms were the very ones that were repudiated by the communists.

When the program of the Popular Front had been formulated in January 1936, the communists had not refrained from criticizing its proposals for economic recovery as partly 'childish and utopian.' Then they had declared they would hold to their own program and continue to fight for the 'French Soviet Republic.' [15] The fact that hardly a year later they had become the most ardent defenders of the Popular Front platform, and regarded it as a maximum program, seems to be due to their constantly growing reluctance to make any pronouncements which they believed might be harmful to the national unity they hoped to promote. They did not even discuss whether the country's potentialities for defense might be furthered by a gradual transition to a planned economy.[16]

On the other hand, the promoters of the CGT plan had no success whatever in arousing popular enthusiasm or even interest for their reform proposals. The more that actual job control slipped away from the unions, and the more their influence was diminished by a falling away of membership, the more unrealistic appeared the bold requests of the plan. It began to be clear that the campaign against the 'two hundred families,' which had been so successful in the elections of 1936, had not succeeded in bringing about an understanding of the impasses of French economy and politics. The initial successes of the Popular Front and the sentimental value of the sudden growth of labor organizations had completely turned away public attention from reform proposals of a more fundamental character.

The report which the executive officers of the CGT submitted to the National Congress at Nantes in the fall of 1938—the first to be held since the Congress of Toulouse—summed up the situation in these words:

Basically, the weakness of the Popular Front is that it did not achieve the fundamental part of its program. Its task was to safeguard democracy from the attacks of fascism, to liberate it from the forces of money, to restore to the country the freedom of its decisions and of its destiny. The Popular Front did not do so, and now the forces of reaction are raising their heads and using the possibilities of action which were left at their disposal.[17]

In Nantes it was no longer with a unanimous vote, as in Toulouse, but only with a majority of votes that the CGT decided to maintain its connection with the Popular Front. An important minority, led by Georges Dumoulin, secretary of the regional union of the Nord, and by André Delmas, secretary of the teachers federation, requested that the CGT leave the Popular Front and become the core of an 'anti-capitalist movement.'[18] But at that period the divergence between majority and minority on this issue was no longer of practical importance. The Popular Front was already dead.

III

By the end of 1938 the rise in earnings which Matignon, collective bargaining, and subsequent awards had obtained for labor was completely wiped out by the rise in prices. Estimates of the annual amount of earned wages and salaries show a total of 87.4 billion francs for 1935 and 133.0 billion for 1938, a rise of 52 per cent. But between November 1935 and November 1938 the cost of living in the whole of France rose by nearly 55 per cent.[19] While in specific industries and skills the increase of earnings was higher than the average, and the rise in living costs was not uniform in every region, on the whole the picture conveyed by these average figures is substantially correct. Thus though the workers still had such important advantages as vacations with pay and, at least for a time, the 40-hour week, in general their real income was no higher than in the worst year of the depression.[20] The inability of the government to keep down the cost of living by effective price control [21] resulted in a general skepticism concerning the repeated announcements that henceforth prices would be frozen at prevailing levels.

The monthly number of workers on strike between October 1936, when the excitement of the wave of sit-down strikes had died down, and February 1938, before Blum came to power a second time, averaged 35,600.[22] This number, a mere 0.44 per cent of all wage earners employed in private industry and trade, was never high enough to explain the unsatisfactory development of production. (The index of industrial production, with 1929 as 100, rose between 1935 and 1938 only from 72.5 to 76.1, while the corresponding figures for Germany were 94.0 and 126.2, and those for Great Britain 105.6 and 115.5.[23]) But the number of strikes was sufficient to put an additional strain on the cohesion of the various organizations gathered in the Popular Front, and soon on that of the CGT itself. Moreover, the strikes were a symbol of a rather considerable unrest among the workers.

There were several factors behind this restlessness. For one thing, the workers were concerned at the progressive loss of the economic advantages they had obtained so shortly before, in the early phase of the Blum experiment. No less important was the unwillingness of management to co-operate with labor and to further the normalization of industrial relations, an attitude which very often bordered on the deliberate provocation of conflicts and seemed to endanger even the more permanent features of the social legislation. Political and psychological conditions also contributed to the unrest. Memory of the easy successes of the June strikes was coupled with genuine disappointment about the fact that the Popular Front majority had fallen from power almost as quickly as had the moderately progressive governments established after the elections of 1924, 1928, and 1932. The 'iron law' of the French republic seemed unalterable—the law that at the polls the voters expressed their sympathy for a left formation which before long had to give way to a government of the right. And, finally, a still further factor was the eagerness of the communists to become the most ardent protagonists of the workers' demands, in order to widen their influence.

As early as April 1937, Jouhaux, in one of his best and most balanced speeches, complained about certain union organizers who did not hesitate to launch strikes without sufficient consideration and preparation, and who did so only in order to make themselves popular and to increase their chances in future elections to important trade-union posts.[24] Jouhaux's remark was clearly aimed at the communists, who no longer sought, as in the June strikes, to exercise a moderating influence on the workers. The communists had not hesitated to pursue their old tactics of 'boring from within,' or 'colonization,' as it was commonly called in France. Also, after the massive influx of new members, they had become very active in promoting the everyday interests of the rank and file, while many of the officials of the old CGT, accustomed to move in the secluded circles of workmen who considered themselves the vanguard of their class, were directing insufficient attention to the needs of a mass organization.

The communists' desire to champion the workers' demands was only apparently in contradiction with their reluctance to agree to any radical reform proposal on the grounds that it might be prejudicial to national unity. Actually, their primary concern was never to lose contact with the masses; for they were confident that as long as they had this contact, they would be able to use their influence to whatever ends were dictated by the interests of the Soviet Union. Some strikes, such as the one of the city workers of Paris in December 1937, which led to a momentary interruption of all urban transportation and caused hostile reactions in public opinion, were regarded by many as a mere demonstration of force by communist-dominated unions.[25]

The situation which arose in March 1938, when Léon Blum, for a second and short time, became head of the government, was typical. In the preceding months disputes had arisen inside and outside of Paris, as a result of the workers' demands for wages adapted to the rising costs of living or of their protests against the dismissal of active union members. A conflict in the metal industry of Paris was smoldering, but it broke out only after the second Blum government came to power. Then, during the two months of March and April, 213,000 workers struck, almost as many as during the entire preceding year. Management showed all its intransigence, in order to create difficulties for the government. But also the communists, whose influence within the Paris metal workers union was predominant, revealed an extraordinary eagerness to see the strike movement expand. Their attitude toward the second Blum government was pronouncedly hostile, because they judged it, not incorrectly, extremely weak at a moment when external tension called for a strong cabinet. While it is true that for a second time Blum had to capitulate before the resistance of the Senate, it is also true that once more the communists joined hands with the Senate in doing everything in their power to make Blum's task impossible. Soon after the installation of Prime Minister Daladier, a favorite with the communists until the day he signed the Munich pact, the social agitation ceased, as if touched by a magician's rod, and without the workers obtaining any advantages. A communist evening paper lyrically spoke of the Easter bells ringing the resurrection of armament production.[26]

The non-communist members in the directing bodies of the CGT and its affiliated organizations, in spite of their deep concern about some of the strikes, never opposed them openly. They did not wish to appear to be either approving the attitude of management or breaking the solidarity of the workers' organization. Actually this solidarity no longer existed. The internal disunity of the CGT, which had become apparent even in the debates at the Congress of Unification, had by 1938 reached in many unions the stage of veritable 'civil war.' But this aspect of the problem is reserved for another chapter.

Not only the rapprochement of the two dominant labor groups but also that of labor and the middle classes was breaking up by the middle of 1938. Urban and rural middle classes had slowly but steadily been alienated from the proletariat, and many of those who had followed the plea of the Popular Front to unite against the 'money wall' and the 'two hundred families' now believed in the existence of a dark plot between the trusts and Blum or Jouhaux.

The social legislation of 1936 had placed a much heavier burden on small and medium-sized enterprises than on the important concerns. Although the CGPF and its affiliated organizations complained about the sharp rise in net costs which the Matignon Agreement caused, the most important industrial enterprises announced for 1937 much higher net profits than in 1936. In the chemical industry the rise amounted to 112 per cent, in the metal industry to 78 per cent, in the food industry to 39 per cent; the average rise for the 122 most important concerns in the country was 36 per cent.[27] Both the working classes and big business were able to offset the increases in prices which the Popular Front had caused. But since production had increased only insignificantly, the costs of the experience had to be borne by others. Persons with fixed incomes and the smaller enterprises were the victims. For the smaller enterprises the difficulties were actually great. Attempts to relieve them by granting special loans were limited by the general credit policy of the banks, for the latter, after a short time, imposed their conditions also on the beneficiaries of these loans.

The June strikes of 1936 had found everywhere the full sympathy of the population. But the recurrence of labor conflicts, which though they scarcely influenced the level of production were often unnecessarily spectacular, aroused the hostility of the middle classes.

For a time the farmers, especially in wheat-growing regions, remained faithful to the Popular Front, which had established the National Wheat Office and assured higher agricultural prices. But the reduction of working time to 40 hours, whatever may have been its economic consequences, was often resented in the countryside. In the eyes of the farmer, collective bargaining and arbitration made it relatively easy for the worker to adapt himself to the rising prices, while the seller of agricultural products was at a disadvantage.

Even after the Popular Front had been broken, inside and outside of Parliament, the forces of militant fascism hardly gained in influence until the outbreak of the war. But a hope had vanished—the hope nurtured by a large part of the population that republican institutions could be affirmed through a rejuvenation of France. The bright expectations of 1936 were followed by a distrustful apathy.

V

The Issue of National Defense

I

A T the outbreak of World War I the French trade-union
movement swung from violent anti-militarism to fervent
patriotism with a suddenness which left many observers per-
plexed and which was unsurpassed even by the simultaneous
turnabout of the German social democrats.

Only a year earlier, Jouhaux, already secretary-general of the
CGT, had proclaimed that French workers would never be naive
enough to die on the battlefields for the interests of the French
capitalists, since they knew that their only enemy was the class
enemy within the borders.[1] The trade unions affiliated with the
CGT had engaged in active anti-militarist propaganda among
French soldiers. Among the workers the belief was aroused that
on the day of mobilization a general strike would not only prevent the outbreak of hostilities but also tear asunder the despised
capitalist state. The government, alarmed by such an attitude,
had prepared a long list, the so-called Carnet B, of 'dangerous elements' that had to be arrested on the first day of mobilization, in
the event of a war. The names of all prominent union leaders
were listed in this carnet.

On the very eve of the war, 30 July 1914, *Le Peuple* had addressed the trade-union members with a dramatic cry of 'Down
with the war.' The next day the Administrative Committee of
the CGT had appealed to the international proletariat to unite
efforts for the preservation of peace. The workers of Paris were
asked to demonstrate against the war on the following day, 1
August.

Four days later, after the general mobilization had been decreed but before the Chamber had voted the military credits, Jouhaux suddenly reversed the previous attitude of the CGT. In a speech at the funeral of the socialist leader Jean Jaurès, who had been assassinated by a reactionary fanatic, Jouhaux declared that the French workers were ready for punitive action against the bloodthirsty rulers of the Central Powers who were responsible for the war. 'We shall be the soldiers of liberty,' he solemnly affirmed. A few hours before the German social democrats voted for the war budget of the Kaiser, the CGT in a new manifesto called upon the French workers to defend the democratic and revolutionary traditions of France against the assault of German militarism.

Later Jouhaux explained his speech at Jaurès' burial in purely sentimental terms which, though probably not quite the whole truth, were characteristic of him. According to his self-analysis he had not known what he was going to say when he went to the funeral. But once he stood before the grave he fell under the spell of the tense atmosphere of those prewar days. He lived through one of those moments, he declared, when long-buried traditions suddenly and unexpectedly come to the fore. While he was delivering his speech, such traditions reemerged and swept away the anti-militarist creed to which French syndicalism had sworn allegiance only a few days before. Another prominent union leader, Georges Dumoulin, offered a different and more cynical explanation: 'Fear is neither syndicalist nor socialist, but human. . . In the CGT we were afraid of possible police action simply because we are human beings.' The fact that several days before the Jaurès funeral, the Minister of Home Affairs, in confidential negotiations with Jouhaux and socialist deputies, had agreed to destroy Carnet B if the CGT would abandon its previous anti-patriotic attitude, makes Dumoulin's explanation more persuasive than that of Jouhaux.[2]

The most important reason, however, for the tergiversation of the French labor movement was not psychological but political. The CGT had not really succeeded in persuading the working class to its point of view. In spite of the violence of its language its anti-patriotic propaganda had actually had but little effect on the masses. The trade-union officials grossly overestimated the success of their efforts. Since they moved almost exclusively within the small circle of convinced internationalists they had never perceived how illusionary it was to expect a revolution to break out on the first day of a war. If the CGT had dared, during the critical days of international tension in 1914, to call for a general strike against the war, the French workers, moved by patriotic sentiments, would most likely have lynched the union leaders without waiting for the action of the police.

Hence the CGT as well as the socialist party entered into a *union sacrée* with all political parties and groups on the first day of the war. When the German invasion plunged the country into grave danger Jouhaux was made a 'Commissaire à la Nation,' in which function he fled with the government to Bordeaux. It was hoped that the creation of such a post would evoke Jacobin traditions, but since the role of propaganda in modern warfare was not very effectively recognized in 1914, Jouhaux's participation in the work of the government never became practical. On the other hand the constitution of a Political Action Committee, formed by representatives of both the CGT and the socialist party, did have a certain significance. The Committee's aim was not only to guarantee the utmost resistance to the enemy from without but also to prevent any attempt at a possible capitulation before the invader. Such a capitulation was judged to be an actual threat after the first grave reverses suffered by the French army.

The entire philosophy of the Charter of Amiens had collapsed. The faith in class warfare was superseded by an affirmation of national defense; alliance with a political party was no longer deemed unclean.

But the conditions under which this change of position took

place had a definite bearing upon the future attitude of the CGT toward national issues. The unexpected conversion was so largely caused by fear and by the obvious impotence of the labor movement that a feeling of shame and betrayal prevented the leadership of the CGT from assessing the significance of the *union sacrée* experience and from defining the place which the labor movement intended to occupy within the nation. Attacks directed against the new orientation of the union movement by a revolutionary minority, relatively strong among the industrial proletariat of Paris, drove the leaders of the CGT even more into the defensive. Spontaneous strikes resulting from the rise in living costs, and later from the growing dissatisfaction about the prolongation of the war, increased the difficulties for a trade-union movement pledged to the maintenance of the *union sacrée*.[3]

Hence the cessation of hostilities in 1918 found the CGT uneasy about the course to follow. Its new program of action— the 'Minimum Program' discussed in the preceding chapter— attempted to outline the conditions under which the labor movement was willing to cooperate in the task of reconstruction. It also, for the first time in French trade-union history, took a definite stand on questions of foreign policy, by giving wholehearted support to the efforts of Woodrow Wilson; it even asked for a participation of workers' representatives at the Peace Conference. But the new program, as was related above, not only met with determined resistance from the employers but also was opposed by the masses of new trade-union members who swelled the ranks of the CGT.

When the labor movement called for powerful demonstrations on May Day 1919, it wanted to display its newly acquired strength; such a manifestation was deemed necessary also in order to express the disgruntled workers' determination to resist the attacks of management against the 8-hour day and the wage level. In Paris the May Day demonstration led, however, to an open clash with the police, and hundreds of workers were injured. As a protest against these events Jouhaux resigned his seat at the

Peace Conference. In a dramatic way the period of the *union sacrée* had ended.

From then on, and even more after the failure of the general strike in 1920, the French labor movement was once more excluded from the national collectivity. But whereas in the period before the war it had been the pride of syndicalism that it owed loyalty only to the cause of the international proletariat, in the postwar period the CGT found itself rejected from the nation's life almost against its will. The unhappy experiences of the *union sacrée*, which eventually led to both the split in the labor movement and the new isolation of labor, estopped the CGT for years from facing the question of its place in the nation. Thus, although it no longer shrank from assuming responsibilities in the framework of the existing social order, the CGT, prior to the Popular Front period, rejected any idea of a National Service law.

II

The conditions of anarchy and improvisation which had prevailed in France at the beginning of World War I in regard to everything outside of purely military mobilization were not entirely forgotten in the years preceding World War II. An empirical handling of the manpower problem and a skyrocketing of war profits, such as had occurred before during the years of France's struggle for survival, were seen as social and political dynamite in the event that the country should once more be obliged to take up arms. As early as 1924 a bill concerning the general organization of the nation for war was submitted to the Parliament. The bill had originated with the Superior Council for National Defense, and it was sponsored by influential members of the French general staff. It was defended before the Parliament by Jean Paul-Boncour, still a member of the socialist party but one of the most ardent and vociferous protagonists of Jacobin traditions.[4] The bill, which was often identified with Paul-Boncour's name, provided for broad powers of requisition which the government could exercise in wartime or in periods of serious international tension, over workers and industrial enterprises.

When the bill was discussed by the Chamber in 1927, its essential provisions were accepted by all parties with the exception of the communists.[5] The speakers for the communist party, which was then in one of its periods of violent insurrectionism, denounced the bill from the tribune of the Chamber as an instrument of war against the Soviet Union, and appealed to workers, peasants, soldiers, and sailors 'to organize and to fight without delay for the transformation of imperialist war into revolutionary class war against the bourgeoisie and its government.' It is not astonishing that the CGTU, already an entirely communist organization, joined in the opposition to the bill, which was denounced as a 'coup de force' against the trade-union movement. 'The CGTU,' read a specially issued manifesto, 'refuses to recognize the legitimacy of national defense under the capitalist system.'[6]

The socialist deputies expressed some misgivings about the bill. But after their fears that it could be used against strikers in peacetime had been soothed by assurances of the government, they voted for the law because it was, they declared, in line with the lessons taught by the socialist leader Jean Jaurès in his famous book on a people's army.[7] The CGT, although it usually followed the lead of the socialist party in legislative matters, did not do so on this occasion, and it refused to countenance the bill. Paul-Boncour declared before the Chamber that the bill aimed at associating the trade unions with national defense, as had been done during the war, but the CGT, in a statement that was marked by hesitations, indeed contradictions, declared that the bill was in opposition to the 'general feelings of the working class,' inasmuch as it 'evoked the ugly spectre of the war and its atrocities.'[8]

A year later, when the bill was debated before the Senate, the socialists no longer voted for it (there were no communist senators at that time). The pretext for this change in attitude was the modifications introduced by the Senate committee, which had eliminated Paul-Boncour's neo-Jacobin phraseology and some of the provisions against war profiteering. Actually the attitude of the socialist senators deviated from that of their colleagues in the Chamber of Deputies because the rank and file of the socialist party had expressed anxiety about the law and the vote of the socialist deputies. Also a great number of left-wing intellectuals, among them many who belonged to the socialist party, had protested against the bill as a serious infringement upon freedom of speech and intellectual independence.[9]

Nothing came of the bill. It should be remembered that that period was the heyday of genuine hope for a pacification of the European continent. Public opinion in France refused to take into account even the possibility of a new war, and thus a law which attempted to prepare for the eventuality of such a war was not viewed with sympathy. Organized labor had expressed its disapproval. But big business, too, was not eager to see a law enacted which could be used for a curtailment of its prerogatives —though the deputies and senators of the right had not been able to oppose the law openly because of the nationalist traditions which at that time were still unanimously adhered to by French conservatives. Hence the bill, in spite of its formal acceptance by vast majorities in both houses, was permitted to fall into oblivion. Technically, the modifications introduced by the Senate made a new debate before the Chamber necessary. Instead, because of the lack of general interest and in the absence of any pressure, the bill was simply shelved for more than ten years.

The measures taken by the Blum government for the strengthening of the French war potential are far less known than the broad social legislation of the Popular Front, probably because of the more controversial character of the social measures. In September 1936 the Popular Front government accepted a new program of national defense which was intended to inaugurate officially a massive rearmament of France.[10] Several months earlier, even before the Matignon Agreement provoked the wave of labor legislation, one of the very first decrees signed by Prime Minister Blum and Minister of War Daladier had established the legal conditions for requisitioning all plants working for national defense. The decree, issued by the council of ministers, stated that on 6 June 1936 the period would commence during which the government was entitled, in accordance with earlier statutes, to require the prestations necessary to supplement the army's needs for supplies.[11] If the government chose to requisition a plant the workers were under a quasi-military obligation to stay on the job. In June 1936, however, no new complications were threatening in the field of foreign relations, whereas mass strikes were sweeping the country and affecting many war industries, and thus the new decree was apparently intended to bring the workers back to work by means of requisition, if this was deemed necessary. Actually the Blum government, for political reasons, did not use this weapon against strikers. It was nevertheless important that the Popular Front government provided the legal basis for requisition procedures. The CGT does not seem to have opposed the issuance of the decree.

A law of 11 August 1936 empowered the government to nationalize the manufacture of war materials not later than 31 March 1937.[12] This authorization, too, was viewed as a means of strengthening the French war effort, and it was immensely popular because of the general aversion to the 'merchants of death' and their profitmaking. Neither the Popular Front nor the Blum government viewed the measure as a first step in the direction of broad nationalization. It was intended solely to control the armament effort of the nation and to prevent the private armament industry from alleged plotting against the cause of peace. Since the law permitted a transfer to public ownership only after the indemnification of the previous owners, the Blum government had to face economic and financial difficulties which considerably limited the extent of nationalization.

The nationalization measures that were taken hampered the

French armament effort much less than is often contended.[13] Here, as in other fields, it was not the boldness of the Popular Front which had a disrupting effect, but the half-heartedness of its measures, which endeavored to alter the mechanism of the existing order without providing new incentives.

The CGT had always favored the complete nationalization of the war industries; its 'plan' warned that limited measures were insufficient and would eventually end in failure. Most of the nationalization procedures enacted by the Blum government provided for the representation of the CGT on the board of directors of the nationalized companies,[14] and thus for the first time the French trade-union movement assumed managerial responsibilities in the production of arms. The share of the CGT in the administration of these companies looked more important on paper, however, than it was in reality.

III

In 1938, when the National Service bill which bore his name was again voted upon by the Chamber, Paul-Boncour was once more Minister of Foreign Affairs, in the second Blum government, though before the Senate took action and the bill became a law, Blum had again fallen from power and the place of the 'Jacobin' Paul-Boncour was occupied by Georges Bonnet, outstanding representative of appeasement tendencies. At that time the situation was fundamentally different from what it had been in 1927 and 1928, when the bill had first been discussed by the Chamber and the Senate. Fascist Italy, after her unresisted successes in Ethiopia, had become blatant in her desire to incorporate French territories in Africa and in Europe. Hitler's remilitarization of the Rhineland had once more brought the French frontier within the range of German guns. The annexation of Austria had upset the balance in Central Europe, where France was bound by international agreements to maintain the status quo. The 'great human peace,' which had seemed assured in the early 1920's and which the Popular Front had vowed to preserve, was threatened anew.

Both houses unanimously approved the National Service law in its entirety.[15] At least outwardly the debates seemed to indicate a high degree of national unity and the full integration of all forces in the face of the imminent threat of war.

The communist Florimond Bonte declared that the deputies of his party would vote for the bill because they desired to spare the country the dangers of improvisation in meeting the demands of war:

The communists want to put the French people in a position that will enable them to resist victoriously from the first day an attack which would try to violate their national independence and integrity. . . The working class is ready, the people are ready. . . Hence the communist deputies will give to their vote on the bill proposing a National Service law the significance of a vibrant appeal for the collaboration of all men of good will in the interest of the defense of peace and security . . . and of a progressive policy which will increase . . . the grandeur of France in the world.

The communist speaker, however, had to face a certain amount of heckling concerning the strikes that were even then breaking out in munitions factories in the Paris region, where the communist influence among the workers was undeniably predominant.

The socialist group in the Chamber declared its unmitigated approval of the bill, which it regarded as insuring an equality of sacrifice for all citizens in the event that France was precipitated into a war of defense. Once more Jaurès was quoted as having subscribed in advance to a National Service law when he wrote: 'We must always possess sufficient strength against our enemies across the borders and sufficient tenderness toward our brothers within. Through your efforts [the French workers] our country must be at the same time an entrenched camp and a garden. It should be said of our beloved France that never under such a strong coat of mail has beat a softer heart.'

The CGT no longer voiced any opposition to a bill which it had so strongly disapproved ten years before. The labor press of all shades did no more, however, than report on the parliamentary debates and on the bill's final ratification. The most far-reaching step ever taken under the Third Republic toward realizing the goal of a nation in arms appeared to be a genuine manifestation of national unity, in which at least the vast majority of the trade-union movement concurred. But the CGT was still so uncertain concerning labor's place within the nation that it approved of the law only inertly. And it did not even see fit to criticize those provisions of the law which could easily be used to sap the foundations of a democratic labor movement.

The law authorized the government to prepare measures for the utilization of the labor force of the nation not only in case of war but also if circumstances should require it in a moment of external tension. All males over 18 years of age could be requisitioned and used either individually or collectively in public services or in any establishment functioning in the interest of the nation. The entire personnel of enterprises considered indispensable in fulfilling the needs of the country could likewise be subjected to requisition. A person whose services were requisitioned was threatened by grave penalties if, without authorization, he left the work to which he had been allocated.

The law provided that such stringent measures should not be taken by the government acting alone. The most representative organizations of management and labor had to consult with the authorities on all questions of importance. It was intended to maintain also in a period of national emergency the significant place which had been given for the first time by the Popular Front legislation to the corporative organizations of both sides. Cooperation of the state and labor and management was to underline the character of the National Service law as a significant expression of national unity.

The generally unsettled state of industrial relations in France, and the events which took place between the enactment of the law and the outbreak of the war, prevented the intentions of the legislators from becoming a reality.

IV

While the Congress of Nantes was in session (14-17 November 1938) the series of enactments known as the Reynaud decree laws were published.[16] The decrees tried to adapt French economy to the situation created by the 'peace of Munich.' Since it was believed that war had been avoided, at least for a considerable time, the plan for economic recovery which the decrees outlined spanned a period of three years.[17] It was obvious that the armament effort of the major European nations would only grow in intensity, and therefore the decrees endeavored to tear down whatever barriers remained in the way of an increase in production. In 1938 production had fallen to a level 25 per cent below that of 1930.

In the blunt language of Paul Reynaud, then Finance Minister and the intellectual father of the entire project, the introduction to the decree stated that 'France has tried budgetary deflation, fiscal strictness, and expansion of credit, one after another. The remedies have varied. The disease, aggravated as it is, remains.' Since the political situation which prevailed in the fall of 1938 did not permit even a thought of seeking a solution in a transformation of the country's economic structure, the new decrees attempted to solve the dilemma by a forthright combination of previously tried policies. The main emphasis was laid on restoration of the confidence of capital in order to overcome the reluctance to invest.

To achieve this goal the 'liberalization' of the 40-hour week was considered by the reports introducing the decree laws to be one of the 'fundamental principles of action.' The work-hour legislation of 1936 was maintained 'in principle,' but actually the decree laws not only sharply condemned the previous schedule of five 8-hour days but also, in effect, removed most of the restrictions on hours of labor.[18] The 40 hours remained merely as the point at which overtime rates became payable. At the same time these rates were reduced, as far as the first 250 hours of overtime a year were concerned, to 10 per cent above the regular hourly rate, notwithstanding contrary provisions in collective agreements which in general had fixed overtime rates at a minimum of time and a quarter. In this respect, therefore, the governmental decree laws interfered directly with the contractual stipulations of employers and workers. The refusal of a worker to work overtime in the interest of national defense was declared a breach of his employment contract, and involved a serious handicap for his future employment. Anyone trying to induce others to refuse to work overtime was liable to imprisonment and a fine.

From the inception of the Popular Front program, management and an important section of the press had maintained that if French production was lagging behind that of other countries, this was due solely to the limitation on working hours, and that work in defense industries was suffering gravely from the new legislation. Actually, however, it is out of the question to lay the major blame for the insufficiency of French production on the legal provisions for the shorter work week.[19]

The influence of the 40-hour legislation on the situation in the labor market had been negligible. If the trade-union movement had hoped for a complete resorption of unemployment by the new legislation, it labored under a misconception of the unemployment problem in France. Between September 1936 and September 1938 the number of (assisted) unemployed had diminished by only 75,000. And when management complained that the 40-hour week caused a dearth of labor in vital activities, its assertions were equally belied by the official statistics. In September 1938 there were in the entire country no more than 4,015 offers of work which could not be filled; in all defense industries the number was no higher than 355.[20] True, the official inquiry into production stated in its final report that while there was no labor shortage in general, some industries found it difficult to obtain certain types of skilled labor. But the same report mentioned as responsible for this situation a long list of factors entirely outside the field of the wage-hour legislation.[21]

General perplexity was created by the fact that the introduction of the 40-hour week had resulted in the five-day week, and that therefore not only employees' hours but also plant hours were limited. But neither the basic statute nor the decrees of application had forbidden employees or plants to work more than five days a week; Prime Minister Léon Blum himself had stated that the five-days-of-eight-hours formula did not seem to him a happy solution.[22] The reason why the trade unions nevertheless pressed for this scheme is that, in their opinion, the organization of work in relays and in rotation might lead to violations of the law on the part of management. It was feared that because of the notorious insufficiency of the labor inspectorate in France— there were no more than 172 inspectors for the entire country —such violations could be forestalled only by closing the plants for two days. The most plausible reason why the five-day work week was favored also by the employers and their organizations is that they were concerned with keeping down costs at a moment when the new labor legislation had caused a notable increase in the cost of production. The failure of French management to seek a more even distribution of costs by a new organization of the work corresponded to its general mentality during this period, to the weakening of 'the creative spirit and the willingness to take risks,' as Paul Reynaud formulated it in his general report introducing the decree laws. It has been maintained, too, that certain employers were eager to see the 40-hour week applied in a way that would discredit it in the eyes of public opinion.

The system that had been adopted permitted additional workers to be employed only in so far as there was extra space available in the plants. The few existing statistics reveal that most industries not only limited the work of men to 40 hours but also worked the machinery only 40 hours, instead of hiring additional workers. In December 1937, when the 40-hour week was at its height, 17 per cent of the labor employed in enterprises of 100 or more workers was working less than 40 hours, and only 0.1 per cent was working more than 40 hours. Six months later, when certain decrees had already begun to make exceptions, the percentage employed for more than 40 hours had not increased, but then 22 per cent were working less than that amount of time.[23]

The rigidities of application and the resulting inflexibility were early complained of by such prominent CGT leaders as Jouhaux and Belin, both of whom warned that the 40-hour principle must be applied to different industries in different ways.[24] In practice little or no advantage was taken even of the possibilities for a more liberal application which the basic statute as well as the various decrees had offered. As to defense work, the new legislation had never placed an upper limit on hours in such industries; the Inquiry into Production admitted that workers' organizations had always agreed to conform with any exception necessary to the interests of defense, and that they asked only for protection against abuses. Nevertheless it was repeatedly stated that the 40-hour week slowed down French defense production; and when Premier Daladier, in August 1938, made a rather violent attack against the work-hour legislation, one of his main arguments was that it was intolerable to see defense industries work only 40 hours.[25]

Actually it was much less the wage-hour legislation of 1936 than the generally unsettled conditions in the field of industrial relations which were detrimental to production. As early as June 1936 Léon Blum had emphasized that for a smooth application of the 40-hour week frequent and direct contacts between labor and management would be indispensable.[26] But organized labor, while on principle inclined to respond to necessities of production, often hesitated to enter upon the path of direct negotiations for fear of 'abuses.' And management refrained from hiring new manpower even when and where it was available, for fear of union control.[27] The slowness and inadequacy of the administrative procedures involved in such matters as the granting of overtime hours, or the extension of provisions in collective trade agreements, only added to the difficulties.

It would be natural to assume that the 40-hour legislation, badly handled though it was, had at least the virtue of increasing labor productivity, by diminishing overwork and fatigue. Actually, however, average productivity declined in almost all branches of industry.[28] Insufficient replacement of obsolete machinery had its share of responsibility for this decline. In addition, the trade-union leadership never clearly faced the issue, and the labor press did not draw attention to the necessity of supplementing the shortening of the work week by an increase in productivity. The 'strike atmosphere' which prevailed in many industrial centers, where communist trade unionists were often eager to launch strikes for political motives, was in some instances detrimental to labor productivity. The decisive factor, however, was again the lack of agreement between the partners in industrial relations, and later the general discouragement into which the disappointing outcome of the Popular Front experiment had thrown the working class. And this decrease in productivity constituted still another reason why the objectives of the 40-hour legislation were defeated.

The Reynaud decrees modified the previous wage-hour legislation at a moment when there was a slow-down in orders, and as an objective observer remarked, this situation by no means called for an abolition of the 40-hour week.[29] Even in February 1939, several months after the decrees were published, only 19 per cent of all workers in establishments with over 100 workers were employed for more than 40 hours. Since the corresponding figure for November 1938 had been 8 per cent,[30] and since the previous legislation would have permitted considerably more overtime work than was actually furnished, it is evident that the decree laws had only small, if any, influence in lengthening the work week. The introductory reports to the decrees mentioned numerous facts which in themselves would have sufficed to explain the unsatisfactory level of production. If, nevertheless, the same reports described the substantial change in the previous wage-hour legislation as a fundamental reform, they did so because with the increasing international tension the question of the 40-hour week had become a political issue. Just as the labor movement, before 1936, had placed considerable hopes on the shortening of the legal work week, in 1938 important sectors of French industry decided to make the *de facto* abolition of the wage-hour legislation the price for their participation in the country's armament effort. The Popular Front government, yielding to various influences and entirely determined by groping empiricism, had permitted the 40-hour week to be applied with harmful rigidity. The Daladier government, desperately trying to obtain the unmitigated support of French industry for the speeding-up of war production, even at the price of alienating organized labor, complied with the demands of management to an extent which was certainly not justified by Paul Reynaud's views on the French crisis.

v

Only against this background can the reactions of the labor movement to the new decrees be explained. During the Czechoslovakian crisis it was explicitly admitted in official publications of the CGT that the trade-union movement was ready to accept a temporary modification of the 40-hour week in certain industries, as a measure for strengthening the defense potential of the country; it was added that the international situation had created problems graver than those of the 40-hour week. The point on which the CGT insisted was that the trade unions should be consulted on these questions.[31]

Hence when Prime Minister Daladier, in his somewhat choleric speech of 22 August 1938, demanded the abolition of the previous legislation and the limitation of overtime rates, and shortly thereafter, when a decree rendered it unnecessary to consult the trade unions in granting exceptions to the 40-hour week,[32] the CGT voiced the sharpest opposition. Its Administrative Committee pointed out that since many undertakings were working much less than 40 hours, the extension of statutory hours was illogical. It stated that employers 'systematically refused to make use of the overtime provided by decrees and agreements,' and it admonished the workers, 'without losing the necessary calm to be ready for the unanimous and disciplined action which the defense of the 40-hour week and of other social gains may possibly require.' One of the communist secretaries of the CGT threatened in a speech that strike action would be taken if the legislation of 1936 were attacked.[33]

But the Reynaud decrees embodied all of Daladier's earlier proposals and definitely abolished any consultation with the labor organizations in regard to the length of the work week in specific industries. Public statements by leading political personages that, as a logical consequence of Munich, France would have to follow the totalitarian pattern in various respects, and would probably have to establish concentration camps for the opponents of the government,[34] made the new decrees appear as the first step in a limitation of civil liberties. The penalties with which the decrees threatened anyone who dissuaded workers from working overtime were regarded as infringing upon the liberty of action of the trade unions.

All through the sessions of the CGT Congress in Nantes the communist delegates loudly voiced their indignation about the new legislation.[35] Since the decrees had just appeared in the *Journal officiel*, since their technicalities were rather intricate, and the consequences they would have on the situation of the workers not easy to measure, it is not astonishing that the actual content of the decrees was hardly discussed. Because of the symbolic significance which the question of the 40-hour week had taken, it was enough to stress the fact that the government considered the modification of the existing legislation a major point in its action. The insistence with which the communists discussed only the decree laws, while their opponents of the *Syndicats* group debated the 'colonization' of the trade-union movement by the communists, gave the latter a welcome occasion to boast that they were the truest defenders of working-class interests.

It was evident in the debates at Nantes that the communists' opposition to the government's foreign policy was at least as great as their wrath about Reynaud's rehabilitation program. In numerous telegrams of protest which communist-influenced trade unions sent to the Congress presidium, as well as in some of the speeches, it was suggested that the decrees be regarded as 'not existing'; the demand for a resort to the ultimate weapon, the general strike, was distinctly raised. And since it was not within the power even of a successful general strike to nullify legislation, the communist plea could have had no other aim than to overthrow, with the aid of a popular movement, the cabinet which had conducted the Munich accord. It was well known that within the Daladier government itself some ministers disapproved of the appeasement policy, and therefore such hopes did not appear wholly far-fetched.

The attitude which the non-communist trade unionists took toward the decree laws and a possible strike varied with their general outlook. The delegates belonging to the *Syndicats* group either avoided the question or voiced certain apprehensions about the consequences of a general strike under prevailing conditions. Jouhaux criticized the decree laws in the name of 'established legality.' The social legislation of 1936 had been voted quasi-unanimously, he argued, by a Parliament elected for four years; it could not be abolished by a merely temporary government.[36] It was well known to Jouhaux, however, that the decree powers had been legally granted to the executive by Parliament, and that therefore only Parliament could nullify the decrees. If the secretary-general of the CGT wished to draw attention to the fact that, exactly as in previous periods, a gap had developed between the way in which the country was actually ruled and the expectations that had been expressed at the preceding elections, he tried to clothe political issues in legal terms.

Jouhaux carefully prevented the Congress from committing the CGT to the calling of a general strike, and arranged that the final responsibility be left to the Administrative Committee. One week later that Committee unanimously decided to call a twenty-four hour demonstration strike on 30 November. On the eve of the strike communist trade-union leaders foretold that the 30th of November would be 'among the most memorable days of French history.' [37] Actually the almost unmitigated failure of the strike made the day memorable only for having accelerated the decline of the labor movement and contributing to the disintegration of the nation.

VI

The Dissolution of Unity

I

UNTIL the spring of 1938 the labor movement's opinions on questions of foreign policy, though increasingly divergent, did not flare into open conflict. During the fifteen years that followed the 1918 armistice there was not even any disagreement, all elements concurring in an attitude of out-and-out pacifism. This position reflected perfectly the feelings of the French working class. The ravages of World War I and the frustration of many hopes in the postwar period only bolstered the genuine aversion of the French workers to any martial adventure and contributed to their sincere horror of another massacre. It is true that it was the villages that suffered most from the carnage of the war, but because of the strong ties that unite city and country in France, the experiences of the rural population and of the urban proletariat were to a great extent mutual.

After the rise of Hitler, however, pacifism was no longer so axiomatic a doctrine. It was in 1935, after the rapprochement between France and the Soviet Union, that the communists began to depart from their previous position and to move in the direction of military preparedness.[1] The non-communist groups were slower to relinquish their uncompromising aversion to war, but among most of them faith in dogmatic pacifism was at least shaken.

This beginning of divergence on international issues was evident at the Unification Congress of Toulouse, held on the eve of Hitler's violation of the Locarno pact. There the speakers of the former CGTU intermingled old and new phraseology in a curious way. During a discussion on the problems of war and peace one of the communists declared, on the one hand, that they were not 'Tolstoyans' and that Jaurès, if he had known the situation that existed in 1936, would certainly have called for the armed defense of Soviet Russia; on the other hand, he did not altogether forget the old gospel when he expressed confidence that if a war broke out the workers would make the best of the situation and use it for their liberation.

At the Toulouse Congress the only outspoken opposition to the communist suggestions came from the old-time syndicalist elements. This faction was no longer strong within the CGT at the time of the reunification of the trade-union movement. Its partisans, however, were scattered throughout the different federations and held strongholds in the trade unions of the postal workers, teachers, proofreaders, and printers. During the debates at the Congress the spokesmen of this group maintained that no agreement between states could change the duty of the working class to oppose any war by all possible means, especially by the general strike. When one of the secretaries of the trade union of postal workers was asked to define what his and his friends' attitude would be in the event of aggression by Nazi Germany, he answered with a frank admission, which was to be reiterated often by intransigent pacifists of the French left: 'Better servitude than war!'

At that period the vast majority of the CGT was much less decided on the question of international affairs than either the communist leadership or the declared pacifists, as was evident from the haphazard way in which the discussions of Toulouse dealt with these problems. There can be no doubt, however, that most of the trade unionists were in full agreement with the position taken by the socialist leader Léon Blum, when he declared before the American Club in May 1936, after Hitler's remilitarization of the Rhineland: 'We do not even think, as our ancestors of 1792 or 1848 did, that war can have its good, its liberating and revolutionary side. It is a good many years since a great man, Jaurès, cured us of that illusion.'[2] That Jaurès' name was used to defend contradictory positions is not surprising. His authority with the labor movement was so great, and his death on the eve of the First World War had left his position toward war and peace so veiled, that both the defenders of isolationism and of internationalism constantly referred to his writings as gospel, thereby often distorting the real issues at stake.

But in the two years that followed the Toulouse Congress of March 1936 the leadership and the rank and file of the labor movement slowly crystallized their ideas on the subject of foreign policy. And the alignment that developed on this issue followed closely the old alignment on the issue of trade-union independence.

During this period preceding Hitler's coup against Austria and his first massing of armed strength against Czechoslovakia, the communists inside and outside the union movement continued to develop their new nationalist line, though it found little sympathy among the non-communists. Shortly after Hitler's remilitarization of the Rhineland in March 1936, a member of the Central Committee of the French communist party had called for the 'unity of the French nation.' After the outbreak of the civil war in Spain, in July, the communists almost completely abandoned the conception of the Popular Front and advocated instead the formation of a 'Front des Français' which would unite all Frenchmen, revolutionary or reactionary, if only they were determined to oppose Nazism and fascism.[3] But the communists, despised by the right and distrusted by most of the left, were totally unable to achieve national unity. The hand that they offered to almost everyone was rejected everywhere. Not only appeasers but also resolute opponents to isolationism denounced the communist efforts as hypocritical, and feared that the new line, based only on the demands of Russia's foreign policy, might be as subject to changes as the old.

On the other hand, despite its lack of success in the nation as a whole, the communist party undoubtedly cemented its ties with its own membership and enlarged its following among the working class by its use of a new, thoroughly nonsectarian approach and language. For the first time in its history the communist party appeared to have become a body in French politics instead of an abstract sect. The new slogan of a 'free, strong and happy France,' the appeal to *joie de vivre* and to fraternity, appealed to many who had previously shunned the party because of its divisionary tactics. A somewhat parochial patriotism was not in contradiction with the unabated dread of a new war. At least until 1938 the communists never conceded that resistance to Hitler could possibly lead to another war; instead, the policy they advocated was presented as the only way to save peace. One of the communist secretaries of the CGT, Julien Racamond, who had always enjoyed the confidence of the Parisian working-class element because of his earthy manners and his apparent lack of cynicism, became a particularly successful propagandist of the new line.[4]

Many leaders of the old CGT reacted to the nationalist accent of the communists with bitter mockery, not quite understanding its potential attraction for the masses. But since the communist efforts to gain support outside the labor movement were unsuccessful, no open conflict arose within the trade-union movement over the question of the communist-sponsored 'Front des Français.'

The government's policy of non-intervention in the Spanish civil war provoked not only the communists but also Jouhaux and many other non-communist trade-union leaders into sharp criticism of Prime Minister Blum and the other socialist cabinet ministers.[5] Blum succeeded in winning over most of the socialist party members to the views he had thought necessary to adopt,[6] but the entire CGT was committed to unconditional aid to the loyalists. Some skirmishes revealed, it is true, that the unity of views was more apparent than real. The majority of the CGT advocated assistance to the republicans as a gesture of international solidarity with a labor movement to which French syndicalists had always felt akin. The communists, on the other hand, with their slogan 'Planes for Spain,' emphasized the military necessities of effective intervention against the Spanish allies of German and Italian fascism. As early as December 1936, André Delmas, of the teachers federation, opposed the communist slogan and warned that military intervention would lead to general war and therefore should not be advocated by the union movement.[7]

The apparent unity of the CGT was still unbroken in March 1938, when Léon Blum, a few hours after Hitler's troops had entered Austria, made a desperate attempt to constitute a government of national unity extending from the extreme right to the communists. 'This will be a National Government around the working class,' he declared, 'directed by the socialists with the participation of the communists and the brotherly support of the CGT.' Unanimously the Administrative Committee of the CGT decided in favor of a 'government of public salvation invested with the confidence of the nation, capable of speaking clearly and of grouping all forces willing to safeguard peace, respect for international agreements, and the independence of the people.'[8] Both the CGT and the communists had revised to a considerable extent the attitude they had taken only two years before, when they had refused Blum's first invitation to the CGT to join the government. In an hour of national emergency both organizations were willing to share governmental responsibilities, or at least to support actively a government representing the entire nation.

But Léon Blum failed no less completely than the communists had failed in their efforts to unite the nation. In dramatic moments which Blum himself considered crucial, it became clear that major political forces in France preferred the triumph of the dictator across the Rhine to the salvation of a republic tainted by the Popular Front.[9] And the apparent unity of views within the trade-union movement did not survive the frustration of its new hopes to see established a government of national unity. After March 1938 the division of opinion on the question of war and peace became a polarization into bitterly opposed factions.

II

From the spring of 1938 every gathering of the French labor movement turned, quite contrary to previous traditions, to problems of foreign policy. At the convention which the socialist party held shortly after the German-Czech tension in May, the fundamental opposition between advocates of appeasement and those who wanted to resist any further expansion of Nazi Germany came into the open. The grave dissensions which were soon to rend the CGT were foreshadowed by the fact that at the socialist convention two delegates who were influential members of the trade-union movement gave voice to the most intransigent isolationism: Ludovic Zoretti, one of the secretaries of the teachers federation, and Georges Lefranc, director of the CGT Institute of Higher Education.[10]

At about the same time the trade-union weekly *Syndicats*, published by René Belin, assistant secretary of the CGT, fell into line with that part of the French press which advocated abandonment of the Czechoslovakian alliance.[11] After the reunification of the CGT the communists had continued to publish the former weekly of the CGTU, *La Vie ouvrière*. In spite of repeated admonitions they had refused to abandon a precious and well-handled instrument for influencing the rank and file, though such practices were certainly in contradiction with the spirit and the letter of the statutes laid down at Toulouse. A number of old-time syndicalists had retaliated by founding their own weekly, *Syndicats*. In addition to Belin these included Pierre Vigne, secretary of the miners federation; Raymond Froideval and Roy, whom the influx of the communists had removed from the direction of the metal workers and construction workers federations;

and Georges Dumoulin. Their paper, in the name of 'trade-union independence,' openly opposed the colonization tactics and often criticized the strike procedures of the communist unions. The 'Friends of *Syndicats*' and the 'Friends of *La Vie ouvrière*' constituted themselves into factions that fought each other on every occasion.[12]

A serious handicap for Belin and his friends was the unrealistic note of their thesis of 'trade-union independence.' Just as during the debates at Toulouse, their opposition to the communist party frequently turned into hostility toward any political activity of organized labor. It was among the leaders of *Syndicats* that the desire to see the CGT withdraw from the Popular Front was most outspoken. Under the pretext that they were seeking a return to purely corporative activities of the trade-union movement, some of them sought and sometimes found a direct contact with management, on the common ground of anti-communism. Such attempts, far from serving to better industrial relations, only further destroyed the cohesion of the labor movement.[13]

But in this period *Syndicats* no longer confined its polemics to a denunciation of the 'colonization' of the trade-union movement by the communists. It now attacked also the stand on foreign policy which the communists had taken, and its columns served as a rallying point for all those, who defended the cause of appeasement in the language of the labor movement. All prominent trade-union leaders who belonged to the *Syndicats* group were willing to sacrifice to the preservation of peace every international agreement by which France was bound. This advocacy of an appeasement policy prevented various other non-communist trade-union leaders, such as Jouhaux and the officials of the civil servants federation, from joining forces with the *Syndicats* group.

The daily of the CGT also mirrored the existing divergencies. One day during the time of the Berchtesgaden conference in September 1938, *Le Peuple* carried a grim comment by its columnist on foreign policy denouncing Chamberlain's 'heartbroken'

trip to Hitler's residence. Shortly thereafter it printed an editorial by Belin stating that a mediocre or even a bad settlement
would still be better than a victorious war.[14]

On 21 September, three days before Chamberlain flew to
Godesberg and before the French government decreed the first
measures of a staggered mobilization, the Administrative Committee of the CGT seemed to have reached unanimity once more. In
a resolution accepted by all members it protested against the pressure which the democracies were bringing upon the Czechoslovak government to give in to Hitler's demands, and decried
the dismemberment of Czechoslovakia, not only as a threat to
the security of France but also as a step that would lead inevitably to a Europe dominated by Hitler Germany.[15] But how little
real agreement existed when this resolution was voted can be
gathered from the fact that immediately after the Munich accord
a prominent member of the isolationist group within the CGT,
speaking for himself and his friends, expressed regret for having
agreed to such a 'worthless' text in order to maintain a sham
unanimity.[16] Actually the pacifists were moved, in 1938, by considerations similar to those which had determined the attitude
of labor leaders at the outbreak of the war in 1914 and which
were to recur in April 1940. At that moment, when an outbreak
of hostilities seemed unavoidable, after the rejection of the London plan by the Czechoslovak government, the isolationists
simply did not dare to declare themselves openly in favor of
capitulation.

During those decisive days, when the almost complete mobilization of France's armed strength made the war appear a cer-
tainty to the French people, the labor movement was thus torn
between conflicting trends and reduced to inactivity. On the
one hand the strongly communist regional union of the Paris
area, without requesting the statutory approval of the CGT,
called for a mass demonstration to express sympathy for the
Czech cause and to threaten a violent response from the working
class if the government should give in to Hitler's demands.[17] On

the other hand the pacifist trade unionists of various shades entered into a working alliance with appeasers outside the labor movement.

Shortly before Munich the revolutionary syndicalists and anarchists assembled their forces, which were partly scattered throughout the CGT and partly concentrated in insignificant labor groups outside the CGT, in a 'Centre Syndical d'Action contre la Guerre,' and this organization established contact with the more moderate pacifists of the *Syndicats* group. It was decided to organize a meeting with the most prominent organization of liberal intellectuals, the 'Comité de Vigilance des Intellectuels Antifascistes,' which had remained faithful to the pacifist traditions of the French intelligentsia developed in the aftermath of the last war. At that meeting not only a representative of the syndicalist postal employees but also Dumoulin and an official of the teachers federation were to protest against armed assistance to the Czechoslovakian republic. The posters announcing the gathering ended their admonitions with a violent 'Down with the guns.' [18] In the end, however, the meeting was forbidden by the government.

The reactionary deputy Pierre-Etienne Flandin, who after Munich was to congratulate Hitler, plastered the streets of Paris with posters urging the people to resist the appeal to arms, and the CGT unions of the teachers and mailmen issued posters of their own proclaiming 'We do not want war.' The signatories asked the French government to 'persevere in the way of negotiations without being discouraged by new difficulties.' The government was urged to 'express during the negotiations the ardent will for peace felt by the French people, who have had so many victims on the battlefields of Europe.' The text was sent all over the country for the signatures of labor leaders, socialists, and anti-fascist intellectuals. For the first time the name of the deputy Marcel Déat appeared along with those of prominent trade-union officials. Within three or four days 150,000 signatures are said to have been assembled. Even before Daladier left for the Munich conference some thousand signatures were brought to his attention.[19]

The 'Centre Syndical' and other pacifist trade unionists, deprived of their meeting, distributed another poster featuring the slogan 'General Mobilization—for the Peace.' This appeal admonished workers and farmers, who would lose everything in a war, to do everything in their power to prevent it.[20] Finally Zoretti, active in both the socialist party and the teachers federation, did not shrink from indulging in anti-semitic utterances. In an article written during the critical days he accused Blum of having provoked the war, if war was to break out. 'The French people,' he concluded, 'do not want to see millions of human beings killed and to see a civilization destroyed in order to render life more agreeable to the 100,000 Jews of the Sudetenland. They know that the high motives presented as reasons for the fight are mere hypocrisy.' [21]

Later some of the prominent members of the *Syndicats* group, and also Delmas, of the teachers federation, did not deny having been in contact with Foreign Minister Bonnet and with Flandin all through the days of mobilization. The pacifist trade-union leaders admitted having followed the suggestions of Bonnet and Flandin for the best way of mobilizing the rank and file of labor against the war. Delmas and his friends boasted of the fact that their tracts against the war had been signed both by a deputy with bonapartist leanings and by a high dignitary of liberal freemasonry, and that Flandin had come to ask the collaboration of the trade-union movement for a realization of the objectives of pacifism.[22] (It was the same Flandin who in March 1938 had most actively sabotaged Blum's effort to establish a government of national unity.)

The CGT leadership could do no more than protest against the breaches of discipline committed by the pacifists and the communists of the Paris area.[23] It had neither power nor sufficient cohesion to silence either of them.

To judge from the general mood and the attitude of the enlisted men who left the cities for the mobilization centers, the chauvinism newly awakened by the communists expressed the feelings of the masses as little as did the desperate attempts of their pacifist counterparts.[24] Wherever isolated communists attempted to give an anti-fascist aura to their departure to the front by the singing of the International, disapproving silence was the answer. But also no significant effort was made by the working classes to resist the call to arms. Isolated instances were recklessly generalized by those who were deluded enough to believe that France's capitulation at Munich had been the result of popular pressure. 'By a spontaneous movement the people forced the leader to enter into negotiations,' declared an official of the teachers federation.[25] Actually, during the days of September 1938 the vast majority of the draftees accepted the war with a calm resolution which, though it may have bordered on resignation, was indicative of a much higher morale than that which prevailed a year later when France declared war on Germany.

III

During the year between Munich and the outbreak of the war the dissension between the pacifists and the communists inside the CGT continued unabated. Like French society as a whole, the French labor movement was divided into friends and foes of Munich, into 'Munichois' and 'Anti-Munichois.'[26]

The two communist secretaries of the CGT, and the trade unions that were under the influence of the communists, had rejected uncompromisingly and from the very beginning the policy which led to Munich. The peace that Munich had saved was criticized by them as a plot of international capitalism and as contrary to the true aspirations of the masses. Continuous policies of appeasement, the communists declared, were as unable to save peace among the nations as capitulation was unable to guarantee social peace within the nation. The communists explicitly refused to allow their actions and attitude toward international problems to be determined by a philosophy conceived ten years earlier. Faced with the accusation of inconsistency, they declared that their critics did not understand how entirely the situation had changed or the extent to which the interests of the workers had become identical with those of the nation.

At a meeting of the Administrative Committee of the CGT in April 1939, the communist secretary Benoît Frachon declared himself in favor of 'an alliance with people who are not revolutionary but who want to defend the nation.'[27] To symbolize the union of all patriots the communists wanted to see the 150th anniversary of the French Revolution observed by a solemn pilgrimage to the battlefield of Valmy. They pressed the CGT to give to the celebration, in truly Jacobin fashion, the significance of an integration of the working class into the nation.

Undoubtedly the open admission that they would have preferred an outbreak of the war in 1938 to the capitulation at Munich cost the communists some of their following inside and outside the trade-union movement. Even some of the communist functionaries turned away when they realized that the policy of firmness advocated by the communists was no guarantee for the maintenance of peace but could possibly lead to war.

The first reaction of the French masses to the accord of Munich was one of relief that the anxiety of the mobilization days had passed without a clash of arms. And the campaign being waged by pacifists of all denominations thrived on such merely sentimental and uninformed feelings. Some of the pacifists within the labor movement based their arguments on the philosophy they had adhered to earlier. Thus leaders who had played a role in the anti-war movement between 1914 and 1918, like Dumoulin, stressed the contention that whether France was faced with an imperial Germany or a Nazi regime, it was contrary to the interests of the French working class to enter into a *union sacrée* and to give its support to any war; on the battlefield French workers would kill their German brothers but not National Socialism. But other pacifist trade unionists, especially those belonging to a younger generation, sought a less doctrinaire approach to the problems with which France was faced. This latter group argued that it was flatly impossible for France to continue to act as if she were still the strong military power she had been in Richelieu's time. She should renounce massive rearmament and seek grandeur only in the field of intellectual achievements and moral generosity. Belin gave expression to his belief that at least twenty-five years of peace and social equilibrium were necessary if France was to survive; to resist fascism successfully she would have to adopt fascist methods herself. Delmas spoke with satisfaction about the growth of isolationist feelings in Belgium, in the Scandinavian countries, in England and the United States, and explained such trends as the natural reaction to the intrinsic difficulties of the situation. At a public banquet uniting many prominent advocates of appeasement, the spokesmen for the *Syndicats* group developed the reasons why they felt much more akin to certain forces commonly called reactionary than to labor elements. Since 'it was no longer true that all pacifists were to the left and all bellicose elements to the right,' since 'anti-fascism was often as intransigent as fascism,' the labor movement had to strive for a fundamental reorientation.[28] Such words well expressed the atmosphere that prevailed among the pacifists of the left. Intransigence had become an entirely negative value and there was practically no limit to the compromises which everybody devoted to the cause of appeasement.

However different their arguments, the pacifist trade unionists thoroughly agreed on their main objective: to see peace maintained even at the price of new concessions to Nazism. Affecting to believe in the sincerity of Hitler's statement that after the cession of the Sudetenland he would have no further demands in Europe, the *Syndicats* group requested that the German claim for colonies be satisfied. A prominent member of the *Syndicats* group hailed Déat when he wrote that no Frenchman should die for Danzig; the teachers federation exhorted the French govern-

ment to bring pressure on the Poles to be moderate in their
answers to the German provocations; Vigne, of the miners federation, in a series of articles published in July 1939 agreed with
the policy pursued by the Comité des Forges in his assertion that
it was insane to ask for the cessation of French pig-iron shipments
to Germany.[29]

It is impossible to explain the attitude of these labor leaders
merely in terms of wilful treachery, personal ambition, or outright corruption. There can be no doubt that many of the campaigns organized by the pacifist trade unionists before and after
Munich, and also their periodical publications, were financed by
sources other than the declining membership dues. The prodigal
generosity of the so-called black funds of the Foreign Office to
all activities in line with Georges Bonnet's policy of appeasement
was notorious. Events since the armistice have shown, too, that
some of the former trade-union officials were quick to become
renegades in order to reach, with the aid of their new contacts,
into spheres of activity from which a labor leader was generally
excluded under the Third Republic. But the main reasons for the
passing of these trade-union officials into the camp of appeasement lay deeper.

Against the background of a sincere hope that new bloodshed
could be spared to a nation still suffering from the last war, very
complex resentment and reasoning had developed. The hatred
of everything communist had gone so far that without examining
whether a specific communist argument was well founded, the
group around *Syndicats* was inclined to accept collaboration
with anyone who was opposed to communism and Soviet Russia.
Moreover, for a labor movement that had cherished internationalist traditions and anti-militarist language it was particularly difficult to tolerate the neochauvinist accents of the communist propaganda.

Also, it is no accident that the trade unionists who at all times
fervently advocated the 'independence' of the labor movement
were the same ones who were addicted to pacifist doctrines. At

the Congress of Nantes the resolution on the problems of war and peace, which was proposed by the isolationists, carried almost exactly the same votes as the one in favor of strictest separation of the trade-union movement from political activity.[30] In so far as the plea for independence was anything more than a mere desire to counterbalance increasing communist influence, it implied an intentional isolation of labor from the institution of the modern state. The counterpart of this isolation within the nation was the isolationism which was preached in foreign affairs. The entire philosophy of trade-union 'independence' was based on an aloofness of labor from happenings outside the sphere of its immediate interests; the problems of politics and especially those of world politics were considered out of bounds. In this orientation were the deepest roots of the inability of many French trade unionists to understand the nature of international fascism, its methods and goals. Their lack of understanding resulted in bewilderment, mistakes, and eventually betrayal of their class and their country.

Between the pacifists of the *Syndicats* group and the communists, Jouhaux and his friends endeavored to maintain an independent position. The strength of this center group cannot be determined but it included the majority of the members of the CGT Central Office, many well-known trade-union officials, and a two-thirds majority of the powerful civil servants federation.[31]

As early as 1936, after the remilitarization of the Rhineland, Jouhaux had shown a clear understanding of the international situation when he criticized as utterly unrealistic the accusations of the revolutionary pacifists that the 'bloody merchants of death' were preparing a new war. Information he had gathered in London, where in March 1936 the International Federation of Trade Unions had adopted a colorless protest against Hitler's violation of the Locarno pact, permitted him to maintain that the forces traditionally characterized as warmongers had become most active in preventing a new war by a continuous appeasement of Nazism and fascism.[32]

During the various crises of 1938 the secretary-general of the CGT had at first sought to bridge the existing differences by slipping once more into emotional vagueness. In March, after Blum had failed to constitute the government of national unity which the CGT had favored, Jouhaux spoke about the necessity of strengthening the ties between 'peoples of common spirit . . . and common social sentiment.'[33] During the days that led to the Munich agreement, Jouhaux was in the United States and had conferred with President Roosevelt on the European crisis. Even before that conversation, but especially after it, the CGT, in spite of its heated controversies, was inclined to reach a unanimous vote whenever it discussed a resolution referring to President Roosevelt's proposals for the settlement of international conflicts, or even invoking his direct intervention.[34] This faith in American aid served to promote, within the ranks of organized labor in France, an illusion concerning the readiness of the United States to participate actively in European politics—an illusion that was not without danger, especially when it continued to be nourished after the outbreak of the war in 1939.

Unlike the communists, Jouhaux and his friends in the Central Office of the CGT did not immediately criticize the Munich agreements. The official bulletin of the CGT saw in the accord a proof that 'action of the great democracies' was capable of 'making Hitler recoil.'[35] Jouhaux admitted that he had lost the courage for whatever action the situation could demand from the labor movement. He no longer believed that war would break out, mainly because a war waged by a France encircled on all sides by hostile regimes was lost in advance.[36]

In regard to the relations which existed between the international and the internal situation, the civil servants federation, backbone of the old CGT and a factor of stability in the fluctuating development of the reunified labor movement, had shown for years a discernment not surpassed by any other group inside or outside organized labor. In its publications the federation had always stressed the fact that reforms of France's economic and social structure were necessary not only to make the Popular Front a success but, even more, in order to guarantee the survival of the French nation in the conflicts to come. As soon as the development of the civil war in Spain had shown unmistakably the intentions of France's totalitarian neighbors, spokesmen for the federation had called for a renovation of the country not by means of an outdated and hypocritical *union sacrée* but by the realization of a higher form of national unity,[37] with a leading part played by the elements that had formed the Popular Front. Even before the Anschluss the majority of the federation spoke about the 'period of public salvation' into which France had entered. 'France awake!' wrote Charles Laurent, secretary-general of the federation, 'Let us reread our history. When our country is in danger, a committee of public salvation is in order. The Popular Front must create it.' [38] After Munich, leading officials of the civil servants federation almost openly accused the *Syndicats* group of belonging to the 'international party of capitulation' and of having become a helpmate of those forces which, by a new split in the labor movement, hoped to deprive the working class of any influence.[39]

In November 1938, at the CGT Congress in Nantes, the center group found a common platform with the communists in regard to questions of foreign policy, thereby uniting with them against the resolution brought forward by the pacifist minority. The majority resolution gave expression to the belief that further appeasement of the aggressor nations would bear no fruit, and that peace could not be saved except by the concerted and firm attitude of the democracies, among which the communists, of course, counted the Soviet Union.

Several factors were responsible for this temporary rapprochement between the communists and the center group. It had rapidly become clear that Munich had been but a mummery, incapable of guaranteeing the permanent peace of Europe. Thus the intentions of the pacifist trade unionists and their activities during the decisive period in September had become highly questionable. Jouhaux and his friends felt in no way akin to the communists, but they denounced the violent anti-communism in which the pacifists indulged as one of the main roads leading eventually to an alliance with reactionary or fascist forces. Even then, in 1938 and 1939, certain trade unionists of *Syndicats* seemed to have some kind of relationship with Jacques Doriot, who had turned from communism to become the leader of the most outspokenly fascist party in France.

But the most important reason why the center group became uncompromising in its attitude against any form of appeasement was the conviction that in the war to come France would be in deadly danger of defeat unless the labor movement was integrated into the national effort. It also had become clear that such an integration was impossible without the clearly manifested will of the working class to see further fascist aggression resisted, if necessary, with the force of arms. Dumoulin, in the name of *Syndicats*, declared to the Congress that it was the sole interest of the working class to see peace maintained at any price, and that the CGT should officially withdraw from the Popular Front. Jouhaux answered him that such proposals, seemingly made in the name of revolutionary and internationalist traditions, would actually but help to realize the hopes of reactionaries and isolationists: to exclude the working class from the national community.[40]

Thus the majority of the Congress voted to remain within the Popular Front organization and to maintain labor's efforts to participate in the nation's destiny. But the Congress of Nantes, as the preceding chapter has shown, was shaken also by the publication of the Reynaud decree laws, which occurred while it was in session. Within only a fortnight after the adjournment of the Congress labor was indeed severed from the affairs of the nation, as a result of the failure of the general strike, decided upon in protest against the decree laws.

IV

In 1937 Jouhaux had endeavored to define the conditions under which a general strike could succeed: it should originate in autonomous action of the trade-union movement, without any outside influence; it should be the ultimate recourse, after a series of actions which had seriously shaken the existing order; and it should be undertaken only if the workers had a concrete plan of how to fill the vacuum that would be created by a successful general strike.[41] None of these conditions existed when the Administrative Committee of the CGT, only one week after the Congress of Nantes, unanimously decided to call for a general strike on 30 November, limited to twenty-four hours.[42] The reluctance to call a general strike, which the non-communist trade unionists had still shown at Nantes, had yielded to pressure.

This pressure came from various directions. The irritation of the communists, and of all those trade unionists who condemned the appeasement policy of the Daladier cabinet, had only increased after the French government, in November, announced the projected conclusion of a Franco-German pact and the visit of Nazi Foreign Minister Ribbentrop to the French capital. A series of strikes had begun to sweep the country; while many of them were traceable to communist inspiration, others were denounced by the trade unions as wildcat demonstrations. The violent means with which the government broke these strikes, such as the use of tear gas and other methods that had been hitherto unknown in France for the solution of labor conflicts, bolstered the opposition also of the non-communist leadership of the CGT. A special kind of pressure was exercised by the probably communist-inspired threat of many affiliated organizations to cease the payment of membership dues to the central organization unless energetic action against the government was forthcoming. In such circumstances the CGT could not evade action if it hoped to remain in control of the various movements of protest and their undercurrents.

There seems to have existed, however, a sincere hope that it would be possible to conclude with the government some transaction that would not only save the face of the CGT but also permit the participation of organized labor in the speeding up of war production. Later the CGT directing personnel was both openly and surreptitiously reproached by some people for having announced its strike decision five days in advance, thereby leaving the government ample time to prepare counter-measures.[43] This delay may indeed have contributed to the failure of the strike, but the CGT officers apparently hoped that the interval could be used to effect an understanding between the government and the labor movement. Even after the decision for a general strike had been made, Jouhaux declared in a public meeting that the CGT was still ready for sincere and confident collaboration with the government in the interest of the community, and that the strike decision was intended only as a means of replacing the provocative policy of the decree laws by a policy of broad cooperation.[44] Probably never before had a general strike been presented in terms of class collaboration. Also the limitation of the movement to twenty-four hours showed that the CGT was far from considering the strike a prelude to revolution.

But in spite of the efforts of some socialist deputies, Daladier refused to enter into negotiations. The Prime Minister was in any case disposed to break openly with the communist party. The government's antagonism to the communist-influenced unions had been increased by the demonstrations which the trade unions of Paris organized during the days of Munich, and the crushing of a general strike which the communists wanted was a welcome occasion for a break. It has even been reported that some of Daladier's advisers would have liked to see the day of the projected general strike turned into a repetition of the bloody repression of the workers of Paris which occurred during the

June days of 1848,[45] in which event it would have been possible for the government to rule during the last phase of rearmament with dictatorial powers.

The failure of the strike was due in part to the lack of purpose and unity which had beset the CGT and in part to the measures which the government took to quell the movement.

The trade-union leaders continued to affirm that the twenty-four hour strike was called as a protest against the decree laws, which by now were in operation. But there was still no clear realization of what the economic and social consequences of the new decree laws would be, and no concrete formulation of what the CGT proposed to replace them. In so far as the 40-hour week had become a question of prestige, it was an issue merely between the CGT and the government; the rank and file of labor, even before the new decree laws, often welcomed overtime work in order to compensate for the decline of real wages.

In the tension that prevailed in the fall of 1938 it was almost impossible, however, for any issue to remain dissociated from the international situation. Thus, although the Administrative Committee of the CGT stated in an open letter to the Prime Minister that the strike was not political, the secretary-general himself declared after the strike, in a private meeting of the League for the Rights of Man: 'The CGT did not call for a general strike in order to protect miserable material interests. We stood up against the decree laws because they are the consequence of the Munich agreements and of a policy which aims at the destruction of the workers' liberties.' [46] The communists admitted almost openly that they considered the strike an action directed against appeasement.

The history of the European labor movement shows that it is not impossible to call a successful general strike with a political purpose. But if this is done it is certainly necessary to declare openly the political aim of the movement, and not deny that such an aim exists. Actually the CGT would never have been able to call a strike as a protest against the policy of Munich.

Not only would such a step have been considered an outward proof that the trade unions were taking orders from a political party, the communists; in addition, a strong minority within the CGT wholeheartedly approved of appeasement and isolationism. Nothwithstanding the public declaration of the CGT that the strike movement was non-political, and notwithstanding the fact that the various federations joined in a unanimous decision to call the strike, the teachers union of Lyons issued a declaration refusing to 'take part in a strike which could be nothing but a protest against pacifism.' [47] For understandable reasons the government gave this declaration widest publicity.

This lack of clear issues made it easy for the government to vilify the threatening strike, in the eyes of the public and the workers, as nothing but an improper means of protest against the policy by which Daladier and Bonnet had saved the peace. But during that period between the calling of the strike and the day that was set for it, the government did not resort to propagandistic means alone. As soon as the CGT announced its decision the government, by decree, requisitioned in rapid sequence the personnel of all the railroads, of the mines and related industries of the Nord and the Haut-Rhin departments, of the potash mines, of maritime transport, and of public and state-licensed enterprises—the *services publics et concédés*, which included such fields as public utilities, health services, and the like.[48] The requisitions were based on the original law of 1877 or the National Service law of 1938, or both, and put into force the grave penalties which these statutes imposed on any employee who did not report for work.

By these means the government intended to discourage the strike at vital points of the country's economic apparatus. It was expected that if the movement was suppressed from the beginning in such activities as transportation and mining, which in previous strikes had always played a somewhat spectacular role, it would collapse elsewhere with relative ease.

These expectations were not disappointed. The workers in

requisitioned enterprises received several days in advance their individual notice of requisition, which was very similar to that of induction into the armed forces. Thereupon the trade unions advised the requisitioned personnel to comply with the orders by reporting for work on the morning of the 30th, but to refuse actual work. It was not astonishing that the men, once on the job and faced with the presence of overwhelming police forces at all important spots, started to work. Hence for all railroad employees and transportation workers the strike orders had to be revoked by the unions themselves, in the very early morning hours. The normal functioning of transportation facilities and other public services discouraged many workers in private industries from striking. On top of everything the CGT, anxious at any cost to avoid a clash between workers and police, had decided to refrain from certain external demonstrations which in the past had been traditional in the strikes of the French labor movement: thus no meetings were held, and it was not required that each union membership card be punched. All this contributed to make the day appear to be a regular working day, whereas it is the aim of every general strike to interfere seriously with the normal activities of the nation.

It was generally conceded that in Paris the number of strikers was insignificant. The CGT maintained that the workers in private industries outside of the capital, especially the sailors and longshoremen and the workers in the printing, metal, and chemical trades, struck in considerable strength.[49] But though estimates differed concerning the percentage of strikers, there could be no doubt that the government's effort to turn the day into a defeat for the labor movement had been entirely successful.

The use of requisitioning as a means toward the solution of labor conflicts was not entirely new in French social history. But before the enactment of the National Service act in 1938 the government had never been able to proceed with such extensive requisitions. Even in August, shortly after the new statute became law, the government had used its provisions to suppress a strike of longshoremen in Marseilles when a conflict about overtime work had arisen.[50] Since the National Service law authorized requisitions not only in the case of open aggression but also in the case of external tension, the government's actions could be legally justified, in spite of the fact that the Foreign Minister of the 'hereditary enemy,' Germany, had just been invited for the signature of a treaty of amity.[51]

Grave doubts were raised, however, about the political advisability of the methods employed. Military circles feared that 'rehearsal' requisitions in peacetime would endanger the smooth mobilization of the labor force in time of war. Moreover, the National Service law had been greeted by all parties as a manifestation of national unity, and its application at a moment of social and political, rather than international, tension was bound to antagonize the working class. As has been mentioned, the statute provided that for the application of all important provisions of the law the government should consult with the representative organizations of labor and management. But the November decrees of application, since they were issued for the express purpose of rendering impossible a strike that had been called by the CGT, naturally omitted any allusion to co-operation with the labor movement. Thus organized labor was simply excluded from the framework of French manpower legislation in wartime.

v

This policy of wilful exclusion of the CGT from national life was continued by the government after the strike. Some of the functions which representatives of the labor movement had assumed in the heyday of the Popular Front were rescinded. Jouhaux was deprived of his post as a member of the General Council of the Bank of France. Though his responsibilities had become more and more nominal, the formal participation of organized labor in the credit policy of the bank of issue was still considered of symbolic importance. The two secretaries of the railwaymen federation were expelled from the administration of the National Railway Company, because, as the government decree expressed it, their functions as administrators were incompatible with the backing they had given the general strike.[52]

The CGT retorted by withdrawing its representatives from all the tripartite boards, councils, and committees through which it had participated in administration and sometimes, in a consultative capacity, in legislation. 'It must be understood that one cannot collaborate with the National Economic Council in an atmosphere of social war,' stated Jouhaux, inviting the Administrative Committee to recommend 'abstention until further notice' from the Council and all similar organizations. Later this decision had to be partly canceled for such bodies as arbitration boards, placement offices, unemployment committees, and the like.[53] The integration of the labor movement into the state had gone too far to permit the sudden discontinuance of every contact. Nevertheless, with the exception of merely technical activities, there existed during the crucial period between the general strike and the outbreak of the war no active collaboration between government and labor or management and labor.

'It is impossible,' was the melancholy summing up of assistant secretary Belin after the failure of the strike, 'to appeal to the law and to violate it at the same time . . . impossible to play simultaneously the so-called reformist and the so-called revolutionary strategist without the risk of losing on both grounds.'[54]

Immediately after the strike one of the spokesmen for the civil servants federation implored employers and government not to turn the defeat of the labor movement into humiliation of the individual workers, for 'wherever there are humiliated or defeated Frenchmen, France herself is in danger of being defeated.'[55] The employer organizations admonished their members not to exploit the situation by any mass dismissal of trade unionists; they even expressed the hope that 30 November might later be regarded as an important step toward social peace.[56] But in spite of such pleas the main activities of the CGT and its affiliates during the months following the general strike consisted of attempts to obtain the return of dismissed workers and shop delegates, to aid in the defense of indicted members before the courts, and to press Parliament to vote an amnesty for those employees with civil-servant status who had been discharged because of their participation in the strike. A statement by the Central Office of the CGT mentioned 'hundreds of thousands' of dismissals.[57]

The Chamber of Deputies, elected in 1936 by a Popular Front majority, refused to vote a general amnesty.[58] The readmission of dismissed workers into private industry proceeded very gradually. It is true that the pacification of industrial relations seemed achieved: between January and the summer of 1939 not a single strike was reported. 'As by enchantment the tumult of demands and assaults which gave French life its troublesome aspect have yielded to an exemplary calm,' stated *Le Temps*.[59] But once again this calm resulted not from a much-needed co-operation between labor and management but from the weakness of the trade-union movement, which had lost, along with its place in the nation, any solid hold on the industrial working class. Union meetings frequently offered the typical appearance of a regressing movement; in many cases they were attended not by shop delegates or workers from the nation's defense industries but by the dismissed and unemployed.

An outer manifestation of this weakness was the decision of the CGT not to call for any stoppage of work on May Day 1939. Jouhaux admitted that such an abandonment of tradition had to be understood as a consequence of the failure of the general strike.[60]

As could be expected in a period of decline, the struggle between the different factions within the CGT only increased in intensity. It remained less and less on a theoretical plane. Scenes of violence, leading sometimes to brutalities, were reported from many union meetings of this period. Union members later attested that in some CGT organizations life had become impossible even before the outbreak of the war. Sometimes an open split, leading to the exclusion of one group by another, destroyed the unity which had formerly been maintained.[61]

The relative strength of the different groups within the CGT is not easy to determine. At the time the war broke out the communists were in complete control of 12 of about 30 industrial federations, among them the important federations of workers in the metal, chemical, construction, textile, electrical, and leather industries and the federation of agricultural workers. Among the most notable regional unions ruled by the communists were that of the Paris area, to which belonged one-fourth of the total CGT membership, that of the Seine-Inférieure (Rouen and Le Havre), that of the Somme (Amiens), and that of the Bas-Rhin (Strasbourg). All these were important industrial centers, with a predominance of defense industries. The communists also dominated the entire Mediterranean coast, from which their influence extended as far as Grenoble.[62]

The only prominent federations in which the communists had not gained notable influence were those of the garment workers, printers, teachers, postmen, miners, civil servants, and the sailors and dockers. In these federations, as well as in the regional unions of Savoie, Doubs, and Calvados, the members of *Syndicats* were dominant. In the important industrial district of the Nord the friends of *Syndicats* succeeded in gaining a majority only after a hard fight.[63]

The resolutions proposed by the *Syndicats* group had obtained about 26 per cent of the votes at the Congress of Nantes.[64] Since the method of designating delegates was disadvantageous to the smaller unions, in which *Syndicats* counted relatively more adherents, it can be estimated that the *Syndicats* group represented at that time only little less than a third of the CGT. The numerical importance of the communists within the CGT cannot be similarly estimated, because at the Congress of Nantes they united in every vote with the center group formed by Jouhaux and his friends. There can be no doubt, however, that the communists were far more numerous than the center group.

But the CGT as a whole had lost a great part of its strength. The last official membership figure before the outbreak of the war—communicated by the CGT to the ILO, as of 1 January 1939—was 3.5 million, based on the 1938 membership; [65] the figure is probably too optimistic even for that period, and it does not take into account the consequences of the general strike. According to other sources no more than 1 million remained. It is most probable that on the eve of the war the membership of the CGT was reduced from its earlier peak of 5.3 million to about 2 million.[66] While certain federations, like that of the civil servants, maintained a rather stable membership, there were great fluctuations in industries which, like building, chemicals, and food, had experienced a mass influx of newcomers in 1936. The organizations of important skills, such as professional workers and technicians, which were won for the trade-union movement in 1936, were almost entirely destroyed by internal dissensions and jurisdictional disputes.[67] This loss in membership caused also very serious financial difficulties to the organizations, whose expenses had been greatly increased during the period of trade-union prosperity.

It has already been mentioned that rises and declines in membership had always been particularly pronounced in the French labor movement. The CGT had known previous defeats and had been able to recover. Never before, however, had the weight of the labor movement as a social force been so great as during the period of the Popular Front. This weight had been thrown into the balance, and to a very large extent it was now lost.

In the particular circumstances that existed during the months preceding the war, the diminution in the influence of the labor movement made for a further restriction of French democracy.

That period, which has been described as *préfascisme français*,[68] derived its ominous significance from the fact that the scope of the democratic process was being continuously narrowed and that the representative organizations of the working class were almost totally excluded from national life.

VII

The Catholic Trade-Union Movement

I

WHEN representatives of the CGPF and the CGT concluded the Matignon Agreement, in June 1936, the CGT refused categorically to allow the Confédération Française des Travailleurs Chrétiens (CFTC) to join in the negotiations. Management was not opposed to a subsequent request from the CFTC to add its signature to the document which had sealed the agreement at Matignon, but Jouhaux declared that proposal equally unacceptable.[1] The CGT felt entitled to speak in the name of the whole of French labor, and it did not wish to share that role with a movement which it considered its adversary rather than its competitor.

The 'phobia' which the entire leadership of the CGT felt in that period for the Christian trade-union movement, and the 'ostracism' which it practiced,[2] were based both on ideological and on practical grounds. The CGT did not deny that the CFTC was a genuine labor movement, so far as its independence from management was concerned. As far back as 1919 the CFTC had united various Catholic trade-union federations and had emphasized the necessity of organizing the wage earners in complete independence of management.[3] As this principle was adhered to in practice, the CGT could not properly identify the Catholic trade unions with the various movements, in French usage commonly referred to as 'yellow' unions, which were organized under the auspices of the employers.[4]

But the confederation of Christian trade unions, though an authentic labor organization, was certainly one that was fundamentally different from the CGT in origin, outlook, and history.

In the CGT the idea of class warfare had always been complemented by outspoken anti-clericalism. Even after World War I, when the concept of class struggle was somewhat forgotten in the day-to-day activity of the trade-union movement, anticlericalism continued almost unabated. Open conflict between the village priest and the teacher belonging to the CGT union was still in many regions a frequent occurrence.

The Christian trade-union group, which in spite of its deliberately chosen name was actually a Catholic organization, had grown out of the general Social Catholic movement. During the troubled infancy of the Third Republic the Social Catholics identified themselves with the principles of counter-revolution and, inspired by the teachings of the Count de Mun, preached a neo-feudalism.[5] Even when the Catholic trade unions reached the full measure of their independence from the Social Catholic movement, the clergy still played an important role in many of the unions, and for a long time membership was restricted to wage earners who were active members of the Catholic church. It was not denied that in all important conflicts the CFTC and its affiliates turned to the church for guidance and advice.[6]

The Catholic trade-union movement was fundamentally opposed to the philosophy of the Charter of Amiens. In accordance with the social teachings of the church as expressed in the papal encyclicals, especially in *Rerum novarum* and *Quadragesimo anno*, it sought to avoid any violent clash between labor and management. It was acknowledged that the interests of the two groups conflicted, but it was believed that a continuous collaboration could and should be established. The institutionalization of this collaboration was sometimes proposed in forms that came close to the formula adopted by modern corporativism. A statement of the principle adopted in 1922, which played a role roughly comparable to that of the Charter of Amiens in the history of the CGT, characterized the movement as 'strongly impregnated by the Catholic doctrine, opposing the endeavors of egoism, of hatred and of revolution from whatever side they come, constituting the double bulwark of equal justice for all and charity dispensed to everyone.' [7]

The social program of the CFTC advocated the development of institutions likely to improve the relations between management and labor. The program centered around proposals for the generalization of collective bargaining and for a compulsory arbitration system, the strike being considered only the ultimate weapon, to be used after the exhaustion of every other means. The reform proposals of the CFTC concerning wage-hour legislation, set forth during the depression of the 1930's, were almost identical with those of the CGT. The 40-hour week and the establishment of minimum wages were advocated. From 1919 a demand for workers' participation in profits and in the management of enterprises also played an important role in the programmatic statements of the Catholic trade-union movement. As this demand was explicitly made in the spirit of class collaboration, it has been suggested that it corresponded to a large extent to the ideals which the French workers' co-operatives developed for the first time in 1848.[8]

In 1934-5, when 'plans' became the *sine qua non* of every social and political movement in France, the CFTC published a plan of its own.[9] The CGT plan was criticized for its exclusively 'materialistic' approach, which neglected the root of the crisis, the diminution of human dignity; as has been mentioned earlier, de Man, one of the initiators of the CGT plan, stressed a similar point. In addition, the plan of the Catholic unions reproached the CGT planners on the ground that their proposals were based on an oversimplified purchasing-power theory. Both plans, however, constituted in effect a blueprint for a planned economy functioning under the National Economic Council, whose powers were to be substantially increased. Both advocated a 'mixed' economic system in which a sector of private enterprise and one of public enterprise were to coexist. The CFTC plan carefully avoided the term 'nationalization' in reference to the industries it would include in the public sector—banks, insurance, transportation, and power—but actually it proposed to submit them to very much the same tripartite administration as that outlined by the CGT. The plans proposed by the two trade-union movements in the period of the reawakening of democratic forces showed a greater unity of views than the two organizations themselves would have acknowledged to exist.

It was in the field of practical action that the sharpest divergencies arose between the two confederations. Not only was the CFTC opposed on principle to general strikes and to any strike movement of political character, but it took pride in having contributed to the failure of the disastrous general strikes that the CGT called in 1920 and 1922.[10] When the Catholic unions boasted of having been the decisive factors in the breakdown of these ill-timed and badly co-ordinated demonstrations they may have overestimated their influence. It is a fact, however, that the defection of the CGT railwaymen, which played an important role in the failure of 1920, directly profited the Catholic railwaymen's union: its membership increased by 500 per cent.

Until 1920 the Catholic trade-union movement was almost exclusively confined to white-collar workers. The CFTC had grown out of their organization, the white-collar unions supplying almost the entire leadership of the confederation. On the eve of the Popular Front, when the CFTC claimed a total membership of 150,000 (15 per cent of the effectives of the reunified CGT), the Catholic federation of white-collar workers numbered 43,200 members, and thus outranked its CGT counterpart. Not only was this the most numerous of the Catholic organizations, but because of its preponderance (23 per cent of the total CFTC membership) it played in the Catholic confederation a role similar to that then held by the civil servants in the CGT. The only other Catholic federations that reached a membership of 10,000 were those of the railwaymen, the textile workers, and the miners.[11]

One of the peculiarities of the Catholic trade-union movement was that none of its federations had a membership distributed over the entire country; they all had only regional importance. In the department of the Nord the weight of the CFTC affiliates was increased by the great influence exercised by the clergy of the Lille diocese, which was strongly in favor of Catholic trade unionism, and also by ties with the Belgian labor movement, where the Christian trade unions had always been relatively strong. Among the workers and employees of the Alsace-Lorraine railroads the Catholic trade unions had an important place because of traditions carried over from the time of the German domination. The preservation of these traditions was favored by the fact that the Alsace-Lorraine railways continued for a long time to be administered separately.

This massing of the CFTC organizations in particular regions gave to the Catholic trade-union movement a greater weight in certain nationally organized tripartite boards and councils, such as the Superior Labor Council and the National Economic Council, than it would have had if its membership had been scattered through the entire country. The regional concentration of its strength also affected its attitude in certain strikes. During the lengthy textile strikes in the Nord region, during the strikes by which white-collar employees attempted to ward off the consequences of the approaching economic depression, and during certain metal workers' strikes, the Catholic trade unions took an active part which was sometimes acknowledged by the CGT and rather violently complained of by Catholic management.[12] In some cases the Catholic unions entered into a 'cartel' with the CGT unions; such an agreement usually provided for a common strike strategy and pledged an end to mutual recriminations. The leadership of the CFTC always saw to it, however, that these cartels did not go too far and did not drive the Catholic unions into activities that would have to be repudiated.[13] In line with its general condemnation of strikes of political character, the

CFTC disapproved of the general strike of twenty-four hours in February 1934 which opened the way to the Popular Front movement.

II

When the elections of 1936 let loose a wave of mass strikes, the CFTC declared its complete agreement with the workers' demands for higher wages, shorter hours, collective bargaining, and shop delegates, but criticized the methods employed, especially the occupation of the plants. Many of the ensuing improvements in labor legislation had already been demanded by the Catholic trade unions, and thus it can be assumed that the CFTC was not simply swept away by the irresistible pressure of the masses when it declared itself in favor of everything that the mass strikes strove to achieve and the new labor legislation realized.

The mass influx of new members to the CGT and the *de facto* monopoly which the new statutes bestowed upon that organization might well be expected to have engulfed a numerically weak movement such as the CFTC. This did not occur, however. The previous decade had shown that the federations affiliated with the CFTC were not subject to great fluctuations of membership; it appeared that they could count upon a regular, though limited, recruitment.[14] But after 1936 this recruitment was suddenly accelerated, and the membership of the CFTC more than trebled, while the number of affiliated unions increased almost as much. The official figure communicated to the ILO, as of 1 January 1938, was 488,000 members.[15] It is true that in comparison with the CGT membership of 5.3 million the relative weight of the CFTC diminished (9 instead of 15 per cent), but a union movement of half a million French wage earners was not totally negligible. This development benefited not only the former strongholds of the Catholic unions; in addition, the movement now extended to such regions as the Pas-de-Calais, the Sambre, the Franche Comté, and the district around St. Etienne, in all of which it held more or less strong minorities among organized working-class elements.[16]

This increase in strength, realized against various and almost overwhelming odds, was due primarily to the general vitality which the Popular Front period had reawakened in the working classes. So powerful was the movement toward overcoming the previous lethargy in industrial relations, so great the hope for a rejuvenation of society, that the development was felt even in a trade-union movement which did not participate in the new formation of the French left. A general upswing of French youth movements occurred during the same period. Thus added strength was acquired by an organization of young Catholic workers, the Jeunesse Ouvrière Chrétienne (JOC), which for some years had been furnishing many active militants to the Catholic trade-union movement and had thereby served to increase the latter's working-class character.[17]

Another reason for the expansion of Catholic trade unionism is undoubtedly to be found in the insistence, and sometimes the brutalities, with which certain elements of the freshly swelled CGT unions tried to force reluctant workers into their ranks.[18] In a country where the closed shop had never become common, these procedures, against which some CGT leaders warned explicitly, aroused so much indignation that they only encouraged the recruiting of organizations outside the CGT. Since many of the workers did not wish to join company unions or 'yellow' organizations, the Catholic unions profited from such reactions. Moreover, the new members who joined out of resentment of the CGT were not necessarily devout Catholics, the rules on admission having been relaxed, and thus the new development brought the Catholic unions more in line with the traditional character of French working-class organizations, which in turn facilitated further recruitment.

The labor legislation of 1936 so largely corresponded to the general conceptions of the Catholic trade-union movement that the latter's adaptation to the new practices was accomplished with particular ease. After the 'pause' was declared in 1937, the CFTC declared that the 'Blum experiment' had realized almost all of the reform proposals of the Catholic trade unions while the more radical requests of the CGT had remained unheeded. Therefore the Popular Front, it was contended, had actually vindicated the moderate views taken by the CFTC.[19]

This did not prevent the Catholic movement from criticizing, and sometimes with more acumen than the CGT, the unwelcome results which some of the new institutions had yielded. The last prewar congress of the CFTC, held in 1939, denounced the growing state intervention in industrial relations with arguments which had never been stated with similar clarity by the spokesmen for the CGT. Thus, in the words of the report:

The collective trade agreements have a tendency to be reduced to a uniform repetition of the clauses which are prescribed by law. Conciliation and arbitration of the first degree are often regarded as mere formalities; for the solution of conflicts only the super-arbiters are relied upon. The sources of such trends are evident: wherever a conflict arises the representatives of labor and management prefer not to take responsibilities and to shift the burden to the umpire. It must be stressed that the professional organizations will never be independent of the government unless they are willing to take their affairs into their own hands: one remains free only by accepting responsibilities.[20]

The active participation of the Catholic trade unions in the practice of collective bargaining was at first only slight. Because of the interpretation given to the term 'most representative organizations' the unions affiliated with the CFTC were originally invested with bargaining power only in a few regions and professions. But legally more than one organization could be 'most representative,' and thus the steady recruitment of the CFTC in well-defined districts and trades, and the decline of the CGT membership after 1937, led to an increasing participation of the Catholic unions in collective bargaining and arbitration. In 1938 the collective trade agreements were renegotiated for the first time, after their validity had previously been repeatedly prolonged, and in numerous instances the Catholic trade unions succeeded in breaking what they described as the monopoly of the CGT. Sometimes these efforts of the Catholic unions gave rise to sharp jurisdictional disputes, but in other instances a smooth functioning of some kind of co-operation between the two organizations was devised. On the eve of the war such collaboration was particularly successful in the department of the Nord, where the CGT secretary Dumoulin was no longer inimical to the Catholic trade-union movement. Catholic writers hoped that these practices were paving the way to a desirable 'pluralism,' a representation of labor's interests by both the trade-union organizations. It should not be overlooked, however, that, although exact statistics are not available, the cases in which such a pluralism was actually accomplished were still the exception.[21]

With the gulf between the CFTC and CGT slowly closing, it remained uncertain whether the development was tending to transform the Catholic trade unions into the moderate wing of a labor movement merged into a single organization,[22] or into a 'third party' between the CGPF management and the CGT. The second alternative was usually preferred by Catholic writers,[23] anxious as they were to preserve the independence of the Catholic labor movement, in accordance with ecclesiastical suggestions. Analogous efforts to organize a Catholic employers' group, the Confédération Française des Professions, met with very little success. It was not possible for a group based on common faith to overcome the centralization and the polarization of professional organizations.

The violent political dissensions which ravaged the CGT unions gave the leadership of the Catholic labor movement a good reason to avoid too close a relationship with the CGT. The CFTC always declined to take any position in political questions, or to transgress the sphere of merely professional activities. This attitude was in conformance with the traditions of French syndicalism, but the motivation was entirely different.

In general the Catholic labor movement, both because of its

relatively minor importance in society and because of the ideological ties which united it, succeeded better than the CGT in maintaining the political neutrality of the organization in the face of divergent tendencies among its members. Thus the CFTC never adhered to the Popular Front. One group of Catholic trade unionists belonged to the Jeune République, an active Catholic movement which supported that political alliance. Others identified themselves with one of the Catholic parties in Parliament, the 'Parti Démocrate Populaire,' which belonged to the center and hardly ever co-operated with the left in the Chamber of Deputies. Still others, and among them the leadership of the important white-collar unions, oriented themselves farther to the right, sometimes indulging in rather violent anti-socialism.[24] In accordance with French parliamentary custom, there existed in the Chamber a 'group for the defense of Christian trade unionism,' comprising deputies of various parties and allegiances.[25] To a certain extent the very existence of such a group belied the claim of Catholic trade unionism that it abstained completely from political activities. But since the Catholic trade-union movement was not important as a pressure group either, the activities of this parliamentary organization were not significant enough to give rise to conflicts.

When the first Popular Front government was forced to resign and the French New Deal was brought to a definite end, the CFTC, once more in conformity with its adopted attitude, did not take a position. As was expected, the Catholic trade unions stigmatized many of the strikes launched thereafter in the Paris region, and also the general strike of November 1938, as political and improper movements.[26] On the other hand, the CFTC did not at all concur with the Daladier-Reynaud plans for the recovery of the country. Its congress in 1939 warned against regarding 'an extension of hours of work as a panacea at a time when unemployment is still rife,' and it accused the government of not attempting to ascertain the real requirements of the national economy and its possibilities of internal and export trade.[27]

In regard to international affairs, the Catholic trade unions merely took pride in their patriotism, and thus they avoided many of the difficulties which the CGT incurred when it attempted to find its place within the nation. At the time of Munich the CFTC, like any other group in French society, included among its members and its leadership both friends and foes of the settlement arrived at. But since the organization as such did not take a position and was not asked to do so, this question hardly affected the activities of the Catholic trade unions. The CFTC congress of 1939 expressed with fervor its agreement with the goal of re-establishing international economic co-operation, and hoped that peace could be maintained on the basis of Van Zeeland's plan and President Roosevelt's appeals.[28]

PART II. WAR

SEPTEMBER 1939—MAY 1940

VIII

The Break with the Communists

ALMOST immediately after the conclusion of the non-aggression
pact between Nazi Germany and Soviet Russia, when it
had become clear that war was unavoidable, there began a realign-
ment of groups and opinions on the French political scene. Those
who had advocated resistance to the rising tide of Hitler imperialism could no longer rely on the support of those who sym-
pathized with Soviet Russia. Conversely, the appeasers of various
denominations could no longer maintain that France was being
driven into war by the propaganda of 'Moscow's agents.'

The CGT was the only organization of importance in which
all current attitudes toward peace and war were represented.
Therefore the events that were precipitated by the conclusion of
the Hitler-Stalin pact were bound to have immediate repercussions upon attitudes and actions of the trade-union movement.

I

During the decisive days before the outbreak of the war, the
Administrative Committee of the CGT was still able to reach
unanimity in certain of its decisions. Immediately after the an-
nouncement of the German-Soviet pact the committee decided
unanimously to address an appeal to President Roosevelt:

At this moment when most threatening events are occurring,
the organizations of French labor appeal to you. We have forgotten neither your previous interventions nor the encouragement and the hopes which those interventions brought to all

those who think that peace is the greatest good and that respect for law is a sacred duty.

Your moral authority as a respected leader of a powerful democratic nation enables you to launch a last appeal for the safeguarding of peace. . . Certain of expressing the feelings of the workers of all countries, the organizations of the French working class ask you to act without delay, and express their respectful confidence in you.[1]

This appeal of the CGT, pinning its hopes on a last-minute intervention by President Roosevelt, was not a mere gesture. Jouhaux, especially after his conversations in Washington in September 1938, actually hoped that the President could bring about something like a 'democratic Munich.'

A few days later the Administrative Committee decided, again unanimously, to address an appeal to the German working class: [2] 'The CGT appeals to your conscience and to your desire for peace. It asks you to prevent, in spite of all the difficulties of such an action, a bloody conflict that would engulf Europe.' The appeal went on to remind the workers in pits and factories of the fraternal relations that had existed between the CGT and the German unions before their destruction by Nazism. While the plea addressed to Roosevelt was based on the belief that the course of events might still be changed, the appeal directed across the Rhine may be considered merely a rhetorical gesture corresponding to the international traditions of the labor movement.

After the German troops had launched their attack against Poland and the French government had decreed total mobilization, the Administrative Committee once more reached unanimity to 'stigmatize the attack on Poland by Hitlerite Germany.'

But it was not possible to achieve unanimity when the majority of the Administrative Committee condemned the Hitler-Stalin pact, at first somewhat hesitantly and then every day more sharply. The communist members of the Central Office and of the Administrative Committee refused to join in a resolution denouncing the pact as 'a threat to the policy of the peace front' and charging it with responsibility for Hitler's assault on Poland.[3] Instead, on 24 August the communist members of the Administrative Committee moved a resolution welcoming 'the initiative taken by the Soviet Union, which by signing the pact . . . achieves a chance to consolidate a true peace front and to hamper the carrying out of the bellicose intentions of the fascist government.'[4]

In the summer of 1939 the communists outside and inside the union movement had reached the highest pitch of nationalist fervor. A few days before the conclusion of the non-aggression pact one of the Paris union leaders had declared: 'We are patriots in the true and complete sense of the word. We love our country and understand that others should love it as we do. We are all out to combat Hitlerism in order to destroy it.'[5]

It is understandable that the non-aggression pact between Hitler and Stalin was judged severely by those who had taken seriously such communist assertions as these, which were made frequently until a few days before the conclusion of the pact. An understanding between the Soviet Union and Hitler Germany was bound to appear as a betrayal of the workers' anti-fascist allegiances. Moreover, the lack of any previous explanation of the change in policy and the fact that the French communists were obviously taken by surprise constituted one more proof that the communist party had no say of its own and was dependent upon the changing outlook of Russian foreign policy; most French workers, with the exception of the oldtime party members, were disposed to resent such a complete disregard of their own objectives, especially in such a crucial situation. Finally, and most important, it was felt that the pact, which preceded Hitler's assault on Poland by only a few days, was immediately responsible for the actual outbreak of hostilities. The communists' simultaneous desertion of the cause of anti-fascism, of the national cause of France, and of the cause of peace was in itself sufficient to turn hundreds of thousands of French workers away from communism.

Some of the communists were themselves baffled during those days of late August, as is evident from a memorandum addressed by Sadoul, French correspondent of *Izvestia*, to the communist senator Cachin:

How is it possible to appraise without rage and indignation the fact that our newspapers celebrate the German-Soviet pact as a providential event for the French people and that they present it as the most precious instrument of peace, as the most powerful obstacle to the outbreak of the war? All this at the very moment when thousands of French citizens are called to the colors, when almost all of them, if not all, are leaving for the frontiers altogether convinced that they are drafted precisely because Stalin refused to sign a defensive pact with France and England and instead signed an agreement with Hitlerite Germany. . .

To the man in the street it appears that the approaching war is a direct result of the German-Soviet pact. And at this very moment *L'Humanité* and *Ce Soir* choose to shout 'The peace is saved, long live Stalin,' without even attempting to give a serious explanation for their extraordinary jubilation.[6]

That the communists were aware of the feelings that their turnabout could arouse among the masses was evident also from the line followed by *La Vie ouvrière* until its disappearance.[7] The communist dailies were suspended on 26 August, immediately after the Hitler-Stalin pact was made public, but the weekly issued by the communists within the CGT continued to be published because the government still hesitated to take measures against a union publication. Hence in that journal the communists strove to explain how they expected to reconcile their anti-Hitler policy of yesterday with the new situation. As the paper naturally attempted not to lose contact with those masses with which the communists had been influential, it had to take into consideration the mood of the anti-fascist workers in industrial centers.

Immediately after the conclusion of the German-Soviet pact, on the very eve of the war, Benoît Frachon, then still a member of the CGT Central Office, wrote an article for *La Vie ouvrière* in which he called for unity against the 'fascist aggressor' and warned the French government against excluding hundreds of thousands of workers from this unity. After the outbreak of hostilities the paper, in spite of the pact, called upon the French workers to fight against Hitler, the 'sworn enemy of social justice.' It asserted its entire agreement with the Prime Minister, Daladier, who in one of his broadcasts had branded Hitler as solely responsible for the war. The democracies, it was also said, should trust the common man who, at the front as well as at home, represents the 'soul of democracy.'

The communist union leaders did not confine themselves to such general declarations. They offered their practical collaboration to the authorities, especially in the Parisian area, where communist influence was predominant in the defense industries. They boasted of their efforts to increase production, and insisted that their activities were most useful in the defense of 'the country and its liberties.' The last issue of *La Vie ouvrière* that was to be published—which appeared on 21 September, a few days after the Russian invasion of Poland, with its columns very much deleted by the censorship—announced for the following number an article on 'Valmy and the Republic.' Hence the nationalist symbol that had been dear to the communists in their Jacobin period was once more invoked, even after the agreement between Russia and Hitler had been supplemented by the division of Poland.

II

After the declaration of war a headline in *Le Peuple* indicated how the CGT envisaged the political nature of the war: 'Against Hitler, not against the German people.' The next day the Central Office transmitted the following declaration to the press:

The inconceivable, the impossible, has happened. The responsibility for it remains entirely with Chancellor Hitler, who, we repeat, immediately after the ratification of the German-Soviet pact, launched his criminal action.

The CGT appeals to the proletariat of the world to condemn this premeditated aggression, this crime against humanity. The CGT tried until the last minute, with all its force, to safeguard peace. It remains at its post, urging the workers who are not drafted to remain in their unions and in their federations. It asks the organizers in unions and federations to fulfil immediately the tasks of reorganization that are necessary and to report the results to the Administrative Committee of the CGT.

During the first days of the war, while the mobilization of 5.5 million men was disorganizing most of the unions and the new wartime legislation was creating considerable difficulties for the labor movement, the CGT as such refrained from taking any action against communist union members. But those unions and federations in which anti-communist feeling had run high, even before the pact and the war, refused at once all collaboration with communist union leaders. Without awaiting any further decision of the central organization, the regional union of the Nord, the miners federation, and the unions of postal employees, telegraph and telephone workers, and seamen, began to exclude prominent communist members.[8]

The invasion of Poland by the Russian troops on 17 September seemed to prove that Soviet Russia had definitely made common cause with the enemy of France. And the day after the Russian move the members of the Central Office of the CGT, with the exception of the two communists, Frachon and Racamond, agreed on a resolution which was endorsed a few days later by a majority of the Administrative Committee and which accomplished the breach with the communists:

Taking cognizance of the invasion of Poland by the Soviet armies, the Central Office declares that the Hitler-Stalin pact, which it has already condemned, reveals its significance as an aid to the aggressor. It is an intentional and outright treachery against the peace. It is a treachery against the proletarians who have been called upon to resist Nazism.

This aid to the aggressor government, which has destroyed all liberty, endangers the lives of millions and more millions of human beings, among them many millions of workers.

In the face of this tragic situation the Central Office of the CGT declares that collaboration is no longer possible with those who could not, or did not wish to, condemn an act that amounts to the negation of the very principles of human solidarity on which the honor of our labor movement is based.

The Central Office trusts all workers, regardless of individual opinion—freedom of opinion not being in question—to remain united shoulder to shoulder in their unions, federations, and regional unions. The Central Office has made its decision out of respect for the codes of honesty and morality.[9]

In an article entitled 'Impossible Collaboration'[10] Jouhaux explained why the decision was believed necessary: 'Stalin's Russia allowed the Reich to let loose the most terrible of all catastrophes. It appears that Russia wanted the war, from which she has decided to profit.' The article asserted that the communist members of the Central Office and of the Administrative Committee of the CGT had not even tried to defend the alliance between Stalinism and Hitlerism,. and instead had spoken only about workers' unity and the independence of the labor movement. 'This is a piece of hypocrisy that cannot be tolerated,' concluded the article. 'If they are incapable of understanding that the labor movement demands liberty, dignity, loyalty, and solidarity, that is their own affair. It is our duty to tell them that there is no longer a place for them in a labor movement that refuses to forget, for the benefit of totalitarian dictatorships, its *raison d'être* and its mission.'

The National Council of the CGT, which met in January 1940 for what proved to be its last assembly before the destruction of the union movement by the Vichy government, took an identical stand on the question of collaboration with the communists. In the meantime Soviet Russia had invaded Finland. In particularly strong terms the resolution voted by the National Council censured this action and the subjugation of the Baltic states by Russia, both having shown in a sinister light, according to the

Council, the warlike intentions of the new Soviet imperialism.[11]

In September 1939, after the break with the communists had been made, René Belin, assistant secretary of the CGT, declared optimistically: 'There will be no split. In every union we will oblige the communist leaders, as distinguished from their followers, to withdraw. And they must withdraw.' [12]

Subsequent events showed not only that Belin's hope was not to be fulfilled but also that it had not been very sincere. There was actually a split, and a split was what Belin and his *Syndicats* friends wanted. During the session of the National Council in January 1940, one of the prominent members of this group declared frankly that life within the union movement had become impossible long before the war. The separation from the communists, he declared, would have been a necessity even without the European conflict. He concluded that any union which did not share this opinion was putting itself outside the ranks of the CGT.[13]

What actually occurred was the expulsion of communists from the leadership and the ranks of the CGT and the expulsion of communist locals and unions at every level from the organizations affiliated with the CGT. Though it varied in form, the adopted procedure was essentially the same everywhere. The Russian invasion of Poland, which had immediately precipitated the breach, no longer played a role. The question put before the members was whether or not they approved of the German-Soviet pact. Those who gave no answer were considered to approve and were excluded. Similar methods were used to expel from their offices in the Bourses du Travail every labor organization which did not openly reject the pact.[14]

Exclusion for adherence to a particular political opinion was an especially difficult operation in a labor movement like the French, which had always declared itself nonpartisan and open to every worker, irrespective of his political creed. Those very union leaders who had always emphasized the necessity for the trade-union movement to keep aloof from political controversies were now expelling members from their organizations for reasons of political belief.

Jouhaux was aware that this procedure disregarded the principles expressed in the Charter of Amiens and confirmed by the resolutions of Toulouse. He tried to contend that the decision reached by the CGT was not directed against communism. Such an action would be impossible, he wrote, for a union movement that was open to all wage earners. The break had been unavoidable only because the labor movement, peaceloving by definition, could not co-operate with advocates of a hostile foreign government and of a pact that had caused the war. To ask an opinion about the German-Soviet pact, Jouhaux argued later, was not to ask an opinion about a political fact, for the war was 'not only' a political fact, and those who refused to condemn the pact were traitors to the cause of peace and of the nation.[15]

Such arguments were considered spurious and futile by Belin and the *Syndicats* group.[16] And their criticism was not wholly unjustified, for Jouhaux's argument was essentially an attempt to interpret the actual facts in such a way as to make them fit the fundamental principles of the French labor movement. The brutal admission of Belin's friends that the exclusions were directed against communism ('They were traitors precisely because they were communists') was certainly a more faithful description of what actually happened.

Now it became clear beyond any doubt that the discussions which had been going on practically ceaselessly since the reunification of the union movement in 1936 had been only a blind. Political issues had been veiled by polemics regarding the acceptance of texts agreed upon more than thirty years earlier, in special historical circumstances. Hence the discussions could not contribute in any way to the clarification of the real divergencies, and they left the rank and file confused or disgusted, or both. In the political situation at the outbreak of the war the previous confusion developed into an entirely hypocritical attitude on all sides. The former advocates of unionist independence betrayed the principles they had defended. The communists, who had always denied that the trade-union movement should be indifferent politically, now protested against their exclusion in the name of the trade-union movement's 'independence.'

Graver than any violation of the dead letter of the Amiens Charter was the role which the expulsion procedure forced upon the CGT in the crucial first months of the war. When Jouhaux wrote about the communists as 'traitors to the national cause,' he touched upon the true reasons for their wholesale expulsion from the labor movement. At the end of September, scarcely more than a week after the CGT Central Office decision to break with the communists, the government had dissolved the communist party and its affiliated organizations.[17] And the CGT, wishing to maintain its status as a legal organization, could not tolerate in its ranks avowed members of organizations that were outlawed by the government. Hence it became willynilly a partner in the governmental policy of repressing a numerically important fraction of the working class.

III

The exclusion of the communists from the CGT and the government's outlawing of all communist organizations and publications forced *La Vie ouvrière* out of existence and made it necessary for communist propaganda to go underground. It is not improbable that if the communist leaders had been given enough freedom to defend the Russian policy they would have lost most of their following and their former adherents would have swung over to active support of the French war effort. As it was, the attitude taken by the government and the CGT undoubtedly made it easier for the communists to cover their change of policy by adopting an air of martyrdom.

Shortly after the banning of *La Vie ouvrière* the communist trade unionists started to publish in Belgium an illegal paper, *Le Monde*, which was secretly introduced into French territory.[18]

It made an appeal for 'trade-union unity' which was signed by most of the well-known communist union leaders who had been excluded from the CGT. The government proceeded to arrest those signatories of the appeal who had not sought refuge on foreign soil. Numerous arrests of other communist union leaders and members followed. Trials of former secretaries of some of the federations resulted in draconian sentences.[19] Little by little what had begun as the elimination of communist organizations deemed dangerous to France's war effort developed into a progressive elimination of civil liberties. Later a special government decree authorized the internment of 'suspects' in concentration camps, without trial.[20] Many thousands were sent to these 'camps des suspects' on a mere denunciation. Very often the police measures were extended to union members who, though they had either broken with the communists or even been hostile to communism, were known for their radicalism. Other decrees limiting the freedom of opinion resulted in the dismissal of numerous civil servants who had been active in the corporative movement but had at all times been opposed to communism. A resolution passed by the League for the Rights of Man complained that all these and similar measures which had the avowed purpose of stamping out communist activities did nothing to hamper the dissemination of Nazi propaganda in France.[21]

Communist propaganda frequently pointed to the fact that this policy compared unfavorably with the course of action followed during World War I, when the Minister of the Interior had left unmolested the three thousand union leaders listed in 'Carnet B.' This gave strength to their argument that the second 'imperialist' war was even worse than its predecessor. Such reasoning concealed, of course, the major difference between the situations prevailing in the labor movement at the outbreak of hostilities in 1914 and in 1939; now the communists called for resistance to an 'imperialist' war, while then the CGT had vowed that its members would become the 'soldiers of liberty.'

The officials of the CGT never approved of the government's practices of suppression. Mild protests were voiced, especially against the arrest of those union members who had broken with communism.[22] With only a few exceptions, however, the trade-union press did not take up the defense of civil liberties, for the government had succeeded in presenting all its measures as serving only the extirpation of communism. One article in *Le Peuple* declared that the labor movement was 'neutral' in regard to the persecution of communists.[23] And since communist organizers and members were not only hounded by the government but also excluded from the CGT, the labor movement was regarded by many as a party to the generally condemned police methods.

Communist underground propaganda made wide use of the confusion that arose out of an ambiguous situation. The leaders of the CGT were attacked as stool-pigeons and informers; they were accused of accelerating the triumph of fascism in France, of using Hitlerian methods, and of serving the interests of the government and of capitalism. The workers' growing dissatisfaction with the inequities of the ill-conceived labor legislation was also exploited by the underground propaganda in order to increase distrust of the legal labor movement. The latter, almost completely excluded from the framework of wartime social legislation, was making continuous though for the most part vain attempts to improve working conditions. But the communists denounced as deliberate collusion with the government what in reality was impotence, and their accusations were believed all the more widely because certain CGT leaders had accepted governmental responsibilities without obtaining any share in power. Secretly distributed leaflets laid the blame for the lowered living standard of the masses on Jouhaux and his 'fellow charlatans, adventurers, and upstarts.' The communist phrase 'reformist traitors,' forgotten since the Seventh International World Congress in Moscow, was vehemently revived.[24]

That the communist propaganda did not remain without influence among members of the unions is evident from the CGT's decision to issue a special weekly, *Les Informations hebdoma-daires*. Jouhaux gave this publication the assignment of replying to 'underground propaganda that is spreading lies and calumnies in accordance with the advice given by Lenin.' From its very aim, the new journal was bound to be defensive in character. Its columns were devoted to repudiating other views rather than to presenting a constructive line of its own. Also, it gave much space to violent criticism of social and political conditions in the Soviet Union,[25] a not very appealing type of propaganda for French workers thoroughly dissatisfied with social and political conditions at home. Quite naturally the publication was written mainly by those within the union movement who had for some time specialized in attacks on the communists: the group around *Syndicats*, whose influence was generally strengthened by the events of those months.

The editors of *Syndicats* had repeatedly asserted that they continued the publication of their journal only because the communists had not ceased publication of *La Vie ouvrière*. With the suppression of the latter, there seemed no longer any justification for a paper like *Syndicats*, which was the mouthpiece of a single faction within the organization. Actually, however, the paper and its sponsoring group expanded their activities, which was proof enough that Belin and his friends aimed at goals beyond the fight against communism in the ranks of the CGT.[26]

Only the representatives of the civil servants federation voiced warnings against the dangers inherent in the course of action that the CGT was taking.[27] This federation's three delegates to the Administrative Committee of the CGT had approved only 'with reserve' the decision taken in September to exclude the communists, and their organization had deferred the exclusion as long as possible. In a private meeting Charles Laurent, their secretary-general, strongly attacked the decision of the CGT as the work of a 'clique of *défaitistes* . . . having no other ambition than to split the union movement.' He added that events had made Jouhaux a prisoner of this clique.

The divergency which became manifest between the *Syndicats* group and the civil servants federation, whose relative weight within the CGT had been considerably increased by the new split, showed how little unity prevailed even after the exclusion of the communists. Robert Lacoste, a secretary of the civil servants federation, had to refute the accusation that he and his friends had hesitated to condemn the Hitler-Stalin pact and the attitude of the communists. Lacoste pointed out that the leadership of his organization had always been entirely free of communist influence and that, as decided foes of Hitlerism, he and his friends had strongly criticized the volte-face of the Soviet Union. What he feared, he explained, was that the CGT's decision might result in its isolation from the working class. He regretted that the labor movement had merely reproved and condemned the communist workers. Instead he wanted to see some simple and clear ideas presented to them, appealing to their real patriotism and offering a positive program of bold social policy. As early as November 1939 Laurent foresaw that the communists would be able to pose as the sole defenders of the workers' rights, and thereby derive more strength than they had ever possessed.

Shortly before the German invasion the official organ of the civil servants federation had to protest once more that it by no means sought to defend communism but that it was more than alarmed by the government's policy of repression: 'We are not living in a totalitarian country,' warned the paper.

During these months of the 'phony war' the communists, appearing to many workers and soldiers not only as martyrs but also as the true champions of social interests and the defenders of civil liberties, regained much of the terrain that they had lost by the volte-face of the Soviet Union. After the outbreak of hostilities and for a short time after the Russian attack on Poland, the majority of French workers had condemned the new policy of the Soviet Union and scorned the new 'line' of the Communist International. But these feelings were soon altered by the hostile

attitude of the Daladier government toward the workers, by the
social realities which the workers faced in the plants, barracks,
and fortifications during the first months of the war, and by
the absence of any serious action on the military front, a situation
that was easily interpreted as proof of some dark plot between
the belligerents.

All this seemed to lend weight to the communists' reasoning on
the character of the war, for which the peoples of Europe had
not, in any case, shown an enthusiasm comparable to the exaltation of August 1914. The new communist line was first defined
in November 1939 by the former communist deputy, André
Marty, in an 'Open letter to Léon Blum': [28]

Why is this war unjust? To answer this question it is necessary
to look not for who started it, but for which forces and which
classes are conducting it, and with what aims. The answer is easy.
    Three imperialist countries—Great Britain, France, the United
States—possess all the essential raw materials and immense economic, financial, and human resources, which they acquired by
war, by looting, and by the exploitation of the workers; the territories of these countries comprise more than half the world.
And they want to keep and to increase these immense territories
and sources of exploitation.
    But three other imperialist countries—Germany, Italy, Japan—
lacking such wealth, want to take away from the former countries their markets, their spheres of influence, and their colonial
empires.
    Like our beloved teachers we shall not cease our struggle
before we have vanquished our enemy—who is within our own
borders.
    Down with the imperialist war!

In their written and oral underground propaganda the communists insisted that this was not a war in the interests of the
peoples, but was solely a war of class interests. As this premise
appeared to be borne out by the policy of the French government, the conclusion, too, was easily accepted. Only the Soviet
Union could wage war in the people's interest because Russia,
not being divided by class interests, was not like other countries.

It was precisely because this war was not in the interest of the world's peoples that the Soviet Union had remained neutral, and her very aloofness revealed this war—until such time as Hitler would choose to attack Russia—as an irretrievably imperialist fracas. Hence no true patriot should take part in it. In 1939 as well as in 1789 the true patriot was he who served no particular class interests but was a revolutionary determined to undermine the foundations of the existing order.[29]

When Russia attacked Finland, at the end of November, the workers' bewilderment about the righteousness of France's cause was increased by the ardor with which the appeasers of yesterday advocated a rupture of diplomatic relations with Soviet Russia, if not a declaration of war. There was much eagerness on the part of these persons to fight the Soviets and to forget about the war with Germany. The Comité des Forges and its spokesmen, who had declared on the eve of the war that it was impossible to suspend shipments of French iron ore to Nazi Germany, now discussed the advantages of an Allied attack on Baku in order to interfere with the shipments of Russian oil to Germany. When it became apparent that the Daladier government, in spite of various pressures brought to bear upon it, could not be induced to declare war on Russia, intrigues started inside and outside the Parliament, with the aim of replacing Daladier by the men who six months later were to constitute the Vichy government.[30]

The resolution approved by the National Council of the CGT in January 1940, sharply censuring the Russian attack on Finland, was entirely in accordance with the traditions of the international labor movement, which had always taken the side of the attacked and condemned the aggressor.[31] But against the background of the political controversies of that period the resolution could easily be represented as proof that the CGT had made common cause with the appeasers and the enemies of the labor movement. Communist propaganda could thus swing to full-fledged *défaitisme* and incite the workers to sabotage the war effort, without appearing to betray the cause of anti-fascism. 'By utilizing all your intelligence and all your technical experience,' declared one of the rather widely distributed communist underground leaflets, 'you should delay the armament production and render its output useless. Frustrate by this method the intentions of the French rulers! . . . Longshoremen . . . you should refuse energetically to load ships with arms and ammunition that are to be sent to the Finnish reactionaries.' [32]

Since such appeals were disseminated among the workers in industrial centers and similar propaganda was spread among soldiers on furlough, the government was bound to intensify its persecution of communism. The severity of police and court action increased considerably, and even in the midst of the battle of France the newspapers announced severe sentences on communist workers.[33]

IX

The Position of Non-Communist Labor

A<small>T</small> the outbreak of World War I the trade-union movement as a whole had held an anti-patriotic and internationalist philosophy, and this had quickly collapsed after the start of hostilities. At the outbreak of World War II only the communists changed their attitude, and this time the swing was in the other direction, from chauvinism to revolutionary internationalism. On the problems of war and peace the other groups within the labor movement still held the same views—firm or equivocal, as the case might be—that they had supported before the war.

I

The revolutionary syndicalists in the CGT, who before the war had formed the 'Centre Syndical d'Action Contre la Guerre,' were too small a group to exert any significant influence. In the days of the Munich crisis they had been backed by elements foreign to the labor movement, but after the outbreak of the war men like Flandin and Bonnet deemed it wiser to shun a group that preached revolutionary resistance to the war. Some of the members of this group, deprived of their former protection, were arrested or sent to concentration camps.[1]

The pacifists of *Syndicats*, on the other hand, had never preached revolutionary resistance to war, and no such action was attempted by them when war broke out. But almost as soon as the war had started, some of the leading personages of *Syndicats*, like certain ministers of Daladier's cabinet (Bonnet and de Monzie) and the leader of the appeasers in the Chamber (Flandin), made desperate attempts to bring about a negotiated peace by means of high diplomacy. While the Nazi troops were bombing Warsaw and its workers' dwellings, Ludovic Zoretti, whose activities after Munich were mentioned in an earlier chapter, established contact with the secretary of a Swiss trade union and with Henri de Man, socialist cabinet minister of Belgium, in order to pave the way for peace negotiations after the anticipated end of the Polish campaign. Also the secretary of the French socialist party, Paul Faure, volunteered his services in connection with this endeavor to use the international connections of the labor movement for the cause of capitulation. Both trade unionists and socialists established relations with Senator Pierre Laval, who even then held the strings of an appeasement plot in his hands.[2]

After the German-Russian conquest of Poland there appeared a widely distributed leaflet, 'Immediate Peace,' which in sentimental terms was openly devoted to the cause of appeasement. As its authors admitted, the leaflet was designed to establish contacts between political and trade-union circles. The signatures of numerous trade unionists of *Syndicats* and its counterpart in Bordeaux, *Septembre* 38, appeared along with that of the deputy Marcel Déat.[3] The best known among the union leaders who signed the leaflet was Pierre Vigne, secretary of the miners federation. At the beginning of the war Vigne had been appointed to a position in the office of the Minister of Labor, and when he signed the manifesto he was the only member of the CGT in an official government position. At about the same time that the leaflet appeared, Pierre-Etienne Flandin, discussing the war before the Foreign Affairs Committee of the Chamber, asked, 'Is it really worth going on with?' The Minister of Labor, Charles Pomaret, also belonged to the appeasement group within the government, and was to vote for capitulation before the invader in that historic cabinet meeting of June 1940, which forced Reynaud into resignation and brought Marshal Pétain to power.

Nevertheless, the signatories of the leaflet were indicted and threatened with court martial. They avoided trial, however, by evasive declarations and probably also through the connivance of their highly placed sympathizers, for Bonnet was still Minister of Justice. The labor advocates of appeasement, after having risked conviction for high treason without preventing the continuation of the 'state of war,' no longer resorted to open action. In World War I the pacifist minority in the labor movement had preached a consistent creed, but the followers of *Syndicats* subscribed to no formulated doctrine of pacifism. An article published by the pacifist socialist, Paul Faure, during Sumner Welles' visit to Paris may be regarded as typical. Faure wrote of the war in oversimplified, purely economic terms. Thus in his article, entitled 'I had a bold dream,' he 'dreamt' of an economic roundtable conference of Hitler, Mussolini, Stalin, Chamberlain, and Daladier, who would successfully discuss the amicable settlement of their differences and the redistribution of raw materials.[4] Such conceptions were shared by many of the prominent members of the *Syndicats* group. But for the time being their 'boldness' remained confined to 'dreams.'

It is true that in the first months of 1940 a certain change of mood seemed to occur. René Belin declared then that while he was still proud of having been among the defenders of the Munich policy, he could no longer hope that peace with Hitler might be based on a contractual agreement.[5] Such statements became more frequent after Reynaud had formed a war-to-the-bitter-end cabinet and all hopes of a negotiated peace seemed to have vanished. During the Norwegian campaign another member of the *Syndicats* group asserted that it was necessary to 'abandon a pacifism that had become merely sentimental and unrealistic, and to favor definitely and openly the victory of the Allies.'[6] But in view of the fact that as soon as the armistice was concluded Belin and the most prominent of his friends either joined Vichy or became fervent collaborationists in Paris, it is likely that their short-lived allegiance to anti-Hitlerism had the same source as that which Georges Dumoulin had ascribed to the unions' attitude in 1914: fear—the fear of being threatened by a government that was likely to take more energetic measures than its predecessors against appeasers of whatever allegiance.

That there was never any real change of mind is evidenced by many statements on apparently secondary issues, of which the real importance could be understood only after the collapse of France. Thus when the deputy Kerillis tried to denounce certain appeasement activities in the highest circles of the republic, and was assailed in the press and in Parliament, Syndicats joined the violent attacks against him.[7] When the Reynaud government made an attempt to discover certain 'fifth columnists,' the secretary of the building workers union asserted flatly that there were no fifth columnists in France except communist agents.[8] When it became known during the days of Dunkerque that Henri de Man, the idol of the French pacifists in the CGT, had been among the first Belgians who offered to 'collaborate' with the invaders of his country, Georges Lefranc published a strange article about de Man. Of course, Lefranc, who at that time was associated with the French Ministry of Information, could only disapprove of de Man's action; he did it, however, in terms that were full of high praise for the Belgian minister and former socialist.[9]

Moreover, all through this period the leaders of the CGT's pacifist faction remained in close touch with those ministers of the Reynaud cabinet whose persistent defeatism soon became evident. De Monzie, for instance, had numerous friends among the old-time union leaders in the Paris region who were now coming again into the foreground.

II

The 'center' group, to which Jouhaux and his friends belonged, was far from subscribing to the philosophy and the activities of Syndicats. But the strength of the center, questionable before the war, was weakened considerably by the new conditions. It became evident to what extent its general political orientation had been affected by the communists, who for opportunist reasons had lent it the support of their well-disciplined followers. Now Jouhaux's associates were only the civil servants federation and certain union officials scattered through the CGT. And the leaders of the civil servants federation, although they had always shown a remarkably clear insight into the international situation, had a necessarily limited influence on the specifically proletarian organizations.

The small amount of support on which the center group could rely made it extremely difficult for it to oppose the ideas propagated by *Syndicats*. In their opposition to the pacifists, Jouhaux and his associates were handicapped also by their reluctance to uncover the extent to which the appeasers actually indulged in treasonable activities. A frontal attack would have meant a serious threat to the infirm reconstruction of the union movement. And on top of everything else, the center had very little opportunity to express itself, for with the advent of the war the financial difficulties of the CGT became almost catastrophic. Thus *Le Peuple* became a weekly instead of a daily, and had to reserve its columns almost entirely for the reports of the unions engaged in rebuilding their organizations. At the same time the size of *Syndicats*, a weekly publication, was hardly affected by the wartime restrictions imposed upon most publications. That *Syndicats* shared this advantage with the organ of the pacifist wing of the socialist party, *Le Pays socialiste*, can hardly be considered a mere coincidence.[10]

The official statements by the CGT on the paramount issues of war and peace reflected the prevailing disunity and uncertainty. The resolutions never used anything but the vaguest and most general terms. Typically enough, a report on the only wartime meeting of the National Council of the CGT remarked that the question of the war was 'treated only incidentally.'[11] This was not due, as the report maintained, to the fact that 'everyone thought a debate on this question was unnecessary.' It was rather an expression of the fact that in the hour of decision the French labor movement was so weak and so disunited that it dared not take a stand on the most burning problems before the nation and its working class. The final resolution unanimously adopted by this meeting dealt briefly with political problems and, in an apparent attempt to conciliate disparate attitudes, declared:

The Council affirms fervently, in spite of the tragedy which once more disturbs the world, its faith in a perfectible humanity, capable of organizing peace and fostering liberty.

It stresses the fact that the union movement unanimously gives its entire support to all hopes for realizing a just and lasting peace. But the National Council asserts that the labor movement's desire for peace should not be interpreted as a desire to yield to the tyrannical totalitarian governments which bear the responsibility for the war.[12]

This colorless text remained the only political declaration of the CGT before the German invasion.

When Jouhaux discussed international problems he gave thought mostly to remote postwar solutions: a new social order, equitable distribution of wealth among nations, international collaboration in order to achieve the best utilization of resources, normalization of industrial relations, development of the International Labour Office.[13]

Only the civil servants federation endeavored to supplement and make more concrete the new social order envisaged by Jouhaux. In accordance with its traditions the federation saw the greatest hopes for the future in the establishment in every country of a planned economy that would lead to a general rise in living standards. Charles Laurent, its secretary-general, did not, however, minimize the fact that one of the main problems would be to reconcile the necessary measures of economic surveillance and control with the maintenance of general freedom.[14]

On the rare occasions when *Le Peuple* discussed political questions of more immediate interest, it indulged in a most unrealistic underestimate of Nazi Germany's strength, a view that was shared, incidentally, by most of the French press of that period. Germany was pictured, even at the very beginning of the war, as having exhausted her economic, financial, and moral forces. Undoubtedly, it was said, her economic plight would rapidly become critical.[15] The fact that France was not invaded during the first months of the war was viewed in unionist as well as in many political circles as proof that the war was practically won for the Allies.

Sweeping generalities and irritating fallacies were not sufficient, however, to interpret to the French workers the character of the war against Hitlerism, and the issues at stake. Therefore it is not surprising that the majority of the organized workers either adhered to the pacifist creed of the appeasement faction or fell entirely under the spell of communist *défaitisme*. As a further attraction the appeasers within the CGT were dexterous enough to use wherever possible the traditional language of internationalism known to the workers from the last war.

After the German invasion of northern France the Central Office of the CGT addressed a patriotic appeal to the working class, emphasizing that the French workers had always made the greatest sacrifices for the cause of liberty. It admonished them to sustain the common effort and to identify themselves with the cause of the nation, since they would be the first victims of a Nazi victory.[16] But once more it was the organ of the civil servants federation which made the most ringing statement, finding the Jacobin accents that the French labor movement had thus far lacked. Under the classical slogan, 'The fatherland is in danger,' Laurent forcefully and significantly wrote:

> Not only is our fatherland in danger but an entire form of civilization is threatened with ruin. We risk being sunk for decades in a period as dark as the Middle Ages. . . Frenchmen will resist to the end, and should be determined to sweep aside all those waverers who may block the path to victory. For months we have been repeating that it is necessary to give back to this country the soul of the French Revolution. . . Sustain-

ing the fight, and vanquishing, demand the total allegiance of workers and farmers and a purification of the political atmosphere of the country.

Enormous mistakes have been committed during these last months, even very recently.[17]

In truly Jacobin fashion Laurent inveighed against the 'sordid avarice of the rich.' 'Why,' he concluded, 'was the indispensable economy of war not created, when it was clear for two years, even to the greatest optimists, that war was coming?'

III

The reconstruction that became necessary in the CGT after the communists were ejected was at best a difficult process. It was made even more difficult by the strictly state-regulated character of the French war economy, which considerably restricted the activity of the labor movement and therefore diminished its possibility of recruitment.

Reorganization was relatively untroublesome in those unions where the communists had not succeeded in penetrating into leading positions—those of the printers and the book trade, the teachers, the postal workers, the miners, dockers, seamen, the clothing industry, the regional union of the Nord, and others. In the federations of the railwaymen and of the lighting industry the former majority was reversed and the communists expelled. But in all other organizations in which the communists had been influential, it became necessary to dissolve the existing unions altogether and to found new ones, which often meant suing before the courts for the surrender of funds, buildings, books, and records. Sometimes the government took it upon itself to dissolve unions by police measures and to deprive them of their property. By such actions the impression was fostered that collusion existed between the leaders of the labor movement and the government. This did not increase the popularity of the newly formed organizations.[18]

Under such conditions reconstruction was necessarily slow, especially on the lower level. The CGT announced as early as the end of October 1939 that at that time the directing bodies of federations and regional unions had been reconstituted, but actually union activities in many important districts and trades were not resumed before the first months of 1940. The first meeting of the new regional union of the Seine (Paris) was held only in March 1940. Many Paris unions, among them those of workers in the armament industries of the suburbs, could not announce a revival of activity until the end of April. The same picture obtained for many other important industrial areas where the communists had been influential. Many groups were so weak that separate trades and districts had to be merged in one organization.

The new organizations had hardly started to function when new troubles arose, from a recrudescence of the old communist tactics of 'boring from within.' Very often the communists had succeeded in entering the new organizations by repudiating the German-Soviet pact, as requested, but once admitted, they engaged in a whispering campaign against the CGT leadership as well as against any aid to the French war effort by the workers. The union officials repeatedly had to warn against such underground activities.[19]

It is impossible to ascertain how the CGT fared numerically in the first months of the war. Its own statistics indicated a total membership of 800,000 at the beginning of 1940.[20] Seven months before the war the civil servants federation, alone, numbered 320,000 members.[21] Since that organization suffered relatively little from mobilization and from the exclusion of the communists, a total of only 800,000 members for the entire CGT would indicate a considerable thinning of the latter's proletarian basis. Jouhaux rightly pointed out that the decline in membership was partly to be explained by the mobilization of more than 5 million soldiers (who, however, came mostly from rural districts) and by the fact that for more than a million workers in defense industries the existing strict legislation did not make union membership attractive, as the unions were prevented from acting in behalf of the workers.

These circumstances, however, do not explain everything. During the preceding war the CGT had considerably increased its membership, but now (even if the figure of 800,000 is assumed as correct) it had returned to its status of the depression years, before the Popular Front and unity had started to swell its ranks. Even less than in the early 1930's was the CGT representative of the majority of the workers. Rather it represented a small traditionalist minority which for decades had formed the backbone of the movement. Those who attended union meetings were almost without exception over fifty years of age.[22]

It is likely that actually the number of members was far less than the official figure. For understandable reasons, prominent union leaders consistently maintained in their public announcements an artificial over-optimism about the progress of union reconstruction.[23] When they were out of the limelight they spoke about the situation in a much more subdued tone. On the very eve of the German invasion one of the assistant secretaries of the regional union of Paris admitted (in a private conversation with the author) that in his long experience as a union organizer he had never known such an anemic condition and such a complete lack of dynamism. The same situation prevailed in industrial regions outside of Paris.

IV

The Catholic trade-union movement did not have to face certain of the difficulties which confronted the CGT after the outbreak of the war. There was no ideological rift within its ranks, nor any organizational split such as that which occurred within the CGT with the exclusion of the communists. On the other hand, the Catholic trade unions, too, suffered from the sudden and massive mobilization of more than 5 million men in the armed forces, and from the strictly state-regulated war economy adopted by the French republic.

According to the official figures published by the CFTC the membership of the Catholic unions did not suffer at all from the outbreak of war, amounting in January 1940 to 488,000, almost exactly the same figure as that reported for the two previous years. During the same period the membership of the CGT declined at least from 5,340,000 to 800,000. If the figures communicated by the CFTC were correct the numerical relation between the two confederations had undergone a radical change; the superiority of the CGT would have dwindled to 1.6 : 1. In view of the undeniable fact that the proportion of civil servants was far lower in the Catholic trade-union movement than in the CGT, the official figures would indicate that during the war the Catholic unions attracted a more important number of wage earners in private industries than the CGT.

It is not likely, however, that the CFTC membership did not suffer at all from general war conditions. A writer closely connected with the Catholic movement admitted that the mobilization gravely affected the organization.[24] Hence it may be assumed that the membership statistics were artificially 'frozen,' at latest at the outbreak of the war, possibly because the general upheaval made it well-nigh impossible for the Central Office of the CFTC to obtain a clear picture of the state of organization.

Despite these uncertainties about the actual figures there is no doubt that the strength of the CFTC increased in relative terms. Perhaps most remarkable was the enhanced attraction which the Catholic trade unions had for the younger generation. As has been mentioned, the CGT was on the whole unable to recruit other elements than the old-time syndicalists, most of them over fifty years of age. But the activity and the dynamism of the Jeunesse Ouvrière Catholique, the Catholic youth organization whose role has been mentioned earlier, only increased with the outbreak of the war. Another impetus was given to the recruitment of the CFTC when French cardinals and archbishops, in

February 1940, officially urged workers and white-collar employees to join the ranks of the Catholic unions.[25]

After Hitler's attack on Poland the traditionally patriotic attitude of the Catholic unions was supplemented by the conception that the war against Hitler was a war for the salvation of Christian civilization. The mental reservations with which an important group within the CGT viewed the war and its avowed aim of putting down Hitlerism did not exist for the Catholic unionists. The meaning of the war was explained by them in terms very similar to those used by the CGT-affiliated civil servants federation. Thus it was held that France and England remained in large part countries of liberal capitalism; the labor movement stood up for their defense because the democracies safeguarded the workers' essential freedom to organize and to defend their interests through the autonomous action of their self-appointed organizations; although the French trade unionists, CFTC and CGT alike, strove to overcome the traditional institutions of capitalist democracy, they did so in a way strikingly different from that of the Nazis, for totalitarianism destroyed every autonomy, be it collective or individual, while organized labor sought to combine the benefits of a planned economy with the independent action of a free labor movement. Hence the war was given another meaning than merely that of a defense of capitalist democracies; it became another phase in the struggle of the western labor movement for the emancipation and the independence of the working class.[26]

Gaston Tessier, secretary-general of the CFTC, joined forces with Jouhaux to list, as foremost among the war aims of French labor, a worldwide federation in the economic as well as in the political domain.[27] This unity of views between the CFTC and the CGT, hitherto unknown in French social history, resulted from a development in the two movements which was accentuated by the war. The CGT, after the exclusion of the communists and its subsequent weakening, became more moderate in expression and in action than ever before. The CFTC, on the other hand, no longer took pride in stressing the differences which separated it from other labor organizations, as it had often done previously. Hence the two movements were drawn together, both ideologically and practically. This change in their relations found expression in numerous contacts and discussions that were maintained during the war. In these discussions one of the participants, a prominent member of the CGT, proposed a common term, 'Syndicalisme Français,' to designate both organizations. The hope was expressed that the common name would be a prelude to a merger of organizations. This was, indeed, a long way from the days of June 1936, when the CGT had refused to see the Catholic unions admitted to Matignon.

This situation and the relative increase in the membership of the CFTC was seized upon by the government to put that organization on an almost equal footing with the CGT wherever collaboration between the government and labor organizations survived. Representatives of the Catholic trade unions asked that they be consulted on all labor questions which would arise under the jurisdiction of the Ministry of Armament.[28] On all boards and committees provided for by the wartime legislation the CFTC was represented by some of its leading officials.

Thus what French management had constantly denounced as the 'monopoly' of the CGT was broken. The principle of the 'most representative organization' was now superseded in every field by what had been called earlier the 'pluralism' of trade-union representation. A Catholic trade-union leader maintained that this pluralism—or rather dualism, for it was only the CGT and the CFTC—had become a reality, and expressed confidence that it was merely a matter of moral and intellectual education to achieve a unified representation of the wage earners' interests.[29] A leading personage in the CGT declared that in his district (the department of the Nord) the Catholic unionists were 'generally recognized and can work in the same direction as the CGT.'[30] This rapprochement between the two organizations was to outlast the French defeat in June 1940.

X

Labor's Position in the War Economy

IN time of war a government has to mobilize the energies of the whole nation behind the common effort. The degree to which it succeeds in speeding up production determines the length, if not the outcome, of the armed conflict. In a war in which the existence of a free labor movement and the survival of democratic liberties are at stake, trade unions have to consider how they can render the maximum contribution to the national effort. The measure of their success in effectively protecting in time of war the interests of their members is indicative of labor's strength ånd of the place it has acquired within the nation. Hence common interests demand the most intimate collaboration between government and trade unions. Under a normally functioning democratic government this collaboration exists at all times. It has to be extended and intensified with the increase in importance which labor derives from war conditions.

Throughout World War I collaboration between the French government and the trade-union movement was most active, and yielded important results in the various fields of social legislation. And before the outbreak of hostilities in 1939 it was believed that in the event of another war the French labor movement would again be required to give fullest assistance to the government.[1] But collaboration between the Daladier regime and the trade-union movement had ceased almost completely after the general strike of November 1938, and when France actually entered the war against her totalitarian neighbor there was no clear-cut change in the policies of her government. At the same time a new body of social legislation exacted the greatest sacrifices from trade-union members and the working class in general.[2]

I

In both world wars France's manpower potential was under a heavy strain, for two reasons. In the first place, she faced an adversary far superior in population, and did so with an ally who could not quickly put an army into the field. And in the second place, the war, both times, proceeded on an entirely different course from what had been expected, and therefore the dispositions initially taken in regard to available manpower had to be hastily adapted to the changing situation.

In 1914 preparations for industrial mobilization were almost entirely lacking, as the possibility of prolonged warfare was not reckoned with. Thus, with most of France's industrial regions invaded, measures to obtain the necessary manpower for the war industries had to be improvised. The administration found itself, understaffed and disorganized as it was, able to cope with its mounting problems only by relying on the active co-operation of employers and trade unions.

In 1939 there seemed to be no need for improvisation. Not only had the National Service law of 11 July 1938 set the framework for the mobilization of human resources; there was even an attempt, on the basis of detailed estimates, to determine the distribution of manpower. Long before the war individual orders had gone out to workers in the armament industries, in the same way as to drafted soldiers.[3] Moreover, in 1939 the war appeared a 'guerre sans guerre.' France had drafted more than 5.5 million men into the armed services to meet an anticipated mass assault from the land and from the air. When this assault did not take place, it was believed in many government circles that a period of at least two years, during which the armament of the belligerents was to be completed, would precede major actions on the military fronts. In the opinion of many, and Raoul Dautry, the

Minister of Armament, was among them, France could hope to obtain tooling machines as well as large quantities of planes and arms from the United States. Such hopes were belied by the launching of the blitzkrieg in western Europe in May 1940, and this change in outlook considerably affected the manpower policy of the French government between the declaration of war and the capitulation.

Since the plans for military mobilization called for the withdrawal of nearly all men between 21 and 40 years of age, constituting more than 40 per cent of the total employed male population, it had been decided from the very outset that in case of war French armament production could not rely on the mechanism of a free labor market, and that voluntary agreement between employers and workers would have to be replaced with a manpower draft, such as was devised by the National Service act of 1938. That act and subsequent decrees [4] provided for the collective requisitioning of all men and women employed in establishments, factories, and undertakings that were engaged in work for army, naval, or air authorities. Wages and salaries of requisitioned personnel were determined in accordance with those in force during the previous employment. When the post was a new one the salary was fixed by reference to that of some comparable peacetime job.

In general the measures of requisition were confined to the employed personnel, and did not affect property relations in the plants. Hence the fact that the workers were being put under quasi-military rule was not mitigated by any simultaneous diminution in the employers' rights. Quite the contrary, the new legislation endowed the employer with new disciplinary authority. If a worker performed his duties unsatisfactorily, was deemed responsible for a slowdown, or lacked discipline, the employer was entitled to make deductions from his wages. It was emphatically stated that this procedure had nothing to do with the fines imposed by employers in former times, inasmuch as the deducted sum was to be paid to a Community War Fund.[5]

For the penalized worker, however, the effect of the deduction was not unlike that of the previous fines, which were regarded as a heritage of the guild age and which the labor movement had for decades been striving to abolish.[6] In graver cases the requisitioned workers could be punished by the courts with imprisonment for violation of their obligations under the National Service act. This means of maintaining discipline among the workers was resorted to rather frequently.[7]

Between the enactment of the National Service act and the beginning of the war, the government, as was discussed above, made use of the requisition provisions as a means of breaking strikes. Hence many of the workers regarded requisitioning not as an indispensable means of speeding up war production but as a device for abolishing the elementary rights of a free labor movement. This resulted in a deep-rooted resentment on the part of the workers against the requisition and its rigid discipline.

At the beginning of the war approximately 1.23 million men and women were employed in war industries. The first requisition measures were very moderate, as it was considered primarily important to mobilize the greatest possible number of men in the armed forces. Thus the military mobilization brought about a decline of about 50 per cent in the number of armament workers. Even by March 1940 the number had risen to only about 1.20 million, not quite the prewar level.[8] This figure alone shows that the respite offered by the months of 'phony war' was not utilized in order to speed up war production.

Only about two-thirds of these 1.2 million workers in defense industries belonged to the category of requisitioned workers (*requis civils*), the remainder being 'specially assigned' (*affectés spéciaux*). Many skilled and semi-skilled workers were at first mobilized as soldiers, and these, under certain conditions of age and dependency and at an order of the military authorities, could become *affectés spéciaux*. The number of conscripts belonging to this category had risen by March 1940 to 450,000.[9] Their wages were determined in the same way as those of requisitioned workers, but their status underwent frequent changes and was definitely established only when the military situation had already become critical.[10] The *affectés spéciaux* were regarded as soldiers. Even when permanently attached to a job they were subject to military rule, and a lack of discipline on their part could be punished as disobedience according to martial law.

The special assignment was granted only at the request of the employer, and different military authorities did not have to follow any established rule in passing upon the requests; the consequence was widespread inequality. There were complaints that some plants had more *affectés spéciaux* than they could use, and others too few. Many thousands of the specially assigned had never been workers before the war.

Most complaints on the part of the workers and their organizations arose from the practices concerning dismissal. The *affectés spéciaux*, though they did not have the right to choose their jobs, could be dismissed by the employers; the *requis civils* were formally dismissed only by the labor inspectors, but the latter acted on the employers' request. If there was to be a 'battlefield' economy, in which workers were shifted and assigned to jobs like soldiers, it was felt that employers should give up their control over firing. Numerous cases became known in which employers saw to it that the special assignment of a worker was canceled, and for no other reason than to get rid of an active union organizer.[11] Dismissal of *affectés spéciaux* almost always led to the workers' return to their military formations. The gates to arbitrary action, and very often to denunciation, were opened all the wider as there was no possibility of appealing a decision which changed the status of a worker. During World War I a Service of Manpower Control had functioned, and the trade unions had had a voice in the decisions of the local boards connected with that office. No comparable services were set up in 1939.

When it became evident that too many men had been mobilized and that more manpower was needed on the farms and in the factories, a third category of semi-military workmen was created: the so-called *compagnies de renforcement*, scheduled to muster more than 100,000 men but probably never attaining quite that number. Many of the workers in these companies were housed in barracks; others returned to their homes. They worked at a fixed remuneration which consisted of the soldiers' pay plus a very insufficient subsistence allotment. The workers belonging to the *compagnies de renforcement* were paid considerably less than the normal wages for the jobs to which they were assigned.[12]

Equality of sacrifice in a war is never attained. It is, however, an important goal toward which government efforts must be directed if the conditions for maximum output are to be realized. The French system of manpower supply only intensified the inequalities. In the shop *requis civils, affectés spéciaux,* and *travailleurs militaires* worked side by side, the first under the authority of the employer, the latter two under military rule. In regard to pay *requis* and *affectés* were treated like workers, the *travailleurs militaires* like soldiers. Still other categories with a special status were formed by foreign workers and by workers from the French colonies, the latter being relied upon in increasing numbers to relieve the shortage of manpower. For most of the trades outside of defense work and public service the free contractual agreement persisted.

These inequalities deeply affected the morale of the workers, and proved a disturbance to defense production. A deputy who never indulged in expressions of excessive radicalism summarized his criticism of the governmental measures in the moderate statement that 'In our internal despair we do not have the impression that things are as they should be, and we are afraid that a change for the better is not impending.' [13] To meet the objection that also the soldiers at the front had to accept, without questioning, the motives of the orders they received, another deputy pertinently remarked that the workers, unlike soldiers, were employed on jobs they knew, and that they could therefore judge for themselves if they were utilized in a sensible way.[14]

Above all, the whole system was so complicated that a survey of available manpower and of the needs of production was unobtainable. Thus poor planning and obvious waste of scarce labor continued. The system left little if any room for the activities of the trade-union movement. There had been proposals to deny *affectés spéciaux* and *requis civils* the right to organize in unions. These plans were finally abandoned, but actually few of the workers in these categories belonged to trade unions. Since working conditions were closely determined by statutory regulation, and since intervention by the labor organizations was practically impossible, membership in the unions seemed pointless to most workers in the defense industries. Moreover, in many localities the holding of trade-union meetings was forbidden.[15]

Participation in the overall planning of the manpower supply was denied to the CGT. As was reported above, the National Service act of 1938 envisaged the institution of regional committees on which management and labor would be represented, but these provisions never emerged from the blueprint stage, as the implementing decrees, which were issued in connection with the general strike in November 1938, refrained from establishing such committees. This was not changed when war broke out, and hence the CGT, despite the wording of the National Service act, was prevented from taking any considerable part in the distribution of the available labor supply on the regional level.

Nationwide employment questions had been attended to before the war by the National Labor Supply Council (Conseil National de la Main d'Oeuvre), whose function it was to supervise the utilization and distribution of labor in general, and more specifically of immigrant labor. On its board the CGT and the Catholic trade-union movement, as well as the employers, had had their representatives. After the outbreak of the war the National Labor Supply Council was suspended by decree and superseded by a National Labor Co-ordination Committee (Commission Nationale de Coordination de la Main d'Oeuvre), composed solely of government officials, with no representatives from either management or labor. Even when this body was enlarged, no such representatives were included.[16] In matters of labor supply the government deliberately clung to a purely bureaucratic solution.

II

There is always a danger that in times of national emergency an indiscriminate lengthening of working hours will be resorted to as the simplest method of increasing production, without consideration for the optimum relation between the extension of the working day and individual output.[17]

The official commentary issued with the French wartime legislation concerning working hours held that there was a need for an 'appreciable extension' of hours in order to furnish 'an enormous effort of production.' All industrial and commercial establishments were permitted to extend working time to 60 hours a week. In defense industries and in all enterprises performing a public service a permit from the labor inspector could increase weekly hours to 72. Hours for women and children were limited to 60 a week, but even this limit could be exceeded on issuance of a special permit. At the same time the weekly rest period and vacations with pay were altogether suspended.[18]

It is generally acknowledged that 60 hours a week is the upper limit of practical working hours for male workers; in various industries even a 60-hour week is considered excessive.[19] Thus in France the government recognized after a relatively short period that lengthening the work week beyond 60 hours decreased individual output. Henceforth, until the invasion of France by Germany, the 60-hour week became the general rule in armament factories. The suspension of the weekly rest period was made permissive rather than mandatory; actually such periods had to be granted regularly, sometimes in rotation. The necessity of returning to the principle of paid vacations was explicitly stressed. It was specified, too, that the 60-hour work week for women should be a rare exception; a 48- to 50-hour week was declared the norm for women and children.[20]

All changes and revisions of the legal work week were made without consultation with the organizations of management and labor. Such consultation had been stipulated in the Labor Code for any change in work-hour legislation, but was abolished at the beginning of the war. Although the Chamber of Deputies Committee on Social Questions urged the government to return to former practices, the latter was unwilling to give any voice to management or labor in these matters.[21] This attitude was all the less understandable as the CGT had never opposed even an indiscriminate lengthening of the work week. It had only insisted that a more rational organization of production would permit of shorter working time.[22] The procedure adopted for the work-hour legislation showed once more the general tendency to dispense with the assistance of the trade-union movement, even in a consultative capacity.

A sound wage policy in a war economy has a twofold aim: first, to prevent the inflationary spiral of prices and wages; and second, to provide the necessary incentives for workers to increase productivity. The two goals are, of course, interconnected, but in some respects they may appear contradictory. This means that a compromise has to be effected, and the skill with which it is achieved determines in large measure the success of economic policy in wartime. After the outbreak of the war the French government did not seek any compromise. It attempted to tackle the first problem and refrained altogether from using wage policy as an incentive for raising output.

The economic and financial policy of Paul Reynaud, Minister of Finance before and after the declaration of war and Prime Minister between the spring of 1940 and the capitulation, was frankly deflationary. The report accompanying the new regulations for working conditions in wartime specified that the armament effort should not place too heavy a burden on the financial system. It thus seemed that the government was guided not only by a desire to avoid an increase in purchasing power but also by a wish to conduct the war in as 'stingy' a way as possible. This stinginess, which prevailed not only in money matters, was generally characteristic of the way in which France tried to fight her totalitarian neighbor.

At the outbreak of the war all money wages were frozen at the prewar level.[23] A stabilization of wholesale and retail prices was to accompany this rigid wage stabilization, but from the very beginning the prices of agricultural products sold by producers, and the wholesale prices of raw materials and articles whose production or importation was supervised by specific ministries, were exempted from the overall regulation.[24]

From the outset, price control met with distrust. Price-control measures had been taken repeatedly since 1936, and nonetheless between June 1936 and the outbreak of the war the cost of living had gone up by more than 50 per cent, even according to the official index, whose accuracy was contested by the labor movement.[25] In the first months of the war, despite official controls, prices rose more sharply than in the comparable period of the earlier war, when no such controls had existed. The official acknowledgment of this fact came in April 1940, when the government decreed for 1 May a new stabilization of all prices at the level then prevailing. It was no longer maintained that the stabilization attempts made eight months earlier had been successful.[26]

One reason for this lack of success was that the several ministries concerned with price control in wartime did not have a uniform interest in determining prices, and there was no superior authority with the power to make decisions when differences developed. Also, the overall ceiling was much too rigorous to succeed. And the enforcement devices, though strengthened in comparison with prewar methods, were still inadequate, especially outside of Paris. Insufficient rationing of food increased the pressure on prices still further.

How important this rise in prices was and how it influenced the cost of living cannot be determined exactly, because with the outbreak of the war the publication of all current price statistics was suspended. Private organizations estimated that between August 1939 and April 1940 the rise in wholesale prices amounted to 50 per cent for imported raw materials, and to 26 per cent for French products; for the same period the price increase in food was estimated at 15 to 20 per cent.[27] Thus the freezing of money wages at the prewar level resulted in a significant lowering of hourly real wages.

Simultaneously new legislation was enacted to prevent the longer work week from resulting in an increase in the purchasing power of the workers. At the outbreak of the war, in order to cut weekly wages, it was provided that the salary hitherto paid for a work week of 40 hours should in the future be paid for a work week of 45 hours; in other words, those working 45 hours or more had to furnish 5 hours without compensation, whether they were war workers or not. Though this regulation seemingly did not touch the hourly rates, it was regarded by the workers as a deliberate cut in their earnings effected by governmental action in the interest of the employers. After one month the government, in order to avoid the impression that the new legislation profited only the employers, provided that all wages for the 40th to the 45th hour of work were to be paid into a National Solidarity Fund which covered part of the allowances for soldiers' families. But since this sum was to be turned over to the fund by the employer, the new procedure was viewed by the workers with equal distrust. At the end of October the system of non-payment for the first 5 hours over 40 was discontinued altogether. It had achieved much less in the way of diminishing spending power than in impairing the confidence of the working class that equality of sacrifices was a goal of the government's wartime social policy.

Even after the first scheme was abandoned, the legislation upheld the principle that overtime wages should be less than the normal rates. At first workers were paid for overtime 75 per cent of the regular rate; soon this was lowered to 66⅔ per cent and eventually to 60 per cent. The difference between the normal wages and the overtime wages was also paid directly by the employer to the National Solidarity Fund.[28]

Such deductions, constituting an overtime tax amounting to from 13 to 18 per cent of total wages, was a unique feature of French wartime labor legislation. In most countries overtime pay was maintained in wartime as a desirable incentive, in spite of the dangers of an increased inflationary gap. Nazi Germany abolished overtime in 1939 but re-established it shortly thereafter. In no country outside of France was it attempted to 'penalize' overtime work. This experiment arose not only from a desire to prevent the dangers of inflation but also from a hope of avoiding resentment on the part of the rural population against the urban working class. Farmers formed a large majority of the French army, and it was feared that their indignation would be aroused if they saw workers making 'big money' in safety.

A notable slackening of output during the first months of the war was due in considerable measure to a system which seemed devised to discourage rather than encourage productivity. In some cases employers clearly recognized the harmful effects of the wage-hour legislation on individual output, and by agreement with the unions fixed the legal work week at 48 instead of 40 hours, thereby making the deductions for the 40 per cent overtime tax begin to operate only with the 49th hour of work.[29]

Characteristically enough, it was not until France's fatal hour in May 1940 that a decree provided that hours above 60 a week were to be paid at normal rates without the 40 per cent deduction hitherto imposed on overtime hours. Not only did this amelioration come too late to effect an improvement, but even then, with the invader rushing toward the Channel and Paris, the French legislator made only partial concessions to the working class.

Meanwhile there was a further tax of 8 per cent of total pay which had to be met by all wage earners. And still another payment exacted from French labor for the costs of war was the

Extraordinary National Contribution, which was in general 5 per cent of earnings and was as high as 15 per cent for men between 18 and 49 who did not belong to a military unit and were not disabled during the previous war. This differentiation, motivated by a desire to disfavor the worker of military age, resulted in gross inequality. Very often two workers doing the same job received different pay. This was considered the more unjust as frequently a father of young children received considerably less than an older worker whose children were self-supporting.

Also these taxes and contributions were deducted by the employer and turned over by him to the Treasury.[30] This method of tax collection was entirely new for France; formerly taxes on wages had been collected by assessment in the following fiscal year. While the pay-as-you-go collection at the source undoubtedly had great advantages, it produced unfortunate psychological results in wartime France. The lack of an adequate information policy reaching the working class population and the confusion aroused by contradictory wartime decrees, especially in matters of overtime pay, left the workers doubtful whether their contributions did not simply benefit the employer rather than flow into the Treasury. In vain the CGT proposed that this attitude of distrust be overcome by giving the workers' organizations at least the possibility of participating in the administration of the Natonal Solidarity Fund.[31]

In view of the fact that, in addition to the various deductions, the rise in the cost of living brought about a lowering of real wages by 10 to 15 per cent, the sacrifice exacted from the working population seems enormous. The increase in weekly earnings that certain categories of workers achieved through overtime work did not essentially change the picture, for in general workers in defense industries were already working overtime before the outbreak of the war and before the enactment of the new legislation.

At the beginning of World War I the French workers had experienced a similar substantial lowering of money and real wages. The first months of the war and invasion had caused disorganization and dislocation of production, and under these conditions the employers in many industries had lowered wage rates. This situation was soon reversed, however, when it became evident that France had to sustain a long war and that armament production could no longer be improvised. In 1915 the socialist Albert Thomas had been made a member of the cabinet in charge of armament production. In close collaboration with the trade-union organizations, which presented the workers' grievances, Thomas pursued a policy of high wages to spur production. Shortly after his appointment he laid down the principles that were to guide his work: 'What method could be better for bringing about maximum production . . . than that of appealing to all private initiatives . . . without being stingy in rewarding the necessary effort and without fear of granting a premium for increased output and for the indispensable creative effort?' [32] The contrast to the policy prevailing in 1939 is obvious.

III

During World War I numerous strikes were called when the rise of prices endangered the living standard of the working class, and usually they were brought to a successful end. In order to ease the conflicts arising between management and labor, a system of wartime arbitration was devised. On the whole, wages kept in step with the rising living costs. In 1939, however, the government not only took it upon itself to lower wages drastically, if not catastrophically, but also denied to the laboring classes, from whom the exigencies of modern war demanded an even greater effort than in 1914-18, any opportunity to participate in the adjustment of grievances.

With the outbreak of the war any strike action was made illegal for the 700,000 to 800,000 workers in plants requisitioned by the government, as well as for the *affectés spéciaux* and other workers placed under military rule. Even where industrial relations were still governed by private ageement, workers could not resort to strikes. The government was in a position to requisition any plant in which a labor conflict threatened, and thereby to make a strike a criminal action. Actually, no strikes on a more than individual scale occurred in wartime France. Where workers struck, they were convicted by military courts to prison terms.

It is important to note that this 'peace' in industrial relations, most desirable in every country at war, was not brought about by any voluntary agreement with the trade-union movement; nor was it due to a non-strike pledge of organized labor. The government had not even attempted to reach such an agreement. It was peace by decree, relying solely on compulsion.

At the very beginning of the war the Daladier government, by decree, suspended for the duration the entire previous legislation concerning industrial arbitration.[33] The government gave no explanation of the reasoning behind this utterly surprising step, but the suspension was certainly due partly to the fact that the system of arbitration had never worked wholly satisfactorily in the prewar period and since its inception had never been wholeheartedly accepted by management, only organized labor giving it full approval. Also a decisive reason for the action taken at the outbreak of the war was the government's determination to 'freeze' social relations at the prewar level and to put them under the sole control of the state. Such freezing was tantamount to denying the very existence of conflicts in the field of industrial relations, and thus arbitration intended to settle such conflicts was deemed superfluous, indeed dangerous to the very principle of French legislation. In spite of the great influence which the state-appointed super-arbiters had gained in the process of industrial arbitration before the war, the representatives of management and labor had continued to play a role in the various stages of mediation and arbitration. The desire to do away with such practices of collaboration between the state and the corporative organizations was one more reason to discontinue the former arbitration procedures.

The decree which abolished arbitration stipulated that existing collective bargaining agreements would remain valid; only such clauses as dealt with the procedure for revision of wages and working conditions were suspended. It was hoped that in this way the complete freezing of the wage level and of labor conditions in general could be realized.

In defense industries a change in wages or working conditions could be brought about by accord between the Minister of Labor and the ministry at whose orders the work in question was being carried out. Thus an exclusively bureaucratic procedure superseded the agreement between management and labor. Outside of defense industries a greater flexibility than that originally devised had to be introduced: early in November new boards were created which were to advise or to decide on the revision of conditions of employment and on the changing of clauses of collective agreements and awards.[34]

Whenever the Minister of Labor wished to amend the clauses of a collective agreement which he deemed incompatible with the needs of production, he could do so after consulting with the Technical Committees which were to be set up on the departmental and national levels as well as *ad hoc* in certain professions. The same procedure was to be followed when the Minister or his representative wished to extend the validity of a collective agreement to all wage earners in a given trade or district. The majority of the members sitting on the various Technical Committees were government officials; representatives of both management and labor remained in a minority, even after their number had been increased by a subsequent decree. None of these representatives was designated by his respective organization; they were appointed either by the Minister of Labor or by the prefects. The activity of these Technical Committees increased somewhat in scope when the rise in living costs led the Minister of Labor to believe that at least in some trades the existing wage rates were 'detrimental under the economic point of view as well as in the interest of maintaining morale,' but the Technical Committees were never given other than consultative functions.[35]

The Higher Committee, which was organized simultaneously with the Technical Committees, was granted the right of decision in the review of conditions of employment and wages. It was designed to function at the request of either or both management and labor if an agreement could not be reached concerning a revision of salaries, general working conditions, vacations with pay or the like. Thus in some respects the Higher Committee (which was somewhat comparable to the War Labor Board in the United States) took the place vacated by the abolished arbitration system. The most important difference between the boards charged with mediation and arbitration in prewar times and the Higher Committee was that the latter was composed solely of high government officials.

When the Minister of Labor was asked in the Chamber of Deputies why the Higher Committee did not include representatives of management and labor, he replied that such representatives had also been absent from the Superior Court of Arbitration which the Higher Committee superseded.[36] This assertion was certainly erroneous. In all cases where the Arbitration Court had to deal with questions of more economic than legal character (*jurisdiction de fond*), its decision was reached with the votes of representatives of management and labor. The very definition of the tasks of the Higher Committee implied that the activities of this body were entirely devoted to a *jurisdiction de fond*.[37]

Moreover, within the fully developed arbitration system of prewar days the Superior Court had been only the last instance. In the decisions of the lower instances the representatives of management and labor had participated more or less actively. Since the Higher Committee was first and last instance at the same time, the fact that no functional representatives sat on its board was tantamount to the complete exclusion of the corporative organizations from the new organ devised to settle disputes. If the war had lasted longer the Higher Committee would undoubtedly have played a role of great importance in the adaptation of the whole system of collective bargaining to the new conditions, and this without even granting a hearing to management and labor.

It is noteworthy that if the Minister of Labor wished to modify existing labor conditions in situations affecting more than one French department, he could avoid consulting the central Technical Committee by requesting the Higher Committee to function in its place. The role played by the representatives of the labor unions in the Technical Committee was certainly rather subdued. Nevertheless, when the Minister feared a clash of opposing interests, he was in a position to shun the advice even of this body, by turning instead to the Higher Committee, which was composed solely of government officials.

The only exception was in regard to miners and quarrymen. On the six-man board of a special Higher Committee, instituted for these vocations, employers and trade unions were represented by one member each. The Minister of Labor, when asked why the two Higher Committees were organized in different ways, was unable to explain.[38]

When the battle of France had already begun, an article in the journalistic organ of the CGT forcefully stressed how grave a mistake had been committed by the abolition of the system of arbitration, and requested a return to former procedures lest the maintenance of social peace be endangered.[39] It was too late then for change.

Under these conditions the trade-union movement had scant possibilities of defending the interests of the wage earners. The only wartime session of the National Council of the CGT acknowledged that 'under wartime legislation most labor questions depend primarily upon the decisions of the public authorities.'[40]

Deprived in most cases of the possibility of even presenting their requests to the employers, to say nothing of the calling of strikes, the trade unions tried to persuade the government that it was in the best interest of the nation to improve working conditions. The spokesmen of the CGT asked the government to make every effort to demonstrate to the workers that while they were fighting Hitler their own social rights would not be sacrificed. Occasionally the CGT stressed the fact that its appeals to the government deserved all the more consideration as the union movement, after Russia's attack on Poland, had so promptly excluded the communists from its ranks. A statement made by René Belin, after only a few weeks of war, was particularly significant:

It would be a fatal error on the part of the political leadership and the employers to believe that the social question has been solved because one group of the labor movement has been weeded out. In order to make the workers believe in liberty, it is necessary that they see behind words a vivid, immediate, and obvious reality. If democracy is nothing but a system in which egoism finds an opportunity to impose once more an inhuman law, the popular classes will not be democratic. . . Where could they then find the incentives, the elements of mysticism, which enable them to withstand the propaganda with which Hitler and Stalin attack the worker's mind through word and sword? [41]

But most of the pleas made by the trade unions remained unheeded. The National Council of the CGT, the meetings of the various federations and unions, as well as the labor press, incessantly clamored for the most urgently needed improvements: adaptation of wages to the rising living costs; alteration of the methods of overtime pay; shortening of working hours for women and children; better organization of the available manpower and of vocational training and retraining; a better protection of *requis civils* and *affectés spéciaux*, especially against dismissal. Particularly at the end of the winter of 1939-40 increasing numbers of union leaders stressed the impossibility of maintaining wages and salaries at the prewar level while all prices were rising. The secretary of the civil servants federation warned that unless energetic action was taken to span the developing gap between wages and prices, a wave of workers' demands would sweep the country.[42]

A few weeks before the invasion of France by the German troops, a secretary of the regional union of Paris sounded strong warnings which showed clearly that since Belin's statement, made six months earlier, little or nothing had been changed:

> If tomorrow the reasons for our sacrifices and for our struggle disappear, if our country takes the appearance of a totalitarian state, there will have been created among the people of this nation the atmosphere which is favorable for Hitler's and Stalin's propaganda. . . It will no longer be possible to rely on the labor movement as a protective shield against *défaitiste* propaganda. . . It is necessary that our sincere collaboration be reciprocated by government and employers. Otherwise our democracy is in deadly risk of being faced by brutal realities and of being overpowered by the dictatorial regimes.[43]

Little more than two months sufficed to turn these dark prophecies into 'brutal realities.'

IV

The exclusion of the labor movement from active co-operation in such vital questions as the regulation of labor supply and wage-hour legislation, and the attribution of only a minor role to organized labor in the new procedure for the adjustment of working conditions, left little room for collaboration between the trade unions and the government. Nevertheless, Charles Pomaret, the Minister of Labor of both the Daladier and the Reynaud governments, declared repeatedly and most emphatically that the social policy of the government was based upon the idea of continuous collaboration between the state, the employers, and the trade unions. Less than ever, he asserted, did the government wish to do away with such practices.[44] Quite rightly, however, a former Minister of Labor, Paul Ramadier, remarked that 'wartime collaboration, placed as it is in the framework of a strictly regulated war economy, calls much more for self-denial than for initiative.' [45]

Actually there were only four areas in which collaboration existed between the union movement and the government. And such joint committees as existed tended to exercise only marginal responsibilities.

The first of these areas of collaboration was a Permanent Economic Committee, set up in October 1939.[46] Four of its twenty-one members were appointed to represent the 'manual and intellectual workers': Jouhaux and Belin of the CGT; Tessier, secretary-general of the CFTC; and the secretary of an organization of intellectual workers. This committee superseded the National Economic Council, which was suspended for the duration of the war as too unwieldy. It is true that the Council, like similar functional bodies organized in various countries after the last war, failed to fulfil the exaggerated hopes that had welcomed it as the foundation stone of a new social democracy. Nevertheless, the French National Economic Council had played an important role in the preparation of legislative texts and in the proposing of administrative regulations pertaining to the economic life of the nation. The Popular Front legislation of 1936 had considerably extended the functions of the Council, on whose board and various subcommittees the labor movement was represented. Hence the dissolution of the National Economic Council shortly after the outbreak of the war was actually a step backward so far as collaboration between government and labor was concerned. The functions of the new Economic Committee were ill-defined. It was supposed to cooperate with the High Commissioner for National Economy,[47] but the Commissioner himself, jammed as he was between the different ministries and agencies concerned with war economy, had somewhat indefinite functions and only limited possibilities of action. This was reflected in the activities of the Permanent Economic Committee, whose role was far less significant than that played by the National Economic Council.

The second area of collaboration between the government and

organized labor was the newly formed Committee for the Study of Social Questions; here too the labor members were Jouhaux, Belin, and Tessier. This body replaced the Superior Labor Council, which, like the National Economic Council, was suspended for the duration of the war.[48] Before the war the Superior Labor Council and its permanent commissions had advised on general working conditions and industrial relations. Nearly all important labor legislation had been threshed out by it in the two decades between the world wars. The Study Committee which superseded the Superior Labor Council was by the very character of French wartime legislation limited to advice on questions of relatively secondary character, such as paid vacations and the remuneration of certain special categories of workers. It is true that the Committee, which met under the presidency of the Minister of Labor or his representative, functioned smoothly and that it fulfilled the important function of bringing labor, management, and government into regular contact. But it was certainly an overstatement for the Minister to assert that never in the last twenty-five years had co-operation between government and the representatives of industry and labor been so regularized, harmonious, and efficient as it was in the Study Committee.[49] Actually the trade unions had formerly been given a far greater share of responsibility, especially during World War I and during the period of the Popular Front.

The third area of co-operation was the Labor Courts, which had been organized according to various trades in order to decide on individual disputes between employers and employees, and were still retained. In peacetime their panels were composed of freely elected representatives of workers and employers. But after the government dissolved all communist organizations, at the end of September 1939, elections of judges for the Labor Courts were suspended and many of the lay judges were deprived of their positions for having been connected with a communist organization. To fill the vacancies the union organization which was 'most representative' in a given trade was invited to submit a list consisting of twice as many candidates as there were vacancies to be filled. From this list the government, without further consultation of the interested unions, was to appoint the judges who would represent the wage earners on the courts.[50]

Finally, a new form of collaboration between government and labor was instituted at the outbreak of the war. Except for a short period at the beginning of World War I no officer of the CGT or of its affiliated organizations had ever accepted a post in the executive branch of the government. Even during the Popular Front period the CGT had refused to share governmental responsibilities, for it was considered contrary to the very principles of syndicalism to serve as a political officer. But in September 1939 Pierre Vigne, secretary of the miners federation, was appointed to the cabinet of the Minister of Labor, to advise on questions of industrial relations.[51] The Minister had at first sought Belin for this post, but the latter, not willing to lose his freedom of action, had declined. Both Belin and Vigne were known as the foremost defenders of appeasement tendencies within the labor movement. It was significant that a trade-union leader who had never concealed his desire to see the war avoided by substantial concessions to Hitler was selected to serve on the first war cabinet. The difference in the roles played by the labor movement in the two world wars is illustrated by the fact that in 1914 the CGT had entered an alliance with the socialist party to frustrate any attempt at capitulation before the enemy, while in 1939 the representative of the CGT utilized his government post to support the forces favoring capitulation, even before hostilities in western Europe had really started.

When the Reynaud cabinet succeeded the Daladier government in March 1940, the same Minister of Labor was retained. In view of the different political orientation of the new government, Pomaret was asked to dispense with the services of a trade-union leader who had definitely committed himself to the cause of appeasement. Pomaret then appointed to his cabinet, in a more formal way than at the beginning of the war, four persons whose duty it was 'to deal with social questions and to maintain contact between the public authorities and the professional organizations.' [52] The two representatives of labor were a member of the CGT and a member of the CFTC; Robert Bothereau, one of the assistant secretaries, was appointed for the CGT. At about the same time the new socialist under-secretary of the Ministry of Armament appointed to his cabinet Robert Lacoste, of the civil servants federation, along with various other socialists.

Both Lacoste and Bothereau belonged to the younger generation of constructive union leaders. They had always opposed every form of appeasement and had shown a clear understanding of the issues at stake in the war against Nazism. But even if their functions had been more clearly defined than they actually were, the time between their appointment and the disorganization of the government apparatus brought about by the German invasion was too short to permit them any extensive activity.

In the Ministry of Information one representative of the CGT and one of the Catholic unions were appointed to the staff after the outbreak of the war. Before the war both these members, Georges Lefranc and Paul Vignaux, had been prominent in the educational work of their respective organizations. Their new duties were to inform the public on labor problems and to devise propaganda intended especially for the workers. Until the invasion their division published a *Bulletin des informations ouvrières* to which officials of both the CGT and the CFTC contributed.

v

The wartime labor legislation of France reveals the odd picture of a system which had abandoned many of the basic features of democratic process without resorting fully to totalitarian practices. Organized labor was no longer given, as in a democratic society, the place of a full partner. If collaboration between labor, management, and government is defined as 'organized co-operation . . . for the determination of conditions of employment, the framing and application of industrial and social legislation, the prevention and settlement of industrial disputes, and the formulation and application of social and economic policies,' [53] then no real collaboration existed in wartime France. In contrast to the conditions prevailing in a free capitalist economy, it was deemed impossible to rely, for the increase of output, upon the incentives offered by higher pay and profits.[54] The government, in its endeavor to speed up production, resorted to compulsion rather than relying on inducements, and in general took over most of the functions which in a pluralist society are attended to by the social groups themselves.

On the other hand, France was not organized to replace the democratic methods she had abandoned with the devices which a full-fledged totalitarian system employs for managing the masses and regulating the economy. The French government deprived the labor movement of its most important functions without creating between government and the working class a transmission organ that would dispense propaganda and enforce terror, like the Labor Front in Nazi Germany. To be sure, courts and police were charged with meting out punishment for breaches of discipline, but in our times a dictatorial rule which is not backed by a mass organization of fanatics is bound to fail.

It is true that great difficulties stood in the way of fully integrating the working class and its organizations in the national effort. In spite of the mutual hatred of the pacifist and the communist factions within the CGT, both groups, though for different motives, were bitterly opposed to the war. With the communists inciting the workers to sabotage the 'imperialist' war and the appeasers devoting their efforts to bringing about a negotiated peace, it would not have been easy for any government to count for support upon the leadership of organized labor. Nor could the more moderate elements in the labor movement fully trust the government. The most prominent representatives of appeasement had been allowed to remain in government posts; persons who favored the totalitarian pattern of restraining civil liberties, establishing concentration camps and tightening the control over labor organizations, continued to play an important political role. The official persecution of the communists, giving them an aura of martyrdom, made it additionally difficult for the moderate representatives of labor to cooperate closely with the government without risking the accusation of being 'stool pigeons' of the bourgeoisie and its political leadership. And the difficulties were increased still further by the methods of *Sitzkrieg* which Hitler decided to impose upon France for eight months, and by the apparent absence of any immediate threat to the country during this period.

When Reynaud became head of the government in March 1940, and gave hope that previous trends of social policy would be at least gradually reversed, time had run short. Only after the crucible of defeat and occupation was it understood to what extent the strength of a state depends upon the organized representatives of employers and workers, and their collaboration with each other and with the institutions of government.

XI

Labor-Management Relations: Divergent Principles

I

IN the months immediately preceding the war there was, as earlier chapters have shown, a progressive deterioration of the relations between trade unions and management. While France was supposed to be girding herself to resist her totalitarian neighbor, still unappeased by the concessions of Munich, armament production was carried on with management and labor unwilling to reach agreement on any problem of industrial relations.

The outbreak of the war did not change this situation, and early in October 1939 the government insisted on bringing together the two partners. The first meetings took place under the auspices of the new Minister of Armament, Raoul Dautry, and resulted in what became known as the 'Majestic Agreement.' The accord received its name from the Hotel Majestic, which housed the Ministry of Armament.

Dautry's career and social philosophy were quite different from those of Albert Thomas, France's first Minister of Armament during World War I. Thomas had been a scholar and a socialist. Dautry, starting as a railroad engineer, had had a brilliant career which culminated in the post of General Director of the French railroads and in the presidency of the Compagnie Générale Transatlantique. After his retirement in 1938 he was elected to the board of nine major concerns operating mainly in the field of transportation and electric power. Hence Dautry could be regarded as enjoying the full confidence of French big business. In labor questions the new Minister of Armament had shown himself inclined toward an attitude of modern paternalism. He clearly recognized the necessity of maintaining a high morale among the workers, but he believed that an atmosphere of sympathy, a wage sufficient to assure a decent living standard, stability of employment, adequate medical care, and attractive housing conditions were the essential conditions for people's happiness. There was no place for labor unions in his scheme, and, although he never came out openly against trade unions, his autobiographic book shows him as regarding certain forms of union activity as undesirable infringements upon the employers' privileges.[1] Nevertheless, Dautry, charged with furnishing indispensable arms to an insufficiently prepared republic, recognized the necessity of improving the relations between management and labor.

Typically enough, the first wartime agreement which was intended to lay the foundation for such improved relations could not be presented as an understanding between the CGT and its counterpart on the employers' side. The employers had always regarded the Matignon Agreement as a shameful defeat won by the 'enemy' (the organized labor movement) through pressure and surprise, and during the three years preceding the war French management had refused to enter any other accord with the CGT. Nor did the war change this reluctance of French business organizations to give formal recognition to the CGT as a full-fledged partner in the adjustment of industrial relations. The strength of the CGT had been gravely affected by the political conditions existent at the outbreak of the war and by the wartime social legislation, and the employers judged it unnecessary to acquiesce in attributing to a weakened labor movement the role and importance they had always attempted to deny to a strong one.

The government managed this difficulty by proposing that an agreement be worked out between Lambert-Ribot and Jouhaux, who were the respective delegates of French employers and workers to the International Labour Office at Geneva. In addition, the industrial branch most directly concerned with the manufacture of arms was given representation, in the persons of Lente, president of the Association of the Metal and Mining Industries, and Maurice Chevalme, secretary of the metal workers federation. In order to avoid even the appearance that the agreement was reached between the regularly constituted organizations of management and labor the official communique issued after the meetings did not contain any reference whatever to the CGT. It was specified that the participants were 'acting in their own names, though certain of expressing the feelings of the groups [*milieux*] to which they belong.' After these reservations the final communique stated that the following declaration of principles had been reached unanimously by those present:

The task of furnishing the armies of the republic with the material means of a victory obtained with the least possible suffering for all, can be accomplished only by a unanimous, profound, and durable accord of hearts and of efforts.

Today there is nothing that stands in the way of such an accord, and the formulas that oppose it are outdated.

Every Frenchman feels, and every citizen of a free nation understands or feels, that France and England fight not for their own sakes but solely for the future of mankind.

Every Frenchman desires that out of the present struggle shall arise not only a better France but a better world. And all citizens of the free nations expect for all humanity an era of progress under freedom, harmony, and respect for individual as well as collective rights.

This social and human progress, which can be attained on the international level only if it is solidly realized on the national level, must be prepared for. Albert Thomas, the first Minister of Armament during the war of 1914 to 1918, and later director of the International Labour Office, gave to that institution the motto: 'If you want peace, provide for justice.'

Actuated by similar feelings in the present circumstances, all Frenchmen unanimously complete this thought by 'If you want liberty in justice, work for victory.'

The communique added that Lambert-Ribot, Jouhaux, Lente, and Chevalme agreed in the belief that 'the achievement of such a program pointing to the future leaves no room either today or tomorrow for the pursuit of selfish interests or for class struggle. Instead it requires a definite accord for a close and complete collaboration.' The communique stated it was also agreed, with the consent of the Minister of Labor, that meetings intended to apply these principles to practical problems would be held among the factory inspectors and the representatives of management and labor in the armament industries.[2]

The wording of the declaration showed clearly the paternity of the various passages. The general terms expressing the hopes for the postwar world corresponded to the philosophy of the labor movement; the CGT also intentionally invoked the memory of Albert Thomas. The representatives of the employers and possibly also Dautry had insisted on the formal abandonment of the class struggle ideology. It was rightly emphasized [3] that the Majestic Agreement was by no means the solemn inauguration of a new policy, as was, for example, Jouhaux's speech at Jaurès' tomb at the beginning of the First World War. Rather it endeavored to reintroduce practices that had been generally resorted to for a quarter of a century but had been discontinued since the general strike in 1938.

The limitations and the possible role of the Majestic Agreement (also referred to in the contemporary French press as the Dautry Agreement) were best expressed by Jouhaux, in what proved an over-optimistic evaluation: 'We entered the war in 1939 with the social atmosphere of 1938 [the year of the general strike]. But prospects are now brighter. Recognition of the trade-union movement by the public authorities has brought about the Majestic Agreement.' [4] It is true that it was only at the insistence of the government that the employers had consented, however reluctantly, to meet with spokesmen of organized labor, and that an agreement between management and labor had been reached. The Matignon Agreement, too, had been realized only by government pressure. But the accord of 1936 had outlined an entire program of reforms which, it was hoped, would accomplish a pacification of the social atmosphere. The wartime accord of 1939, while not entirely clear in its wording, was but a 'declaration of principle.' The only programmatic part of this declaration was the promise that other meetings would be held between representatives of management and labor.

II

The principle of 'class co-operation' embodied in the Majestic Agreement was wholly accepted by the CGT and its affiliated unions. But the problems involved in such collaboration gave rise to a great deal of enervating theoretical consideration. They formed the main topic of discussion at the only wartime session of the CGT National Council. Spokesmen of organized labor devoted numerous articles to the subject in union papers and the general press,[5] several periodicals all but specializing in a detailed consideration of the theory and practice of collaboration. Among these a number had in prewar times been closely connected with the *Syndicats* school of thought.[6]

It may appear astonishing that the problems of co-operation between unions and management were viewed by so many union leaders as an entirely new issue. As earlier chapters have shown, however, the implications of the transformation undergone by the French labor movement since the beginning of World War I had never been fully realized by the unions themselves. At least in terminology most of the official declarations issued by the union movement had denounced the principle of union-management co-operation as often as possible. As late as 1936 the final resolution of the Congress of Toulouse had protested that none of the activities of the CGT should be regarded as an 'integration of the labor movement in the state or as a collaboration with management.' The same convention had explicitly confirmed the 'absolute opposition which exists between the interests of the

wage earners, whose defense is the mission of the labor movement, and the interests of capitalism, to whose destruction the
labor movement is committed.' [7]

One of the reasons why the programmatic statements of the
CGT, throughout the period between the wars, carefully avoided
any modification of the syndicalist point of view on industrial
relations, is to be found in the split of the labor movement into
a reformist and a communist wing. Accused by the communists
of having capitulated before the capitalist state and of collaborating with the employers, the leaders of the CGT defended
themselves by denying that they indulged in any kind of 'class
collaboration.' With the formal reunification of the trade-union
movement in 1936, the communist attacks, though different in
form and content, did not cease. Internal polemics, often conducted on sham issues, prevented the trade-union movement from
revising its earlier philosophy. The few union leaders who attempted to redefine the philosophy of the union movement and
to confront organized labor with its new tasks were not heeded.
Their thesis did not even give rise to a thorough discussion.

The unsatisfactory state of industrial relations before and after
Matignon were equally detrimental to a frank facing of the problem of union-management collaboration. Since French management in general shunned co-operation and agreement with the
union movement, and since the philosophy and activities of the
unions are always likely to reflect the policies and actions of
management, the leadership of the CGT never discussed the implications which the new labor legislation and the organizational
drives of both the CGT and the CGPF might have on union-
management relations.

That even as late as 1938 the idea of collaboration between the
two partners of industrial relations was by no means generally
accepted is evident from the so-called 'Pontigny Affair.' In the
summer of that year a conference was held on the neutral
grounds of the Abbey of Pontigny, which was no longer devoted

to ecclesiastical purposes but was a frequent meeting place for roundtable discussions. The session of 1938 was devoted to the study of industrial relations in Sweden. Among those attending were Swedish industrialists and labor leaders, representatives of French big business, and a few union officials of the CGT and the CFTC. Most of the French businessmen were connected with the electrical or chemical industries; the executives in these fields were traditionally inclined to social experiments somewhat more than their colleagues.

This rather inconspicuous meeting, which would have gone unnoticed in other countries, was considered sensational by many French newspapers. It was saluted by some as the dawn of a new social experiment in France, and decried by others as a despicable betrayal of syndicalist principles. All the CGT leaders who took part in it, among them Robert Lacoste and Georges Lefranc, declared that they did so only in their own names and not as representatives of the organizations to which they belonged. They were almost apologetic in their explanations, declaring that nobody thought of regarding the meeting at Pontigny as a kind of super-Matignon, and that even in Sweden 'the class struggle was not abolished.' It was only after the outbreak of the war, when the Majestic Agreement had placed the problem of collaboration in the foreground, that a writer who had earlier tried to belittle the importance of the Pontigny meeting described it as a most significant manifestation of the changes which the French labor movement had undergone.[8]

The crisis in which the CGT found itself at the beginning of the war was serious enough to force the unions to overhaul their philosophy. Communist criticism seemed no longer to be feared. But the principle of collaboration between unions and management was so novel, the discussion of labor's role in society had so long been delayed, that once the CGT started on the new path there seemed to exist no limit for the revision of previous beliefs.

III

A *union sacrée,* as it had been conceived in Europe during World War I, left the social structure of a country fundamentally untouched and made no attempt to modify existing class relations. It merely attempted, in order to facilitate the conduct of the war, to alter the expression to be given by the various social groups to their particular interests, and did so without denying that these interests might be antagonistic.

In 1939 there was a small group of French union leaders who still maintained that the class struggle was a natural phenomenon of social life which could not possibly be decreed out of existence, even by the most perfect agreement. All that could be achieved, these writers agreed, was to submit the class struggle to the rules of fair play and reason. The urgency of the situation was not denied. Robert Lacoste and Jean Zyromski, the principal defenders of this thesis,[9] were prominent leaders of the union movement and active members of the socialist party, and they had always objected to the political isolationism of many syndicalists, maintaining that the democracies should make themselves strong in order to withstand the expansionist imperialism of the fascist nations. They merely insisted that in finding the solution the facts of the class struggle could not be overlooked.

Jouhaux, in his discussion of the problem of co-operation, gave less emphasis to the issue of class struggle. He asserted, quite rightly, that co-operation with management was nothing new for French labor, and contended that the very existence of an organized union movement was based on belief in the possible normalization of industrial relations through negotiation and co-operation. In Jouhaux's definition, however, collaboration meant the distribution of responsibilities among state, labor, and management. He pictured a nation in which these three forces would assume equal responsibilities, not only in the field of social policy but in every sphere of national life, even in that of foreign affairs. By maintaining that labor had to play a role beyond the promotion of its immediate interests he turned away from the political isolationism which the CGT had affected for so long. But his interpretation of the phenomenon of collaboration did not imply any fundamentally new social vision, as is evident from the examples he used in order to clarify his thought. He referred to the bipartite and tripartite committees that had come into existence in many countries, and mentioned explicitly the pattern set by such committees in Great Britain and by the International Labour Office in Geneva.[10]

Jouhaux's thesis that state, labor, and management should seek the compromise solution which corresponded best to the 'general interest,' and that the reaching of such a compromise would permit the French nation to emerge victoriously from the war, was in accordance with the pluralist conception of society. To conceive the state not as a sovereign unit but as one agency among others was a typical defense attitude against the rigid state regulation which was characteristic of the wartime social policy of the French republic. But a pluralistic and democratic system such as that proposed by Jouhaux can work only if there exists some fundamental basis of understanding among the social groups involved,[11] and in France such a basis of understanding did not exist.

Belin and his friends from *Syndicats* made far more radical departures from traditional European trade unionism. Unlike Jouhaux, they contended that union-management co-operation was a new social experiment, of decisive importance for the future development of French labor. Unlike Lacoste and Zyromski, they discarded the whole doctrine of class struggle, terming it an 'indigestible pill.' Dumoulin, traditionally a revolutionary syndicalist and during the last war an opponent of any *union sacrée*, declared that classes could no longer be clearly distinguished. The general tenor of the discussions at the National Council of the CGT showed clearly that most unions had drifted from the class struggle ideology to which the CGT Congress of Toulouse had still paid at least lip service in 1936.[12]

To many union leaders the giving up of this position seemed not only a necessary consequence of previous developments but also a necessary precondition for the salvation of the French labor movement. 'The dilemma placed before a great number of trade unionists in September 1939 was not collaboration or class struggle, but collaboration or disappearance,' remarked one observer.[13] These trade-union leaders did not wish to see a revival of the *union sacrée*, preferring to seek more permanent and more thorough changes in industrial relations. They contended that events had maneuvered the CGT into a blind alley.

Actually the reunification of the trade-union movement and the accomplishments of the Popular Front had thoroughly changed the structure of the CGT: from a union movement embracing only a minority of the working class, it had been converted into a mass movement. As such, however, it had never won the full recognition of French management. Relations between the two partners had hardly anywhere been stabilized, except in certain special spheres of industrial activity. Instead, the CGT had relied heavily on the support of the government, which had essentially improved the position of the wage earners, but only temporarily. The period of rise and strength was followed by a period of very conspicuous decline.

Curiously enough, the years during which the CGT had enjoyed the position of a mass movement were described now by many of these 'revisionist' union leaders as a kind of nightmare and a most unhappy experience of mass demagoguery. Their statements suggested that they viewed the contraction of the trade-union movement almost with joy. They deemed it impossible, however, to return to the practices and beliefs of the pre-1936 period, which were now regarded as either antiquated or incompatible with war conditions, and in any case altogether unfitted for extracting the labor movement from the extreme weakness and ossification into which it had lapsed. Belin insisted on what he had emphasized before the war: the very day the trade-union movement had accepted the institution of compulsory arbitration it had engaged upon a new path, for that institution thoroughly transformed the character of industrial relations and the role of organized labor.

It was hoped and expected by the union leaders connected with *Syndicats* that successful co-operation between unions and management would furnish the needed impetus to the labor movement. 'By throwing overboard exaggerated demagoguery . . . traditional, abused, and old-fashioned clichés, . . . by abandoning sectarianism, rigid doctrines, and outmoded conceptions,' the CGT, it was hoped, would be reborn as a strong, 'enthusiastic, non-sectarian, undoctrinal, and constructive' organization, capable of attracting the younger generations.[14] These expectations were far from reality, but they indicate the willingness to hammer out an entirely new ideology if this seemed necessary.

Belin and his friends frequently criticized the term 'collaboration,' deploring its lack of precision.[15] But their own definitions and explanations were equally vague and contradictory until an article in *Syndicats* revealed the direction of their thinking. 'Whoever speaks about collaboration,' it declared, 'thinks inevitably of the "organized profession" [*profession organisée*]. Collaboration presupposes this organization of the professions, without which the word collaboration would lose its real significance. And collaboration also presupposes a thorough reform of our economic system.'[16] That this thorough reform was not sought in the direction of an abolition of the capitalist system was evident from the praise that the same article gave to the social schemes of certain 'modern-minded' employers. Not only were these employers among those who had been actively favoring the reorganization of French economy on a basis of corporativism, but the very term 'organized profession' had been widely and exclusively used in the prewar discussion on corporativism.

IV

An organization of 'the profession' is fundamentally different from the autonomous organization of either labor or capital. Trade unions and employer associations guard their autonomy, even if they enter, at various levels, committees on which both labor and capital are represented. The 'organized profession,' on the other hand, comprises all persons connected with the same trade: employers, workers, white-collar employees, technicians. After the profession is duly organized, it is, in the scheme of the corporativists, granted the power of economic and social regulation. All those engaged in the profession are subject to this regulation, whether or not they joined the organization willingly. There is no autonomous organization of the various groups.

It is obvious that such a system destroys the two aspects of freedom to which the French labor movement had always attributed the utmost importance: the individual is no longer free to join or not to join an organization, and the trade union is no longer free to remain autonomous or to affiliate itself with that national organization, federation, or confederation which corresponds best to the leanings of its members.

The corporative doctrine in its modern form had first been developed in France in the latter part of the nineteenth century, by Catholic traditionalists who preferred the feudalist organization of the Middle Ages to the social structure of the French republic. La Tour du Pin, a most outspoken advocate of a corporative system and a staunch monarchist,[17] had influenced the social doctrines of the Action Française. If it had not been for the profound crisis into which Europe was plunged during the interwar period, the corporative philosophy might never have spread outside the narrow circle of the French monarchists and traditionalists. The great vogue that it actually enjoyed in France, especially at the beginning of the 1930's, is explainable by the special character of that crisis and the psychological reactions thereby produced.[18] The breakdown of laissez-faire economy left the individual helplessly facing the growing intervention of the state, and at the same time the increasing strength of the pressure groups threatened to destroy the unity of the nation. The generous dreams of the corporativists seemed to assure the individual the protection of the 'organized profession,' a society in miniature, and thus to satisfy his nostalgia for a feeling of community.[19] Corporative principles appeared to mean a diminution of state interference, inasmuch as the corporations would assume many of the regulatory functions of the state. They also promised a disciplinary effect on the various social groups, by amalgamating them in the higher unity of the corporation. Finally, as a result of the fallacious assertion that Mussolini's fascism had translated the corporative ideas into reality, many French critics of democracy looked upon corporativism as a specifically 'Latin' means of wrecking despised liberties and overcoming democratic institutions.

In 1933-4, when the republic had seemed ready for destruction but no fascist party was available for the establishment of a totalitarian dictatorship, the circle of those who pinned highest hopes on a corporative solution was no longer restricted to the monarchists of the Action Française. Marcel Déat, who had only shortly before severed his connection with the socialist party, remarked that all possibilities for a rejuvenation of the state centered around the corporative ideas.[20] The 'Movement of the July 9th Plan,' which united under the guidance of Jules Romains a wide range of social and political groups of France, from the fascist Croix de Feu to the then still leftist neo-socialists, believed in the necessity of a corporative reorganization. The columns of newspapers and the pages of learned magazines were filled with proposals for a reorganization of society on a corporative basis.

Then one force had insistently, unanimously, and successfully resisted the corporative ideology and proposals: the labor movement. Both the political organizations of labor and the trade-union movement itself, in spite of their apparent weakness at that moment, had declared their implacable opposition to corporativism.

In a widely discussed speech in the Chamber, the socialist deputy Spinasse rejected the idea of establishing functional representation through a corporative legislative body. 'It is for the political power alone to foresee and to arbitrate,' he declared.[21] After World War I the CGT had favored some kind of functional representation, and had taken an active part in the work of the National Economic Council when it was established in 1925. And the institution of a national assembly of occupations is, to be sure, an important feature of most corporative schemes. But those who favor the establishment of such an institution are not necessarily advocates of corporativism, as long as they wish to maintain a parliament elected by national suffrage and do not attempt to infringe upon the autonomy of professional organizations.[22] The CGT, though it was favorably disposed toward the National Economic Council, had never, before the outbreak of the war, advocated corporative principles.

In 1934, at the height of the corporative discussions, various writers prominent in the CGT had explained their unmitigated opposition to any kind of organization that would detract from the autonomy of labor unions. 'Between trade unionism and corporativism you have to choose. Our choice is made. We are trade unionists.' [23] Later even the American New Deal was criticized in the official magazine of the CGT, on the grounds that it might open the way to an authoritarian corporativism. When the CGT plan was published it was stressed over and over again that the corporative formula was the very antithesis of the goals of planism. In these discussions the spokesmen of the CGT produced some of the most penetrating criticism of corporativism.

It was pointed out that to abandon universal suffrage under the prevailing economic system and to supersede the political organization of the state by the hierarchy cherished by the corporativists would result in the undisputed rule of the economic oligarchies. Even in 1939 the official comments on the new edition of the plan stressed that the CGT was not favorably disposed toward an increase in the functions of the National Economic Council as long as no thorough changes had been achieved in the economic structure of French capitalism. Without such reforms it would only increase corporative tendencies if greater influence were given to the Council, and corporativism, it was explicitly warned, had led everywhere to the suppression of political and social liberties.[24]

In 1934 the refusal of the CGT to accede to corporative principles had helped to save the political and social liberties of the French people. In 1940 the most prominent weekly published by leading officials of the same CGT accepted basic formulas of corporativism, such as the 'organized profession,' without even explaining the shift in position.

The crisis into which the war had thrown French labor was only one reason for this development. The atmosphere that prevailed in France during the first months of the war was highly favorable to authoritarian conceptions. There was no freely expressed public opinion, the labor press was muzzled by a strict censorship, the workers were regimented almost as much as under a dictatorship, the unions themselves were deprived of most of their democratic functions. Many trade-union leaders had become separated from the rank and file of the membership and were no longer subject to its control. Among the union officials who had earlier attempted to stem the rising influence of communism, a strange and almost conspiratorial solidarity had developed. After the expulsion of the communists this solidarity culminated in a frantic endeavor to destroy all ideological bridges with the former position of the trade-union movement.

The great influence that Proudhon had always had on the CGT has already been emphasized. His formula, 'The workshop will replace the government,' had been regarded as the essence of the revolutionary aim of the working class. The stress that he put on economic emancipation, and his contempt for 'meaningless' political struggle and 'sterile' political discussion, had always appealed to the syndicalists. It was in conformance with this point of view that Pierre Vigne, of the miners federation, remarked shortly after his appointment to the cabinet of the Minister of Labor, in September 1939, that 'political matters should cease to taint labor matters.' [25]

But in the situation created by the war Proudhon's conception was quickly emptied of all revolutionary content and fitted into the corporative pattern. Actually, this was not too difficult. The corporativists shared with Proudhon illusions about the possibility of solving the social conflict in the economic domain alone. One can easily recognize in the corporative scheme Proudhon's conception of an economic society that would be balanced inwardly, functioning by exchange and contract, without the intervention of the domineering power of the state.[26] Proudhon, not unlike the later protagonists of corporativism, had often maintained that classes could be merged on the level of economic questions, and that only unnecessary political controversies divided the national collectivity.[27]

The interwar period, and especially the Popular Front experience, had increased the diffidence felt by many of the CGT leaders toward political activities. The experiences of these years were seen not as an indication of how much the conservation of labor's gains depends on the attitude of the political organization, the state, but merely as one more proof that the labor movement had nothing to gain from participation in the political struggle.

Yet another factor made some of the leading union officials favorably disposed toward the ideological pattern of corporativism. Although syndicalism and classical trade unionism had always preserved an international outlook, stressing the workers' common interests, the trade-union officials connected with the *Syndicats* group had little by little sacrificed internationalism to their craving for the maintenance of peace at any price. Their espousal of the cause of appeasement had forced them to forsake any solidarity with the labor movements of countries that were threatened with or actually overrun by fascist aggression. After the outbreak of the war, Belin, however cautiously, even criticized the conferences being held between British labor and the representatives of the French labor movement.[28] And this abandonment of internationalist traditions facilitated the transition to corporativism, which promoted a scheme of class harmony in the framework of the national state, and had always appealed to a strictly nationalistic philosophy.

It must be stressed that by no means the entire CGT leadership shifted to corporative principles. Jouhaux, for example, forcefully pointed out that collaboration should not be realized by a corporative system, and added that 'some people' had been tempted to give to the Majestic Agreement and to the principle of co-operation a meaning which neither had. His intention was equally clear when he warned against the maneuvering of certain trade unionists who were endangering the ideological unity of the movement.[29]

V

The Catholic trade-union movement also accepted the idea of union-management collaboration as expressed in the Majestic Agreement. From its very inception in November 1919 the CFTC had declared that it aimed at a social transformation 'not by class struggle but by the education and the collaboration of the productive elements.' These elements, the declaration had stated, were to be organized in distinct groups of employers and wage earners, but the organizations of the two sides would be bridged by a mixed body. Throughout the interwar period the CFTC, in contrast with the CGT, had maintained its adherence to the principle of class collaboration.[30] After the outbreak of war in 1939 the Administrative Committee of the CFTC gave its assent to any form of union-management co-operation which would not infringe upon the independence of the trade unions, and shortly before the German invasion one of its leaders once more emphasized that in effecting the recommended collaboration it was essential that the independent action of the union movement be safeguarded.[31] It is not without significance that this point was emphasized so much by the Catholic unions, which had often been accused by the CGT of not being sufficiently eager to defend the independence of the labor movement.

In the CFTC, too, there were various nuances of opinion in the profuse and often confused discussions of union-management collaboration. Some of the Catholics explicitly admitted that the acceptance of co-operation did not imply a belief that conflicting social interests had ceased to exist; on the contrary, collaboration between the partners of industrial relations was to be sought in spite of the validity and force of the prevailing antagonism. These writers regarded collaboration as an important foundation of a 'federated society,' a term that corresponds roughly to what is termed a pluralist society in Anglo-Saxon countries. Hence the position of these Catholic authors did not differ essentially from that maintained at the same time by Jouhaux.[32]

Other Catholic writers equally connected with the CFTC, but closer to the Parti Démocrate Populaire, criticized Jouhaux for defining collaboration between unions and management as a confrontation of opposite views rather than as a common striving for a common goal.[33] That party's declaration of wartime principles, which centered around the definition of collaboration, maintained that the 1936 legislation concerning collective bargaining and shop stewards had clearly failed to transform industrial relations, and that therefore job security should be granted to the workers by making them 'civil servants not of the state but of the enterprise or of their profession.' [34] This formula is decidedly in the corporative line. If the wage earners are bound by statute to the enterprise or the profession, instead of having a contractual relationship with the employers, the profession or the enterprise must be organized as an entity; it becomes a 'communion of labor' in which the workers are integrated. But unionism integrated in a 'communion of labor' is not free; it is protected against lockouts but it is also deprived of the possibility of striking.[35]

By a slow process of clarification the CFTC had separated itself from the corporative formulas of the Catholic traditionalists who, like La Tour du Pin, advocated a return to feudal forms of organization. Its main criticism of the traditionalists was that in their system trade unions would cease to exist. To symbolize the disagreement on this point the spokesmen for the CFTC preferred the formula of 'organized profession' to the term 'corporativism,' and in the years immediately preceding the war they completed this formula by speaking about a 'free union in an organized profession.'[36]

But the attempts to clarify the issues were not wholly successful. The discussions at the 'Semaines Sociales,' annual gatherings held by those interested in Social Catholicism and frequently devoted to a discussion of modern corporativism, were invariably confused and ambiguous.[37] The Catholic trade unionists were never able to explain how trade unions could remain 'free' within the framework of an 'organized profession.' They did not deny their entire agreement with the corporative principle that both of the productive factors (capital and labor) which contribute to a particular undertaking 'must be grouped in the same community.'[38] But they could not show how this compulsory organization, vested with the right to regulate the content of industrial relations, was to be reconciled with their insistence on free trade unions.

Even in 1939 a report on the problems of professional organization, presented at the last peacetime convention of the CFTC, showed an insistence on the autonomy of the trade-union movement. This report, which represented the point of view of what one is tempted to call the 'leftists' among the Catholic unionists, warned against the dangers of a corporative state and favored collective bargaining as a means of co-operation between employers and workers, rather than corporative boards with ill-defined functions. Parts of this report were incorporated in the final resolutions of the convention.[39] It is noteworthy that in their attitude toward the organizational implications of union-management collaboration the leaders of the CFTC, however gropingly, tried to solve some of the objections to corporativism, while the *Syndicats* group of the CGT did not hesitate to make the step from syndicalism to corporative principles. At about the same time that *Syndicats* was accepting without qualification the slogan of the 'organized profession,' a Catholic unionist was declaring that all that could be expected from co-operation was a reform of the legal relations of employers, workers, and the state.[40] The CFTC and the *Syndicats* group of the CGT moved in opposite directions from originally opposite poles. During the first months of the war their ideologies met and had much in common, but after the armistice they diverged again, the Catholic movement standing up for the defense of a free union movement, and the *Syndicats* group providing the Vichy regime with its 'labor wing.'

VI

French management and its press had high praise for the Majestic Agreement, regarding it as the CGT's first official relinquishment of the class-conflict idea in labor-management relations. The *Bulletin quotidien,* sponsored by the Comité des Forges, hoped that 'a death-blow had been dealt to the false and pernicious doctrine which was conceived artificially and which was never based on the actuality of human relations.' If this doctrine could be abandoned once and for all, if employers and workers would regard each other only as fellow citizens, co-operation would be possible in peace as well as in wartime.[41] But the discussions among the leaders of organized labor regarding the problems of union-management co-operation were viewed with considerable misgivings by most of French big business. Only those groups within French management which had long since adhered to corporative beliefs approved of the attempts to redefine the fundamental position of labor and capital. It is not an accident that almost all of these businessmen belonged to the 'distressed' branches of industry, such as textiles and leather. These poor relations in the family of French business had feared, at least since the crisis in the early years of the decade, that they would be less able than the highly organized and cartellized branches, such as mining and heavy industry, to sustain further social conflicts. The insufficiently rationalized consumer goods industries could no longer face long strikes and lockouts; arbitration awards often proved less satisfactory to them than to the producer goods industries. Since the early 1930's the corporative system had been advocated as a basis of economic reconstruction by certain industrialists of the northern departments, among them Pierre Mathon, president of the Central Committee of the Wool Industry, and Maurice Olivier, president of a trade association. The Comité Central de l'Organisation Professionnelle (CCOP), in which most of these industrial branches were represented, elaborated detailed blueprints showing how the professions could be organized as entities.[42]

The same persons and organizations were among those that *Syndicats* praised as 'modern-minded employers' when it performed its swing to corporativism. Olivier, who took an active part in union-management co-operation in northern France, had addressed a letter to Belin in which he outlined a social program of collaboration for war and peace. The workers were to be granted a share of the profits and a voice in the management of all social institutions, such as housing projects and consumers' co-operatives. This program, which openly favored the 'organization of the profession,' was enthusiastically received by *Syndicats* as inspired by 'neither paternalism nor state interventionism.'[43] The CCOP and Olivier were often referred to as the 'leftist' wing of French management, but actually their 'revolutionary' views were a replica of the corporative principles advocated by the *Syndicats* wing of the union movement.

There is another reason why the acceptance of Olivier's program by Belin was noteworthy. Olivier had stated that in his belief the workers wished only to participate in the management of welfare institutions connected with the plant, and were not at all interested in the conduct of the enterprise; hence economic and financial responsibility was to remain solely with the employer. Traditionally, the French trade unionists had never acknowledged the legitimacy of private ownership, and had always clamored for the transfer of the means of production, however much the CGT plan had modified this conception in regard to other than key industries.[44] That Belin accepted Olivier's views on this point without criticism was one more evidence of his radical departure from the former social philosophy of the French trade-union movement.

French heavy industry and the CGPF viewed with hostility the accord that was apparently growing up between men like Belin and Olivier. The influential Comité des Forges and the mining industry had habitually criticized schemes of corporativism no less than requests for the nationalization of industry. Now, under the guise of a defense of free enterprise, the spokesmen for these industries again rejected any shackling of industrial society by other fetters than those set by the cartels and monopolies. Marcel Tardy, who before the war, under the auspices of the Comité des Forges, had written a violent diatribe against corporativism,[45] reported weekly in Le Temps on the climate of industrial relations. While he viewed as a happy symptom the willingness of the CGT to give up class ideologies and to embrace openly the cause of union-management co-operation, he nonetheless advised the labor movement that 'memories of the past,' class violence, and the threats of social revolution could not be suddenly forgotten. The tone of his reporting was frequently that of admonitions addressed to a criminal on parole.[46]

In a polemic against the moderate ideas advanced by Jouhaux in regard to union-management co-operation, Le Temps made it clear that the industrial circles which it represented did not consider organized labor a full-fledged partner in society. To Jouhaux's contention that collaboration meant the distribution of responsibilities among the state, labor, and capital, *Le Temps* replied that only the state should assume responsibilities. The pressure groups should only be consulted by the government, and should never be allowed to make the private interests which they represented prevail over the public interest represented by the state. The labor movement, instead of indulging in a dangerous interpretation of 'collaboration' and in discussions of whether wartime taxation and wage policy corresponded to the principles of social justice, should be made to understand that its supreme duty in wartime was discipline.

Le Temps maintained that by condemning the aspirations of the labor movement it was upholding liberal and democratic principles. This is true only if democracy and liberalism are regarded as identical with the ideas promoted by the French Revolution. The theory which *Le Temps* defended in 1940 corresponded almost exactly to Le Chapelier's famous declaration of 14 June 1791: 'The individual owes allegiance solely and exclusively to the state, and to no one else.' *Le Temps*, which Jaurès had once called 'the bourgeoisie transformed into a newspaper,' might have pondered the fact that the occasion on which Le Chapelier made his declaration was the confirmation of the French law prohibiting trade unions. The outlawing of trade unions was the logical conclusion of the conception defended by *Le Temps*.

Thus Jouhaux was not unjustified when he remarked that this philosophy would set back the cause of labor more than a century. He also criticized *Le Temps* for invoking the monolithic power of the state every time that management saw fit to oppose needed reforms asked for by the labor movement, while the same paper decried undue state intervention whenever reforms were decided upon by the government. What *Le Temps* proposed, concluded Jouhaux, was to exclude the labor movement, if not the working class, from the national collectivity. Under that conception the collaboration envisaged by the Majestic Agreement would be deprived of all significance.[47]

The extent to which the discussions on union-management co-operation were overshadowed by the social events of the preceding decades was made even clearer by a speech delivered at an official meeting of the CGPF. The speaker, an influential industrialist, ridiculed what he termed the 'discovery' of the Majestic Agreement. French management, he said, apparently provoked also by Dautry's circular letter (to be discussed in the next chapter), could organize assistance for mobilized workers and introduce devices for industrial hygiene without calling meetings with the representatives of labor or sitting on bipartite committees. As long as the statutes of the CGT continued to clamor for the abolition of private property and of the wage system, the speaker declared amid applause, he would regard the wartime conversion of the trade unions as purely temporary. The former sins of the CGT, such as the strikes of 1910 and 1917, the Popular Front and the general strike of 1938, would never be forgotten. Referring to his 'excellent memory' the speaker concluded by denouncing the CGT as having always been inimical to social peace and contemptuous of the glorious traditions of France.[48]

With such utterances made in the name of the most important employers' association the discussions of union-management co-operation obviously reached a dead end. That they were made hardly a month before the German onslaught is indicative of the role that the rift between classes and groups was to play in the defeat of France. The union movement had hoped that labor-management co-operation would show a way out of the blind alley in which the CGT found itself at the outbreak of the war. After a few months it was evident that the discussions between the union movement and French management had only led into another blind alley. The spokesmen of big business had clearly indicated the price which labor would have to pay to be acceptable: a complete and open abandonment of its traditional role.

XII

Labor-Management Relations: The Actuality

I

IN the nine months that followed the declaration of war there was not only no agreement on the principles of collaboration but also an almost complete lack of any actual co-operation between capital and labor. For the most part any co-operation that existed was 'selective' on both sides. The workers and their representatives regarded the majority of employers as falling in one of two categories: those who deliberately attempted to provoke their workers, and those who stubbornly opposed every request. They abandoned any hope of coming to an understanding with either type, and reconciled themselves to the fact that normal union-management relations could be developed only with the handful of employers who showed real understanding for the difficulties into which the war had plunged the workers.[1] Similarly, management selected the union leaders whom it considered acceptable for some form of collaboration. The CGT had repeatedly insisted that union-management collaboration should be practiced with the legitimate workers' organizations themselves, rather than with individuals connected with the union movement, but its demands were not heeded. The union leaders with whom French management chose to deal belonged without exception to the *Syndicats* group. The same men, such as Dumoulin, Belin, Froideval, Vigne, Roy, Savoie, were later, after the armistice, among those who collaborated with the Pétain regime or the occupation authorities.

The closest approach to actual co-operation between unions

and management occurred in the industrial region of the Nord department. There, however, regular contacts between management and unions had never ceased, and had been frequent even on the eve of the war. In the trade organizations of this district the old type of hard-boiled fighters ('patrons de combat,' in the terminology of the French labor movement) no longer existed; the social ideas of many of the employers represented a mixture of corporativism and old-time paternalism. And in this region the officials of the CGT were almost without exception strongly anti-communist. In prewar days the relations between trade unions and management had sometimes grown out of a common opposition to communism.

These contacts were regularized and intensified after the central agreement had been reached at the Majestic. Under the chairmanship of the prefect of the Nord department representatives of important industries met with corresponding numbers of trade-union leaders. Frequently the labor movement was represented not only by the CGT but also by the Catholic and the so-called 'free' unions, which had not previously been recognized by the courts as a genuine labor movement. When Dumoulin, the then uncontested leader of the CGT in the Nord department, was questioned about these meetings, he defended the presence of at least the Catholic unions as having developed naturally and without contention.[2] Other participants in the meetings were the representatives of the foremen and technicians, whom the CGT had vainly attempted to organize within its ranks.

At the conclusion of the first of these meetings, which was held in Lille in November 1939, a communique was published which stressed the necessity of close collaboration of employers, workers, and white-collar employees. It was particularly emphasized that this collaboration should be based on mutual respect and on respect for the existent labor legislation and the previously concluded collective agreements. A permanent committee of coordination was set up in Lille, and bipartite meetings in several important industrial localities of the department followed. In general they functioned satisfactorily, particularly in the adjustment of grievances for which the labor legislation, since the suspension of arbitration procedures, no longer provided a sufficient outlet.

On a smaller scale, similar methods of co-operation were pursued in the metal industry of Paris, with the aid of the Minister of Labor and certain members of his staff. A committee composed of representatives of industry and labor was set up, and it met regularly to settle rising conflicts and to discuss current problems of industrial relations.[3] Similarly, in an important northwestern department employers and workers in the building trade asked the prefect to preside over their meetings, which dealt primarily with the application of clauses in collective agreements.

These cases, however, remained exceptional. Elsewhere no formal agreements between unions and management were concluded. Hopes expressed by the Minister of Labor[4] that other trades would follow the example of the metal industry in Paris were not fulfilled. With the few exceptions in the northern regions, industrial relations were particularly tense in the larger enterprises; in the small shops complaints were less frequent.

A new and urgent appeal was made by the Minister of Armament in a New Year's letter to the industrialists:

Whether we wanted it or not, we are bound to have the same destiny. We are more than united, we are welded together. It is necessary to transpose this unity to the psychological plane, and to transform your men into a fighting crew ardently devoted to victory. You will be able to overcome moral obstacles under one condition: nobody must have the right to believe that you are moved by political resentment or intentions of social reaction. Everybody must be compelled to acknowledge that you are devoted solely to the fulfilment of your role as leader.

After making concrete suggestions on how to improve conditions of industrial hygiene, the Minister admonished the employers to 'collaborate sincerely and cordially with the representatives of the personnel.'[5]

This plea not only was characteristic of Dautry's social philosophy, but also pointed clearly, if not bluntly, to the vulnerable spots in the labor-management relationship during the first months of the war. The feeling on the part of the workers that the employers were actuated by 'political resentment' and 'intentions of social reaction' did not further successful union-management agreements. In accordance with Dautry's outlook, his letter avoided any mention of the trade unions. Apparently he deemed it wiser to appeal for collaboration with 'the representatives of the personnel,' a term that could refer either to the representatives of the trade unions or to the shop stewards. As a matter of fact, the institution of shop stewards became a test for the possibility of improving industrial relations and achieving the desired collaboration between labor and management.

II

In the prewar period, as was shown above, the institution of shop stewards had not functioned as smoothly as had been hoped, and sometimes industrial peace was more harmed than furthered by the election and the activities of the workers' delegates in the plants. But the institution had become so important a part of French labor legislation that after the outbreak of the war the Minister of Labor repeatedly declared an abolition of the shop stewards out of the question.[6]

After September 1939, however, the activities of the shop stewards were practically suspended, especially in defense industries and wherever communists or communist sympathizers had held the posts as delegates. Therefore new regulations were asked for by the union movement.[7] When the government issued them it was stressed that it was unthinkable to shelve for the duration of hostilities an institution that had been created during the last war and was then found highly beneficial to the improvement of industrial relations.[8] But in spite of these assertions the new provisions eliminated the shop stewards in a great number of enterprises: while previously their election had been obligatory in all firms where more than ten persons were employed, they were now to function only in enterprises with a personnel of more than one hundred. Moreover, the new regulations maintained the requirement that only persons who had been employed for at least one year could be chosen as shop stewards. With the very widespread shifting of personnel caused by the war and by the gearing of production to a new armament program, this provision considerably narrowed down the number of workers eligible to the post.

The mandate of the previously elected shop stewards was declared to have expired, and the 'Permanent Workers' Committees,' which had been functioning in a role similar to that of shop stewards in the mining enterprises of eastern France, were suspended.[9] These measures were motivated mainly by the desire to rid the plants of communist stewards. In order to prevent the election of undesirable candidates in the future, the system of having the stewards designated by free elections was altogether abandoned. Instead it was provided that the 'most representative' legally constituted professional organization of the employees in a given enterprise should nominate the new shop stewards. In enterprises working for national defense the nominations had to be approved by the Minister of Labor. By thus linking the shop stewards with the professional organizations, that is, the trade-union movement, the new decree intended to eliminate the duplication of shop stewards and union representatives in the same plant. In the report accompanying the new regulations such duplication was described as harmful to the cause of industrial peace, which it was hoped the shop stewards would unswervingly serve in the future.

The CGT greeted the new regulations with unmitigated approval. During the first war both unions and government had been uneasy about the drifting away of the shop stewards from union control. Especially after the events in Russia in 1917 it was feared that the institution would turn into a rule of soviets. The Congress of Toulouse in 1936 had made a proposal similar to the scheme that was now adopted for the nomination of shop stewards, but that proposal had not been followed in the legislation originating from the Matignon Agreement, which provided only that the workers' delegates in the plants could seek the assistance of a representative of the union.

Early in 1940 Maurice Chevalme, who had participated in the Majestic meetings, expressed his belief that the CGT, through the institution of the shop stewards, would be able to transform itself and find the way toward constructive action.[10] René Belin saw in the new mode of designation a hopeful possibility of sounder co-operation between trade unions and management. He believed that acceptance of the nominations and of the redefined functions of the shop stewards should be considered a touchstone for the willingness of management to come to an understanding with the trade unions. From the outset Belin welcomed the idea that in the future the employers would no longer deal with delegates who, instead of being subject to union control, were sustained by the 'sometimes demagogical forces that every electoral body can let loose.'[11] With this remark he clearly indicated that in his opinion the labor movement, where it had to choose between elections and the direct rule of professional organizations, should prefer the latter.

In other countries, too, organized labor had been critical of a possible dualism between the shop stewards and the representatives of the trade unions. Almost everywhere, however, an actual unity had been possible, both in views and in action, through the strength of the trade unions in the plants; all that the state did was to sanction by statute an existing situation. The situation that existed in wartime France was significantly different. Hence Belin and the other CGT spokesmen, when they approved the new legislation, were expressing satisfaction not with a monopoly obtained by the labor movement but with a monopoly created by the state without consultation of those concerned: the wage earners of a given enterprise.

The position of the government was very similar to that expressed by Belin. The outlawing of the communist party and of its sympathizers in the union movement, and the general suspension of the democratic system of elections left only one alternative to the procedure adopted for the nomination of shop stewards: to abolish the institution altogether and to resort in every detail of industrial relations to direct state interference. Even the totalitarian regimes did not consider this alternative practicable in a highly developed industrial society. Hence the French government was obliged to rely on the existing professional organizations for the nomination of the workers' delegates. The minor role granted to the organized labor movement by the wartime labor legislation in general showed that the new regulation concerning shop stewards was by no means born out of a governmental predilection for the CGT.

Management and its representatives reacted very unfavorably to the decree providing for the nomination of the shop stewards by the trade unions. Some spokesmen based their opposition on the contention that the new regulations were contrary to the principles of liberty and of a free economy. Le Temps, still a protagonist of an economic system which had altogether vanished with the French wartime legislation, criticized the decree in terms almost identical with those in which it had opposed the introduction of arbitration procedures during the last war.[12]

In most cases, however, the opposition of the employers was based on the contention that in too many instances the proposed scheme gave the nomination into the hands of unions affiliated with the CGT, for in many industries and trades these organizations still retained the character of 'most representative' organization. It was argued that in the absence of elections it was not possible to determine the most representative organization, and that in the prevailing situation the candidates of the CGT unions would automatically be nominated.[13]

A circular letter from the Minister of Labor to the labor inspectors endeavored to appease the employers and anyone else who objected to the decree. It was made clear that all non-communist organizations would be regarded as 'legally constituted.' In determining the 'most representative' organization the last election of shop stewards prior to the war was to serve only as an indication. It was specifically stressed that where there was reason to believe that the workers had changed their minds since the last elections, or where the personnel of the enterprise had changed, the yardstick of the last elections could be abandoned. In such cases it was considered possible that two or more organizations would share in the nomination of several delegates. The circular letter added that even organizations not 'strictly union' in character could be considered entitled to nominate delegates, as long as their 'independence' seemed certain. This suggestion clearly referred to the so-called 'Amicales d'Entreprise,' company unions which had received every encouragement from numerous employers since the outbreak of the war.

While the decree providing for the nomination of shop stewards had stipulated that the nomination should take place within two months, the circular letter warned against resorting to 'undue haste.' Where it was believed that it was not yet possible to ascertain the most representative organization, the nomination could be postponed.

These modifications of the original ruling went very far toward meeting the criticism of the employers. They left the door wide open to an indefinite postponement of the nomination and to breaking any 'monopoly' of the CGT that may still have survived. Nevertheless, even in this interpretation the decree on the nomination of shop stewards was not welcomed by the majority of employers. In March 1940 one of the official spokesmen of the CGPF, at a meeting of that organization, called the method of nomination a 'strange' one; he denounced the 'influences from without' which would be brought to bear on the workers, and regretted that the delegates would be responsible not to their colleagues but to 'irresponsible clubs' [14]—a startling designation for a spokesman of the central employers' organization to use in reference to the CGT unions, after half a century of trade-union development in France. Belin called this opposition of French industry and its press to the new shop steward law alarming. 'If *Le Temps*,' he wrote, 'states that one cannot have confidence in the CGT for the designation of the shop stewards, that paper raises another question which it does not explicitly ask but which I want to ask. When and where is it still possible for the spokesmen of management to have confidence in the CGT?' [15]

Alarm over the employers' opposition was not confined to the CGT. In a declaration of the very moderate Catholic Parti Démocrate Populaire, French management was almost implored not to indulge itself, in the all-important matter of the nomination of shop stewards, in a hostility which could be interpreted by the workers as vengefulness. In order to purify the atmosphere, the declaration stated, employers should solemnly repudiate the so-called 'Amicales d'Entreprises,' the company unions which were all too often formed with the sole aim of preventing the designation of genuine trade-union representatives affiliated with the CGT or the CGTF.[16]

Actually, in numerous enterprises the nominations were long delayed. As late as May 1940 union representatives brought complaints before the Minister of Labor that in spite of their strenuous efforts hardly any shop stewards had been nominated in the all-important metal industry.[17] The same situation prevailed in other industries. It is true, however, that in many cases the unions themselves were unable to make adequate proposals for nomination. The trade-union movement had not recovered from the crisis into which it was plunged by the expulsion of the communists and the outbreak of hostilities. In addition, it often happened that a candidate did not wish to accept his nomination; experience had taught the workers that frequently the shop stewards merely exposed themselves to severe sanctions from the employers without being able to obtain substantial advantages for their colleagues from a management unwilling to co-operate with the representatives of the personnel.

It has been mentioned that in case of dismissal the shop stewards had no recourse other than the regular arbitration procedures. The wartime legislation abolished the system of arbitration, and thus the stewards were now left without any protection against dismissal. Because of the close link that now existed between the shop stewards and the unions, dismissal of the stewards was frequently tantamount to a weeding out of those workers who had been the backbone of the unions in the plants. The CGT made many protests, but it was unable to prevent sanctions being taken against shop stewards.[18] Thus there were many vital plants in which the personnel was practically without representation, for the former shop stewards had ceased to function with the enactment of the decree of November 1939.

The institution of shop stewards, which had been looked upon as an effective instrument of union-management co-operation, remained on the whole without effect. It even worked against its expressed purpose of bettering industrial relations, as a result of the impetus that the new wartime legislation gave to the formation of company unions, and hence to ill feelings on the part of organized labor.

III

Those employers who saw no advantage in the normalization of industrial relations could use the extreme intricacy of the wartime legislation for successfully evading their obligations and for interpreting the regulations in the way most unfavorable for labor. Just as ways were found to render the new shop-steward legislation innocuous, many of the important enterprises ignored official communications on the application of the very few wartime provisions protecting the health and furthering the morale of the workers. Remonstrances of the workers were generally rejected, sometimes with brutality. The 'iron discipline' exercised by the employers in former times was once more applied in many enterprises. The regulations governing the employment of *requis* and *affectés* made it all the easier to enforce such discipline, for the employers could rid their plants of all undesired workers simply by having them sent to the army. Many instances became known where this was done without much consideration for the need of skilled labor for war production.[19]

In such circumstances the promises made by the Majestic Agreement became worthless and hypocritical in the eyes of the workers. The exceptions to the general dissatisfaction counted but little. Daily experience impressed upon the majority of the workers the conviction that the promises had been a fraud and that the fraud had been deliberate. By the spring of 1940 such feelings had reached proportions which made the workers susceptible to the incessant and adroit communist underground propaganda, and provoked strong warnings from most moderate observers. The workers' complaints even found an echo, however feeble, in a memorandum which the Minister of Labor addressed to industrialists and labor inspectors in April 1940.[20]

A warning voiced by Paul Ramadier, a former Minister of Labor who had never excelled in radical views, was almost pathetic. He stated bluntly that the majority of employers had seen in the offer of organized labor to collaborate with management nothing but an admission of weakness. Management hoped to use the offer as a means of getting rid of trade unions altogether. Even minor concessions were made by management only when it was compelled to do so by the government. Ramadier warned that under conditions aggravated by the sacrifices and sufferings of the war, a resurgence of 'extremism' was to be feared. 'If we don't do anything to avoid it, an explosion is bound to occur,' he concluded, writing exactly one week before the German invasion of western Europe.[21]

In the same period Jouhaux, denouncing the sanctions taken by employers against many workers, declared, 'The *malaise* threatens to become very great.'[22] Belin, who had made so many ideological sacrifices to defend the cause of collaboration between

unions and management, admitted in April 1940, shortly after
Reynaud's ministry was installed, that for months the problem
of normalizing industrial relations had not made the slightest
progress. Most of the time, Belin wrote, the CGPF had remained
silent, in spite of all the attempts made by the CGT. 'Its silence
is by no means neutral, but covertly hostile. . . . All this is serious,
very serious,' he added. 'If both partners remain what they have
been, the violent social clash, blind and senseless as it is, will recur
at the first occasion.' [23] Savoie, prominent in the *Syndicats* group
and secretary of the federation of workers in the food industries,
openly voiced what was an almost general opinion among his
friends. It would be a mere waste of time, he wrote, to go on
hoping for voluntary co-operation between unions and management. The elimination of the strike weapon and the stubbornness
of the majority of the employers made it necessary to supersede
contractual agreements by 'compulsory relations' (*rapports
obligés*). The state should intervene and establish the necessary
equilibrium of social forces by regulation. The writer was well
aware of the fact that the adoption of such procedures meant
the definite end of democracy. 'Of course liberty is endangered
thereby,' he admitted, 'but there is no other way.' [24]

Those labor leaders who saw co-operation between unions and
management as dependent on some form of corporative organization had to acknowledge that the state was essential for protection. They had to acknowledge that the 'organized profession'
was unable to achieve its ends except through the most stringent
intervention of the state in economic affairs and industrial relations. What had already become evident from the corporative
experiences of other lands had to be realized in France under the
influence of war and the approaching catastrophe: corporativism
was a method for integrating the forces of production into the
totalitarian state. Savoie and his friends, compelled to decide between liberty and 'order,' saw no other way but the sacrifice of
liberty.[25]

Such was the social atmosphere that prevailed when France experienced the onslaught of the invader.

At the hour of supreme danger, in the midst of the battle of France and shortly after the capitulation of Belgium, representatives of the CGT and the CGPF met again. In its last number to appear, Le Peuple, central organ of the CGT, published the text of the new agreement, which was described as having been concluded spontaneously without any government pressure:

At this moment, when France is engaged in a war on which depend simultaneously her own existence, that of numerous oppressed peoples, and the very principles of civilization, there exists for all Frenchmen but one duty: to contribute with all their efforts to the defense of the country and the defeat of the aggressor.

The CGPF and the CGT have signed the following declaration.

All trade unions and all organizations of employers, workers, handicraftsmen, middle classes, engineers, technicians, foremen, intellectuals, representing all and every productive force of France, have adhered to this declaration and have signed it.

They affirm their unalterable decision that everything shall be done for total, efficient, and lasting victory, out of which a new world, based on justice, shall rise.

They unite in this collaboration in an atmosphere of mutual esteem and confidence.

To the hour of the greatest dangers, the hour of greatest duties should correspond. In the struggle for independence which republican France must sustain, there is no room for selfish interests or for class actions or doctrines.

Employers and workers become collaborators, inspired by the same desire for unity and social peace, indispensable for victory. They vow that they will bring a common endeavor to the reconstruction and reorganization which must follow the war in order that they may secure for the future generation a better, fuller, and more secure life.[26]

Under the pressure of growing panic French labor and management sought to achieve the *union sacrée* they had hitherto been reluctant to agree upon. The employers seemed to have abandoned most of their former reservations, but Jouhaux admitted in an article commenting on the common declaration that even at that moment the agreement was not as complete as the CGT wanted to see it. Even as it stood, however, it was certainly a radical departure from the methods adhered to during the months of 'phony war.'

But here again the reversal had come too late. 'Republican France,' which the CGPF and the CGT had sworn to defend, succumbed to blows which became mortal because of the lack of moral, military, and economic preparation. Too late the organizations of labor and capital had endeavored to strike at the roots of national disunity.

PART III. VICHY

JUNE 1940—AUGUST 1944

XIII

Collaboration and Resistance

I T is not yet possible to present a social history of Pétain's 'French state.' Contemporary documents alone—and little further evidence is now available—cannot reveal the actual status of industrial relations during that period. The artificial atmosphere created by a satellite regime, such as that residing in Vichy, generally results in a steadily widening gap between the laws on the statute books and social reality. Moreover, even now after some of the main collaborators have stood trial, most of the judicial archives which will reveal the implications of their collaboration are still closed; and industrial relations in Vichy France, influenced in every aspect by economic and political collaboration between the German and the French authorities, will not be fully understood until the records of such activities can be read and interpreted by the historian.

The evidence of the underground press is equally inadequate. The labor movement's renascence under conditions of illegality was by no means a consistent development, either in action or in philosophy. It varied according to regional differences, traditions, the hazard of personal contacts, and very often the conditions created by Gestapo terror or Vichy militia. To weigh the importance of tendencies and groups which emerged during the Vichy period, to ascertain the opinions and desires of the rank and file of labor, it will be necessary to go farther than a mere examination of the underground press. At present, however, the testimony of the participants in the illegal labor movement has not yet been collected and evaluated.

Thus the concluding chapters of this study will not attempt to trace in detail the history of the French labor movement between the capitulation of France in the summer of 1940 and the liberation of the country four years later. It does seem desirable, however, to present at least the main trends of labor history during the Vichy period. In the first place, some of the developments that have been traced in the foregoing chapters reached their logical conclusion after the capitulation of Bordeaux. Tendencies toward corporativism and isolationism, for example, which had come to life during the last years of the republic and were accentuated during the first months of the war, assumed more definite form under the pressure of defeat and change of regime, and thus shed a new light on previous phases of trade-union orientation.

Moreover, it would seem unjust to close the record of French trade-union history with the Franco-German armistice. This record was often one of confusion and aimlessness, of dissension, and even of treacherous abandonment of labor's cause and that of the nation. The decay of republican institutions, which had been noticeable since 1934 and had been accelerated after the failure of the Popular Front, particularly during the first months of the war, subjected certain sectors of the labor movement to a corresponding process of disintegration. But almost immediately after the official burial of the republic, French labor, reverting to the sources of its strength, redeemed itself from many of its past errors. It is hoped that a report on these developments, while necessarily incomplete, will afford a more balanced view of French labor history than would an account that closed with the momentary triumph of reaction and fascism in France.

I

During the first months of its existence, the actions of the Pétain government were guided by the assumptions that had led to the capitulation before the invader at Bordeaux: a rapid defeat of the British Isles would result in a *pax hitleriana* and the un-contested rule of Europe by Nazi Germany. The more quickly France could adopt the governmental system of the victor and condition herself to the moral climate of totalitarianism, the better, it was believed, would be her chances of being allowed to partake in some of the spoils of the 'New Order.' The com-plete bewilderment, heedlessness, and apathy which the lightning victory of the invading armies had provoked, the dispersion of the civilian population throughout the country, the severance of almost all organizational ties, seemed to provide favorable condi-tions for imposing speedily upon the country a new social system in harmony with the views of the Vichy government.

In those first days of defeat, organized labor was not yet fully aware of the tasks that awaited it.[1] One month after the armistice the members of the Central Office of the CGT, all of whom sojourned in the then unoccupied portion of the country, called together the National Council. This meeting, which was to be the last session of the supreme organ of the CGT, took place in Toulouse, where the reunified trade-union movement had given itself a new constitution scarcely more than four years before. There the representatives of 24 federations and 28 regional unions who were available in unoccupied territory voted, in view of the 'immense disaster' that had befallen the country, in favor of the establishment of a 'French Community of Labor.' In somewhat ambiguous terms the resolution which was adopted sought to institute a 'permanent co-ordination' of capital and labor, as the 'logical development' of previous agreements, such as the Ma-jestic accord and the Paris accord of May 1940. The resolution adopted at Toulouse declared that

The immediate tasks of the French Community of Labor should be to put the country back to work by actively reorganizing and normalizing as much as possible the economic life of the nation, by rearranging the transportation system on a national scale, by pursuing a general policy in the field of electric power, by de-veloping intensely agricultural production, by re-establishing the industries of consumer goods, the shortage of which is already making itself felt on the market and creating anxiety among the masses.[2]

But French management, looking forward to the establishment of authoritarian corporativism, did not even consider the offer of the labor movement.

In Toulouse the CGT also declared its determination to continue co-operation with the Catholic unions. Both Jouhaux and the secretary-general of the CFTC, the latter from Paris, instructed their affiliated organizations wherever possible to make common cause for the salvation of a free labor movement.

Of greater importance, however, than the discussions at Toulouse concerning the future orientation of the trade-union movement was the refusal of those present to endorse the recent appointment of Belin, a prominent member of their Central Office, to the post of Minister of Production and Labor in the Pétain cabinet. The issue was presented in somewhat personal terms, but this decision of the delegates at Toulouse was actually a first notice that the trade-union movement refused to be integrated within the new French state or to be represented in its councils.

Belin was the logical choice of those elements that had sought since the outbreak of the war, even before the launching of Hitler's blitzkrieg in the west, to form a government of capitulation under Pétain's leadership. Belin had been an outspoken advocate of appeasement before and after Munich. His violent anti-communism, while it had called forth the suspicion of many of his colleagues within the CGT, had also opened to him new contacts among political leaders of the extreme right and among certain influential industrialists and bankers.[3] His social philosophy had developed strongly in the direction of corporativism. Moreover, he was well known to his new associates as a man of unbridled ambition with a rancor against the traditional leadership of the CGT as represented by Jouhaux.[4]

Those who had maneuvered the formation of the Vichy regime

hoped that the inclusion of Belin in the cabinet would secure the alignment of labor with the new government. Belin found himself not only presiding over the Labor Ministry but also in charge of production. The actual direction of the Ministry soon rested, however, with Belin's chief of cabinet, a director of the Worms bank, which was foremost among the appeasement and collaborationist forces of France.

Belin knew that he would never be able to convert such elements as the leaders of the civil servants federation to his conception of an authoritarian corporative state or to a break with the leadership of Jouhaux and his group. But he mistakenly believed that as a result of the partial marasmus which had befallen the CGT under the threefold burden of ideological confusion, expulsion of the communists, and wartime regulations, he could easily dispense with the central organization of the trade-union movement and still be successful in the task that was assigned to him: to intégrate the French working class into the new state.

One of the early laws promulgated by the Vichy regime, in August 1940, presaged the liquidation of the CGT.[5] This statute, which proposed to create the provisional framework for the economic and social reorganization of the defeated country, followed a strictly authoritarian pattern. For each industry a so-called 'Organization Committee' was formed, which was charged with the formulating of general rules for industrial operations, the distribution of raw materials, and the 'suggestion' of prices to the government. The members of these bodies were nominated by the government and were chosen almost exclusively from the leading persons in the most influential concerns and trusts.[6]

The dissolution of the CGT, foreshadowed in the law of August, became official in November.[7] Both legislative acts bear the signature of Belin. It was left to Vichy's Minister of Labor to preside over the legal dissolution of the organization of which he had been secretary for years. The CFTC was also outlawed. The simultaneous liquidation of the CGPF, the national organization of management, and of the Comité des Forges and similar

associations served merely propagandistic purposes, as the Organization Committees permitted French big business to exercise
its influence more directly than before.

In general the new regulations did not touch either the federations or the union locals affiliated with the CGT and the CFTC,
but an important exception to this rule was the immediate liquidation of the civil servants federation.[8] This measure not only once
more denied to public officials the long-contested right to organize; it also decreed the dispersal of an organization which in
many respects had become the vanguard of the French labor
movement.

In a series of articles and declarations to the press Belin attempted to explain the principles that guided his actions.[9] He did
not conceal the authoritarian character of the new structure,
which was to serve the ends of a planned economy directed according to the 'interests of all.' But while thus using formulas
reminiscent of the Nazis' *Gemeinnutz geht vor Eigennutz,* the
former labor leader explicitly promised the rebirth of trade-union
activity in the framework of a new Labor Charter.

II

It was generally expected that the Labor Charter would soon
become law. Actually the discussions which were to prepare the
legislative text unearthed fundamental controversies about the
role to be assigned to labor in the new French state, and more
than a year passed before the Charter was promulgated. The
commission which prepared the text and the introductory report
to Marshal Pétain comprised, besides representatives of the government, a number of employers and some former trade-union
leaders who had chosen to heed Belin's appeal for collaboration.
The chairman of the commission was Henri Moysset, foremost
French authority on Proudhon. It is interesting to note that
Proudhon and his disciples were not only honored at Vichy but

also frequently extolled by the collaborationist press of the occupied zone.[10]

The Charter, which was finally adopted in October 1941, was presented by Vichy as one of the 'constitutional laws of the new France.' [11] A German paper published in Paris remarked that it could be considered a synthesis of the fascist corporative system and the German Labor Front, but that it would hardly function effectively until the one-party system was established in France.[12] This statement, which was a blunt admission that the true function of the Labor Front was to serve as auxiliary for the regimentation and indoctrination of labor under totalitarian rule, correctly predicted the eventual failure of the French Labor Charter.

The principal cells of the new social organism which the Charter sought to establish were the Social Committees. These were to be established at all levels. On the factory level they were created in agreement with the employer, which meant that the members of the individual committees were actually appointed by him. On the local, regional, and national levels, where committees were organized for each branch of industry or trade, the committees were given broad powers in occupational affairs. They were supposed to fix wages and to conclude collective agreements, and they were to discuss problems of technical training, apprenticeship, hiring and firing, hygiene and safety. In the language of the Charter, which borrowed freely from the teachings and the terminology of the Catholic traditionalists, all the duties of the committees pertained to the 'professional family.' Actually they were all matters that had formerly been included in the province of trade-union activity.

The Social Committees were composed in equal proportions of representatives of management, of the technical personnel (cadres), and of manual or white-collar workers. The threefold division was devised in order to undermine wherever possible the solidarity between the two categories of wage earners which had made common cause in the days of the Popular Front. The influence of the state was brought to bear by the presence of a government commissioner on each of the national Social Committees. His decision was to be invoked in all questions where final arbitration of rising conflicts was necessary. As a matter of course strikes were outlawed, and remained so.

The representatives of labor were to be designated by the trade unions, either locals or federations, but only one union was to represent each branch or profession. Membership in the single union became compulsory for each wage earner. Thereby two traditional aspects of freedom of organization in France were eradicated: the wage earners were no longer free to join or not to join a union; and they could no longer choose the union of their liking. By abolishing all labor organizations that cut across the professions the Charter did away with the organizations that traditionally represented the collective interests of the workers as a class, such as the regional unions.

State control of the existing trade unions was to be continuously exercised at each level: the union locals were compelled to expel members if 'reasons of public order' demanded it; the nomination of every union official had to be sanctioned by public authorities; all the activities of union locals and federations were to be supervised by the Social Committees; statutes of the unions had to be approved either by the same committees or by the Minister of Labor. René Belin and the members of the *Syndicats* group, who in prewar times had unceasingly preached the 'independence' of the trade-union movement and had sometimes taken anachronistic pride in deploring the interference of the modern state in labor affairs, now sought to establish a labor organization entirely dominated by the state.

That the Labor Charter was tantamount to the end of free trade unionism was intentional. But for two reasons the Charter itself defeated its purpose of integrating a state-controlled labor movement within the new state. Since the Social Committees and the state were given all functions traditionally assigned to the trade unions, the latter were deprived of their *raison d'être*. In addition, the Charter made no attempt to define the relationship between the Social Committees and the well-entrenched Organization Committees, established by the law of 1940. High government officials did not conceal the fact that the definition and organization of a rapport between the two was essential for the functioning of the Charter,[13] but any attempt to gear the new statute of industrial relations to the untrammeled rule of the trusts as established by Vichy proved well-nigh impossible. The same difficulties had threatened to arise in Germany, between the Labor Front and the National Economic Chamber, and there the National Socialist regime had cut the Gordian knot by depriving the Labor Front of all economic activities.[14] Since the corporativists of Vichy, and among them the trade-union leaders collaborating with Belin, were seeking legislation that would render the one-party rule unnecessary, this solution was not available in France.

What the Labor Charter and its authors had not foreseen was the resistance to the corporative experiment which was provoked among the workers and their organizations, legal or illegal. From a criticism that was at first somewhat hesitating this opposition grew to a resolute refusal and a determination to sabotage the new set-up by every available means.

Crippled by its internal contradictions and obstructed by hostility from without, the Labor Charter could be saved neither by new decrees, setting more detailed rules for the establishment of compulsory trade unions,[15] nor by a rapid succession of labor ministers. In April 1942 the position of Belin, who had already lost to representatives of big business all his functions in the field of production, had become untenable. His successor, Hubert Lagardelle, had in earlier years been a disciple of revolutionary syndicalism, but subsequently followed his teacher and friend, Georges Sorel, into admiration of Mussolini. In the fall of 1943 the failure of the new experiment had become so obvious that a 'technician,' Bichelonne, took over Lagardelle's post, thereby ending even the appearance of the co-operation of labor representatives.

Two years after the promulgation of the Labor Charter the newspapers of both the northern and southern zones had to admit that the organization of labor interests had made little progress, and that the stiffened resistance of management rendered impossible any adjustment of industrial relations along the desired corporative lines.[16] For the activities of the Social Committees, which were unable to function, the government had to substitute direct intervention in industrial relations. The Labor Charter was dead even before the downfall of the Vichy regime.

III

In the early days of his activities in the Pétain government Belin succeeded in obtaining the collaboration of a certain number of former trade-union leaders. All of them had belonged to the *Syndicats* group within the CGT; all had shared both Belin's violent anti-communism and his pacifist creed. The commission that prepared the Labor Charter counted among its labor representatives the general secretaries of the federations of the food industries, the miners, and the garment workers, and one of the secretaries of the federation of metal workers. In a so-called 'Trade-Union Co-ordination Committee' of Vichy origin the co-authors of the Labor Charter were joined by other officials of trade unions formerly affiliated with the CGT, including the secretaries of fairly important federations, such as those of the railwaymen, the white-collar workers, the printing trade, the leather workers, the hatmakers, the government workers without civil-service status. They all endeavored to give to the new regime a halo of sympathy for the workers' cause; after the promulgation of the Labor Charter they volunteered their services for supplying the Social Committees with labor representatives.[17]

All these men had been active in the trade-union movement

for many years. Some of them, however, had lost their functions after 1936 through the wave of communist 'colonization,' and had been able to reoccupy their former posts only after the new split in 1939. These developments, which accounted in part for their anti-communism, had brought them into early contact with the *Syndicats* group.

It is not wholly surprising that most of the trade-union leaders who advocated collaboration with the Germans after the armistice, and an establishment of a corporative system, had been the protagonists of planning within the prewar CGT. For many of them the idea of planned economy had become a value in itself. The question of the political framework into which the planning would be fitted was given little or no consideration by trade unionists who had always scorned political issues. After Hitler's rapid victories the 'New Order,' with its thoroughly centralized and regimented economy, seemed to these labor leaders at least to approximate the schemes of their blueprints, and to represent a higher form of economic organization.

The extent to which the members of the Co-ordination Committee could still speak in the names of their organizations was doubtful from the outset. As was mentioned above, after the outbreak of the war the majority of trade-union officials were more or less out of contact with the rank and file. After the armistice the severance of organizational ties was almost complete for those labor leaders who sojourned in the south of France, for the central offices of all federations had been in Paris and the trade unions had naturally recruited most of their members in the industrial regions, then occupied by the Germans. Hence a considerable number of the secretaries of federations who participated in the endeavors of the Co-ordination Committee acted merely in their own names and not as true representatives of their organizations. In addition, some ten former secretaries of regional unions, all of which were located in unoccupied France, had joined the Co-ordination Committee. For geographical reasons these trade-union officials were in closer contact with their organizations than were the secretaries of federations, but in view of the fact that there were more than eighty regional unions in prewar France it is evident that those who pledged allegiance to the Vichy ventures represented but a small minority. Moreover, since the Labor Charter had dissolved the regional unions, and since this dissolution had been accepted without resistance by Belin's friends, their mandate was as dubious as that of their colleagues.

Bertin, formerly secretary of one of the regional unions, published in Savoie a weekly paper known as *Au Travail*. Among his collaborators were members of the Co-ordination Committee, the director and co-director of the former CGT Institute of Higher Education, some pacifist intellectuals, and writers of syndicalist leanings. Most of them had been working together for the cause of appeasement since the days that preceded the Munich pact. The paper indulged occasionally in frankly anti-capitalist propaganda, but since the authorities regarded it as a ready medium for reaching the working classes its tirades against the trusts were permitted by the Vichy censorship. This tolerance was paid for by the collaborators of *Au Travail* with praises of Pétain and Laval and of their 'National Revolution,' and even with exhortations to the workers to accept work in Germany.[18]

Much more violent in its collaborationism was another paper published by former trade unionists in the occupied zone. As early as December 1940 *L'Atelier* started publication in Paris, under the unmistakable sponsorship of the Germans. At that time the development of the European war had changed the role that the Germans had assigned to France. With the vanishing of hopes for an early peace, Nazi Germany became less interested in the growth of an indigenous French authoritarianism, which would have lent a vestige of justification to the German claim to leadership in a happy concert of united European nations. Instead, it became increasingly important to gear the entire life of France to the needs of the German war economy. Since France was the most important reservoir for skilled manpower, one of Germany's greatest needs, the interest of the Germans was quite naturally directed toward the French working class. With the co-operation of genuine labor organizations, it was hoped that the labor reserve represented by the French prisoners of war could be put to better use, that scores of thousands of new recruits would stream into the German factories, and that the output of French plants working for the German war machine could be greatly increased.

The Germans seem never to have had great illusions about the usefulness of such men as Doriot, who had long since lost contact with the French industrial workers, and thus their choice for collaborators fell upon those authentic labor leaders of the *Syndicats* group who resided in occupied territory. Most notable among them was Dumoulin, who had been, before World War I, assistant secretary of the CGT, during that war a protagonist of revolutionary internationalism, and later at times the most respected spokesman of the industrial proletariat of northern France. Disappointed, however, by the shortcomings and failures of the labor movement during the interwar period, and embittered by frustrated ambitions, he had increasingly abandoned himself to cynicism, finally turning from violent red-baiting to glowing praise of Nazism.[19] With him on *L'Atelier* were Vigne, former secretary of the miners federation and during the war an official of the Labor Ministry, Zoretti, a leader of the teachers federation, and some oldtime syndicalists. Thus on the whole both the corporativists at Vichy and the collaborationists at Paris were recruited from labor leaders of similar tendencies.

At first *L'Atelier* was careful to use oldtime terminology. Affecting indifference to the military outcome of the war, it declared that the unavoidable 'social revolution' was its unique concern. Collaboration with Germany was presented as the fulfilment of old aspirations of the French left. After a tour of Nazi Germany Dumoulin and his fellow travelers reported enthusiastically on the 'strict equality' which prevailed there in industrial relations. The German Labor Front was termed an 'extraordinary success.' Soon thereafter the paper began to urge French workers to sign contracts for work in Germany, where excellent working conditions were said to await them.[20]

L'Atelier joined the former deputy Déat in his efforts to convert France to full-fledged totalitarianism, and in his attacks against the Vichy government, which was accused of lack of fervor in its collaboration with Germany. Especially after the Allied invasion of North Africa anti-semitism and violent anti-British feelings were aroused, as a part of the battle against the 'plutocracies.' After Laval's pledge, in 1942, to furnish more and more contingents of French workers for the German war machine, the paper's appeals to the workers to do their duty for the 'reconstruction of France' became increasingly insistent.[21] The small group of editors and contributors to *L'Atelier* worked through numerous committees, welfare organizations, and similar agencies, all easily convertible into recruitment bureaus for manpower needed in Germany.

These fascist proselytes first established a 'Committee of Trade-Union Propaganda' and later a 'Labor Committee of Immediate Help.' The latter was housed in the former administration building of the CGT in Paris, and was openly aided by the German authorities with funds expropriated from the Jewish population. An attempt to co-ordinate the activities of sympathetic labor leaders in the occupied and unoccupied zones was made by the establishment of a 'Committee of Labor and Social Information,' which had the avowed aim of helping Laval recruit an ever-increasing number of French workers.[22]

Dumoulin and his friends were no more successful, however, than Belin and his appointees. The trade-union movement to which these men had belonged refused to follow them. Universal contempt and complete isolation were their lot. Their only claim to historical importance is that they hastened the rebirth of a genuine labor movement which arose in opposition to their betrayal of democratic traditions.

IV

The resurrection of the French trade-union movement during the four years of the Vichy regime was swift and complete. In 1940 the bewildered and seriously divided labor movement lived at best on the margin of the nation. In 1944, on the eve of liberation, the trade unions had recovered organizational and ideological cohesion; labor was regarded as having formed the very core of the national resistance movement inside France; its program and plans for the future of the country had very wide approval; in the councils of London and Algiers its representatives were respected and influential partners. A number of factors contributed to this complete reversal of the situation.

In 1940 neither the consequences of the defeat nor the implications of the change of regime were fully grasped by the French population. The republic, after a prolonged period of disintegration and estrangement, had not stood the test of battle, and to those who ignored the true intentions of the rulers at Vichy, the new order of things seemed to offer the possibility of national survival. Promises made by the man who had been the 'hero of Verdun' were, if not readily accepted, at least looked upon as a ray of hope in an otherwise hopeless situation. The demarcation line which divided the nation in two, and the absence of almost two million prisoners of war, belonging to the most active part of the population, made it difficult to understand what France had to expect from a future under a totalitarian regime.

A gradual awakening followed Pétain's meeting with Hitler in Montoire. The relentlessness with which cherished symbols of freedom were attacked by the new government was bitterly resented. The voice of the London radio, eagerly listened to, dispersed many illusions about the true state of French affairs and the happenings in the outside world.

But if there was protest, its manifestations were at first only passive. A refusal to believe in official assurances, or to take part in ceremonies staged by eager imitators of Nazi propaganda methods, was at first the sole form in which disagreement could find expression. The rallying of public opinion was made all but impossible by the lack of communication facilities, for old channels of intercourse had been blocked by the destruction of republican institutions and new ones were not yet established.

In this situation the working class, as a result of its natural cohesion, had an immense advantage over other groups of the population. In the interest of the German war machine industrial production had to be maintained and even stepped up as far as possible, and therefore workers could not be prevented from communicating with each other and from manifesting solidarity. Thus before increased police surveillance could crush the resistance movement of the workers, they were able, with inventiveness and courage, to make use of the possibilities of organization offered by Vichy's illusional scheme of a corporative state.

The economic policies of the new French state affected no other group so severely as the wage earners, and especially the urban proletariat. There was often actual misery in the midst of the business boom created by German orders. The official wage policy attempted at first to cling to the wartime practice of freezing all wages and salaries, but adjustments had to be made. These proved wholly insufficient, and eventually a new system was adopted by which minimum and maximum hourly wages were fixed within each zone and for each class of activity; the maximum wages were not to exceed the minimum by more than 15 per cent.[23] The rise of prices taxed the workers' budgets so heavily that the decline of real wages was estimated to have reached 20 per cent by July 1942; on the eve of liberation living costs were estimated to have risen by 200 per cent, while wage rates had been increased by no more than 18 per cent.[24]

This development not only gave the workers a concrete object for their opposition to the Vichy regime but also permitted their propaganda among the general population to point to the fallacies of the 'National Revolution.' Even the collaborationist pseudo-labor press was obliged to depict repeatedly a state of affairs in which the workers saw themselves denied their requests for a revalorization of wages and for measures of industrial hygiene and security while corrupt practices were rampant among government officials and employers.[25]

The general attitude of French big business was yet another factor in forging the unity of labor and giving it a role in the vanguard of the resistance movement. It had long been whispered that many industrialists, because of their hatred for the France of the Popular Front, preferred Hitler and defeat to the despised republic. Such suspicions seemed justified by the unmitigated readiness of many of the larger concerns to engage in economic collaboration with the invader. Only a handful of former labor leaders, soon without any following, aligned themselves with the Germans or their Vichy satellites, but in all major fields of industrial production and trade there was frank and fruitful collaboration.[26] While there were undoubtedly employers who supported the resistance movement, there were many cases in which employers rid their plants of active labor organizers and trade-union members by facilitating their deportation to forced labor in Germany.[27]

This attitude of the French trusts that were represented in Vichy's Organization Committees seemed to the public a *post-hoc* justification of the labor movement's earlier campaign against the 'two hundred families.' Since big business engaged in activities that were generally regarded as treasonable, its antagonist, the labor movement, was considered vindicated in its earlier denunciation.

Finally, the conscription of labor by the French and German governments made labor truly the core of resistance. What later became known as the Maquis—there was a Maquis in the big cities as well as in the mountain regions—was born when an increasing number of workers and employees answered the call to work in Germany by hiding themselves and inflicting the greatest possible damage on the enemy. Quite naturally this class of resisters was composed almost exclusively of workingmen of all categories. By helping to organize, by co-ordinating and supporting this highly efficient form of national resistance, the trade-union movement showed the full measure of its regeneration.

v

After the armistice, when French trade unionism took off for a new start, a clarification of its philosophy and a redefinition of its basic conceptions appeared necessary. It was essential that the labor movement overcome the ideological confusion which had overshadowed the last period of the CGT's legal existence and had culminated in the capitulation of the Belin and Dumoulin groups.

On 15 November 1940, only about a week after the dissolution of the CGT and the CFTC had become official, twelve leading French trade unionists, opposed to the social experiment of the new French state, attempted to define the guiding principles of an autonomous labor movement. Among the authors of the manifesto, who wrote from occupied territory, were officers of the federations of metal, transport, building and wood, and textile workers, of civil servants and of white-collar workers, all formerly affiliated with the CGT, and the secretary-general and two assistant secretaries of the CFTC.

The document, which was to be known as the 'Manifesto of the Twelve,' [28] first assessed the responsibilities for the situation into which the country had fallen: 'It is wrong to pretend today that the defeat of our country was caused by the exercise of freedom by its citizens, while actually it was due to the incompetence of our General Staff, to the softness of our administration, and the anarchy of industrial production.' Recalling the repeated but unheeded warnings and the concrete reform proposals of the trade-union movement, the manifesto cleared organized labor from a share in the responsibilities, but admitted grave mistakes. Organized labor was accused of having too often sacrificed the search for general economic solutions to the satisfaction of immediate demands, and of having permitted sectarianism to disturb working-class unity.

After asserting the necessarily anti-capitalist character of trade unionism, the authors of the document emphasized that labor, while taking its full place in the state, should not let the state interfere with the organizational life and the activities of trade unions. The manifesto forcefully denounced the dissolution of the two confederations of labor, already decided upon by the Vichy government. At a moment when Germany, with the aid of French quislings, was attempting to lead the country into the orbit of Nazism, the manifesto bluntly stated that French trade unionism could not tolerate 'anti-semitism, religious persecution, limitation of freedom of opinion, privileges of wealth.'

The authors' attempt to define the relationship of unions and management still bore the marks of the confusion which characterized previous discussions of this point. In a concession to the philosophy that had been developed mainly by the Catholic movement, the document stated that 'the choice is not between trade unionism and corporativism; the two are equally necessary,' and arrived at the equivocal formula, 'a free trade union, within an organized profession, under the sovereign state.' The main reason for the ambiguity in regard to the problem of corporativism was that at that time the discussion was still on the theoretical level. Faced later with the actual danger, in the form of the Labor Charter, the trade-union movement rejected every form of corporativism.

When Marshal Pétain stated, in 1941, that it was the aim of the new social organization to 'put an end to the vindictive spirit which ruined us,' twenty-one secretaries of federations answered him that organized labor had been vindictive only 'by the nature of things and the exigencies of life.' [29] The positive achievements of the trade-union movement during the interwar period, especially in the field of labor legislation, were extolled and analyzed

by various semi-legal and illegal publications.[30] The promulgation of the Labor Charter in October 1941 afforded an opportunity to proclaim that organized labor could function normally
only in a climate of freedom:

In order to exist, trade unionism must be free, in a free country.
Its climate should be democracy. The conditions of its development should be free institutions. . . Because it did not know
these truths, the commission called by the powers to draw up
the new Labor Charter has wasted its time. . . The workers are
militantly united against this effort to enslave the labor movement.[31]

At once, therefore, the opposition to the Labor Charter
became an opposition to the existing political order. The often
futile and misleading pre-armistice discussions on the 'independence' of the labor movement acquired now a new and much
more concrete significance. Independence was conceived of as
the absence of state tutelage over the formation and the internal
life of trade unions, the selection of officials and the determination of activities. But independence no longer meant political
aloofness.[32] The political tinge of labor propaganda became so
pronounced that some observers spoke about a blend of trade
unionism and 'neo-Jacobinism' pervading the new movement.[33]

At the same time what had previously been termed, often in a
confused and loose way, collaboration—with the employers on
the one hand, with the state on the other—was newly conceived.
Such co-operation was not rejected in general, but it was regarded
as amounting to sheer hypocrisy if there was not full autonomy
for the labor movement and if the state protected the special interests of the trusts, 'changed into professional Organization
Committees by the men of Vichy, directing the economy and
exploiting the nation, under the protection and for the benefit
of the invader.' [34]

The conception of combining ·a corporative system and a
genuine trade-union movement vanished completely. Soon after
the issuance of the 'Manifesto of the Twelve' in November 1940,

its signers formed the Committee of Economic and Trade-Union Studies. All through the period of illegality this group made a valuable effort to clarify the issues. Its work is particularly noteworthy as the group included the most prominent leaders of both CGT and CFTC, among them Louis Saillant, who became head of the CGT after the liberation and before Léon Jouhaux's return from a German prison. In the fall of 1941 the same trade-union leaders who had only one year before subscribed to the manifesto declaring trade unionism and corporativism equally necessary, joined in an appeal of the CGT which declared: 'There can be no choice between trade unions and corporations. The formula of the future consists of industrial trade unions in a sovereign state.' [35]

The secretary of one of the federations, in a letter to Georges Lefranc, the former director of the CGT Institute of Higher Education and now an apostle of corporativism, pointed to the hostile stand that the CGT and Lefranc himself had previously taken against corporativism. In an effective way and with persuasive arguments the corporative formula was contrasted with the enduring characteristics of French trade-union history: on the one hand, the impractical blueprints of men who dabbled in social engineering, on the other the empirical, close-to-life approach of men who, as the writer stated, 'throughout our country, among our multiple trades, professions, and industries, for years and years . . . have used their leisure, their family life, their rest, their health, all their hours and all their strength, after their work or during their work, to raise up other beaten men and souls that are downtrodden and weakened.' [36]

In this and similar documents which were widely used in labor's underground propaganda there was perceptible both a return to cherished and viable traditions of the CGT and a realistic awareness of the tasks awaiting a trade-union movement under new conditions.

XIV

Resistance and Regeneration

I

THE framework set up to carry on trade-union activities during the Vichy period consisted in an ingenious interlocking of legal and illegal organizations.[1] Those organizations that had been prohibited either by special legislative act or by the Labor Charter reconstituted themselves underground as soon as feasible. Former trade-union officials or active members emerging from the rank and file established contacts which war and dispersion had disrupted, and formed directing bodies.

The Central Office of the CGT was itself able to function after not too long an interruption. It was composed almost entirely of its old members, who were joined by a few younger trade-union leaders. The previous experience of these men had not in the least prepared them for the beyond-the-law existence to which they were now forced in order to shield their activities from German and Vichy surveillance. Under such conditions it was obviously impossible for Léon Jouhaux to resume his former position of leadership. But his mere name and authority were considered such a threat to the new state that in the latter part of 1941 he was confined by the government, of which his former assistant Belin was still a member. Subsequently Jouhaux was delivered by the Vichy police to the Germans, who put him in a German prison, along with other French political personages.

Once its illegal Central Office was re-established, the CGT attempted, through special regional delegates, to restore the entire chain of trade-union organizations, whether the new regime had decreed their discontinuance or permitted their survival. Among the first to be revived were the regional unions, traditionally the strongest expression of inter-professional interests within the CGT. Through 1942 and 1943 these regional unions and their directing bodies were re-established as illegal organizations, in every part of the then wholly German-occupied country.[2]

A more complicated situation was confronted by the federations and the union locals, both of which the government hoped to fit into the Social Committees of the Labor Charter. Where the leadership of such unions was in the hands of officials who had chosen to collaborate with Vichy or the Germans, the workers were as a rule reluctant to be identified with them. Thus the membership of such federations as those of the railwaymen, the miners, and the metal workers dwindled very rapidly, because these organizations were closely controlled by the government.[3] Sometimes the rank and file was successful in ousting leaders who had allied themselves with the new rulers of France. As early as the fall of 1941 Dumoulin and Vigne were dismissed by a majority vote from the posts they held in the trade-union movement, and they were eventually ousted from their organizations.[4] In this determined way the union membership in occupied territory ostracized the very men with whom the occupation authorities had chosen to co-operate.

With the increasing influence of the illegal directing bodies of the CGT and its regional unions, labor leaders made frequent and urgent appeals to the workers to join the legally existing union locals. At the end of 1943 the Central Office of the CGT admonished the workers to re-enter en masse the surviving trade unions, and to create new ones where the old organizations had disappeared. The workers were encouraged to resist the check-off system which Vichy had introduced for the collection of union dues, and to contribute on a voluntary basis to the defraying of costs incurred by the organizations. They were explicitly exhorted not to refrain from joining because certain unions were still dominated by 'felonious' elements, but rather to join and co-operate with those who were trying to oust the traitors.[5]

Almost everywhere the membership of the legal unions heeded the orders from clandestine organizations—the CGT itself or the directing bodies of the regional unions, or the so-called 'Popular Committees' which were organized in many regions to co-ordinate workers' resistance. In some organizations there existed a double leadership: one composed of Vichy followers and an illegal one which actually suggested the line of action to be taken by the rank and file. It was not rare for a legally constituted union local to follow the directives given by an underground paper. A similar situation obtained in the plants themselves. On the initiative of the CGT, trade-union factory committees sprang up where the Labor Charter had hoped to see peaceful 'professional families.' [6]

Early in 1944 the Vichy government, and especially the arch-collaborator Déat, tried to correct this situation by having its state-appointed labor leaders prepare the reconstitution of a nationwide trade-union organization.[7] But it was too late to prevent the genuine CGT from controlling and using for its own ends either simultaneously or alternately the illegal and legal organizations of labor. The attitude of the genuine trade-union leaders toward such official attempts was typified by a sharp declaration made by the Central Office of the CGT concerning the Labor Charter:

Absolutely opposed to the paternalistic spirit and the reactionary content of the Labor Charter, which is but a child of the capitalist desire for revenge for the reforms of 1936, the Central Office affirms once more that this Charter is intended to muffle and to destroy the genuine trade-union movement, expression of the true intention of the wage earners, and it points to the general opposition in principle as well as to the practical opposition to the Charter demonstrated by the workers. The success of this opposition is recognized and proclaimed, even by the promoter of the Charter. Trade-union members should persevere in their opposition and extend it even farther. The publication in the *Journal officiel* of lists of so-called unique trade unions [*syndicats uniques*] will not hide the emptiness of these unions, which exist only on paper.[8]

The interlocking of legal and illegal organizations as a means of working-class resistance to a dictatorship has a notable tradition in France. During the dictatorship of Napoleon III, from the coup d'état until the granting of the right of association in 1864, both the social policy of the Empire and the workers' methods of opposition showed a striking resemblance to the situation that prevailed under the Vichy regime. It need not be stressed, of course, that after 1940 neither the workers nor their leaders were motivated in their actions by historical reminiscences. What happened was rather that after an interval of ninety years a similar situation produced similar reactions on the part of a working class which was often slow to join the established union movement but excelled in inventiveness and initiative.

The 'Societies of Mutual Aid,' dear to the Emperor, were supposed to serve the same aims which Marshal Pétain assigned to the Social Committees of the Labor Charter. Contrary to official hopes the workers found, a few years after the establishment of the Empire, a way of using these organizations as a means of joining forces for the presentation of their claims. Often the societies seemed to heed the orders of the forces of 'anarchy' which were thought to have been definitely overcome. There were instances in which the government-installed directors were suddenly replaced by men of the workers' own choice. Subsequent developments proved that Louis Bonaparte's hopes of taking the political sting out of the workers' efforts to better their positions were thwarted to the same extent as those cherished by Pétain.[9]

During the German occupation there was a high degree of coordination between the activities of the trade unions and the political resistance movement. Before the latter's unification the trade unions and their illegal leaders maintained close contacts with the two principal resistance groups, 'Libération' and 'Libération Nationale.'[10] After the first organized contacts between de Gaulle's London Committee and the resistance movement in France had been established, through the Libération group, it became known that certain prominent trade-union leaders were participating in the activities of Libération. The trade-union movement did not, however, sacrifice any of its independence, nor did it entirely control the Libération group.[11]

When the National Council of Resistance, comprising all resistance groups, including right-wing organizations, was founded in France in May 1943, the CGT was prominently represented on it, and also on the Departmental Committee of Liberation, which aimed to co-ordinate the resistance movements of various denominations all over the country. Saillant, the new leader of the CGT, was chosen president of the all-embracing and influential National Council of Resistance. The importance to which the CGT had risen could not be better demonstrated. At the same time the relations between the CGT and the French Committee of National Liberation in London became increasingly close. At the beginning of 1944 the members of the illegal Central Office of the CGT, in an appeal to the French people, explicitly greeted the committee presided over by General de Gaulle, hoping thereby to manifest 'the longing of the working masses of our country for a French resurrection in national independence and liberty.'[12]

Prior to this declaration the CGT had been granted a prominent representation in the Provisional Assembly set up at Algiers to assist the Committee of National Liberation. Charles Laurent, before the armistice the leader of the civil servants federation and in the period of illegality treasurer of the CGT, became the president of the Finance Committee of the Algiers Assembly. Georges Buisson, one of the assistant secretaries of the CGT and, like Laurent, a participant in the clandestine activities of the trade unions inside France until 1943, was made a member of the Assembly, as was also the secretary of the federation of metal workers, a communist who had been expelled from the CGT during the days of the Hitler-Stalin pact.

II

During the first year after the conclusion of the Franco-German armistice the attitude of the communists toward the war changed but little from the stand taken by them at the outbreak of the war in 1939. Both *L'Humanité* and *La Vie ouvrière* continued to appear underground, the first intended for the communist reader in general, the latter for trade unionists with communist leanings. On 28 August 1940 *L'Humanité* celebrated the anniversary of the German-Soviet pact, which 'consolidated peace in eastern Europe.' Shortly afterward an editorial by prominent communist leaders indulged in the boast, 'The French people understand, see that we were right in opposing the imperialist war, that war which led our country to catastrophe, to defeat, to occupation by the enemy.' Not to take sides in the imperialist war was still the catchword of all communist-inspired propaganda. 'Our party is adamant against any attempt to renew the slaughter of Frenchmen, be it under the standards of de Gaulle's Cross of Lorraine or under the swastika,' wrote *L'Humanité* on 7 November 1940.[13]

This attitude was somewhat modified, however, by what had for some time been the paramount concern of French communist organizations—never to lose contact with the masses. Well aware of the rise of nationalist feelings among the people of France, and of the growing hatred for both the invader and the Vichy regime, the communist propaganda made more and more use of patriotic slogans. The same declarations which defended the German-Soviet pact vowed that the French nation would never become a people of slaves, and that the hopes of national and social liberation resided in the working class.[14] Wherever possible, appeals to French popular patriotism were linked up with advocacy of close friendship for Soviet Russia. The party presented itself as the instrument for the resurrection of an independent France. As early as May 1941 the idea of a National

Battlefront for the Independence of France was launched by the communist underground press, which, however, made no concrete statement on the aims of this organization.

With Hitler's attack on Russia the avowed indifference toward the outcome of the war was suddenly ended. The patriotic propaganda line, already inaugurated, was increasingly stressed, and communist appeals for a National Front cited the need for unity against the Nazi efforts to separate Frenchmen. On the whole the communists were back to the attitude they had taken in 1936 when they advocated a 'Front des Français,' though their attitude toward the de Gaulle Committee in London was pronouncedly more friendly than that they had manifested for the Blum government. Relations between the communists and the French Committee of National Liberation were regularized by the delegation of a prominent communist leader to London and, in April 1944, by the entrance of two communists as members of the committee which was soon thereafter to become the Provisional Government of the French Republic.[15]

The communist groups inside France, such as the 'Francs Tireurs' and the 'Partisans,' most often emphasized military activities. They successfully tried to institute sabotage and guerilla warfare in the rear of the enemy on the widest possible scale. But the deportation policy of Sauckel and Laval, which made the working class the primary element in the resistance movement, led the communists to pay increasing attention to trade-union activities.

In 1943 they began to agitate for the reintegration in the CGT of all communist elements, leaders as well as the rank and file. In line with previous practices they formed a National Committee of Trade-Union Unity and Action, with affiliates in many trades and regions. It was composed solely of communist sympathizers, and it was determined to achieve the greatest possible agreement on the readmission of the communists to the CGT organization.

From the outset this aim seemed justifiable. The exclusion of the communists from the trade unions in 1939 had been effected for a political reason: their refusal to disapprove of the German-Soviet treaty. With the outbreak of the war between Germany and Soviet Russia and the wholehearted return of the French communists to the cause of patriotism, the exclusion of 1939 had lost its justification. As has been mentioned, this new split in the trade-union movement had never been popular; it had coincided with the persecution of the communists by the government, and therefore the CGT was easily though unjustifiably reproached for having become the accomplice of a government generally unfriendly to labor's cause.

Moreover, after the armistice a good number of those who had been most active in anti-communist propaganda, and had ardently favored the exclusion of the communists, passed into the camp of collaborationists in Vichy or Paris. The communists now emphasized that if they had had their way at the last CGT Congress in Nantes, all those who had become traitors would have been excluded from the trade unions, or at least deprived of their leading positions. As for their own record, the communists could point to the ruthless persecution to which their adherents were subjected both by the Gestapo and by the Vichy police. Communist underground papers published frequent accounts of the martyrdom of prominent leaders or courageous members of their organizations. The political and military activities of the communist underground were widely known and admired.[16]

All these factors so strengthened the position of the communist trade unionists that when the split of 1939 was mended, they obtained a stronger representation than they had had in 1936. At the top the formal reunification was achieved in May 1943, by an agreement among four underground leaders, two from each side. The accord read, in its essential parts:

1. The confederal trade-union movement is reunited by a return to the physiognomy the movement had in September 1939.
2. Unity is re-established first at the level of the Central Office. The fundamental principles of the Confederal Committee of

Nantes will be the basis for this reorganization. Consequently the Central Office will be composed of three representatives of one tendency [the communists] and of five representatives of the other tendency . . .

3. Unity will be realized according to identical principles in the regional unions and the federations. The proportions which existed between the various tendencies in September 1939 will be re-established.[17]

Actually this scheme granted the communists a greater numerical representation in the Central Office than they had had before the war. It appears that during their period of ostracism they had won a stronger position than they had held at the time which was considered by many observers the apogee of their influence within the CGT.

At the end of 1943 the enlarged Central Office of the CGT urged all federations and regional and local unions to readmit in their directing bodies, legal and illegal, those who had been excluded 'for political reasons.' At the same time the communist rank and file was to be readmitted. The process of reunification, not unlike that which occurred during 1935, was greatly furthered by pressure from the membership, which was eager to amalgamate forces in the face of repression. On the other hand, among the leaders of the various organizations, especially at the regional level, the old distrust was not easily overcome. Difficulties arose in many instances, and the CGT repeatedly had to admonish its affiliates to manifest a spirit of true unity. The communist press insisted that the reunification of the trade-union movement should 'not be just a small gesture taking place unnoticed, like the reconciliation of a few individuals. It must be a great public gesture, on the level of the sentiments of thousands of workers whose desire it expresses.'[18] In many instances provisional 'unity committees' had to be formed, in order to prepare the way for unification. On the eve of liberation, however, the process of reunification was practically completed.

It is scarcely surprising that the communists would not

abandon their resolve to act as a well-disciplined faction within the trade-union movement.[19] They maintained their own underground paper, which emphasized above all the need for unity, just as in the period of the Popular Front. But when the communists disagreed with the majority of the CGT on points of rather considerable importance concerning plans for the post-liberation period, the communist members of the Central Office did not hesitate to publish their own version. The communists also openly expressed their dislike of one of the delegates whom the CGT had sent to London before the reunification, and eventually they obtained his demotion.

III

The close relationship between Catholic and lay unionism, initiated by both sides after the armistice, outlasted the dissolution of the two trade-union confederations by the Vichy government. A remarkable similarity of views, already evident in the recent development of the CGT and the CFTC, obtained in the attitudes of the two movements toward political developments as well as in their practical activities.

The establishment of the Vichy regime put the Catholic trade unions in a grave dilemma.[20] From the first the leaders of the ecclesiastical hierarchy not only supported Pétain as the legitimate power, but praised him as a providential gift made to France by God. In addition, many prominent members of the Social Catholic movement, whose close relations with the CFTC have been mentioned, actively defended the social policy inaugurated by Vichy. A number of priests who had for years been the spiritual advisers of Catholic trade unionism became propagandists for the new social and allegedly Christian order which defeat had brought upon their country.[21] If the Catholic union leaders wished to reach an understanding with the CGT they had to achieve this in opposition to the wishes of leading members of the ecclesiastical hierarchy.

It was, however, only a small group of Catholic trade unionists, organized under the auspices of the 'Equipes d'Action Ouvrière,' which joined with Belin in efforts to integrate the legitimate labor movement in Vichy's corporative scheme. The large majority followed the leader of the CFTC, first in the 'Manifesto of the Twelve' and later in the Committee of Economic and Trade-Union Studies, co-operating with the most clearsighted CGT leaders in defining and upholding the principles of free trade unionism against those embodied in the Labor Charter. The opposition of the Catholics to the system of compulsory and single unionism was, if anything, even more decided than that of the CGT. Since the Catholic unions had always been numerically weaker than the CGT organizations, their stake in what was still called trade-union pluralism was particularly great.

In their opposition to the monolithic and authoritarian system devised by the Labor Charter the Catholic trade unionists eventually found the support of the highest ecclesiastics. On May Day 1941, which Vichy made an official holiday, in imitation of Nazi practices, the archbishop of Toulouse declared in a public address that he was hoping and praying for free unionism. Later the primate of Gaul and Cardinal Liénart from enemy-occupied Lille appealed to Pétain to maintain the independence of labor organizations.[22] When such appeals remained unheeded, because of the government's resolve to break the cohesion of the working class with totalitarian means, Catholic trade unionism turned to complete abstention from any legal activity within the framework of the Labor Charter.

In a declaration of Catholic trade-union leaders, which embodied the guiding principles of their action throughout the years of occupation, opposition was affirmed to 'doctrines which, whatever their form, attack the very foundation of Christian civilization by introducing the spirit of totalitarianism.' The hope was expressed that 'unionists of all tendencies, conscious of the perils of division at this moment,' would agree to 'carry on in heart and spirit the great French labor movement, pending the liberation of the nation which will permit its physical realization.' [23]

In accordance with this attitude the Catholic trade unions and their leaders engaged, like the CGT, in a patient work of underground organization and propaganda. They, too, succeeded to a certain extent in co-ordinating legal and illegal activities for the betterment of working conditions and for the spreading of opposition to the deportation policies of the invader and his satellites. When the resistance movement became nationally and regionally organized, the CFTC was represented on many of its directing bodies. The Catholic unions delegated one of their prominent leaders to the Algiers Assembly.

The complete departure of the CFTC from its origins in the Social Catholic movement and the disavowal of its corporative heritage have a twofold explanation. Even before the war, and also during it, the Catholic trade-union movement, under the influence of a younger generation of leaders and taught by its own experience, had been led to clarify its philosophies and overhaul its beliefs in corporative solutions. Experience after the armistice with the actualities of a corporative experiment clearly showed even to the Catholic unions the futility of previous expectations and the close relationship existing between corporativism and fascism.[24]

Even more important is the fact that it soon became evident how strongly the entire working class, practicing Catholics or not, was opposed to the Vichy regime and the Nazi new order. If the CFTC and its affiliates wished to remain a genuine labor organization there was no other way than that of active resistance. It is significant that the Catholic youth organization, despite its moderate political outlook, never hesitated in its opposition to Vichy.[25] More than ever before the Catholic trade unions recruited their members from the ranks of the JOC.

Hopes were expressed that the increasing rapprochement of the two trade-union movements would end in a fusion of the CGT and the CFTC.[26] Indeed, in September 1943 the Central

Office of the CGT made to the corresponding organ of the CFTC a definite proposal for the establishment of complete unity between the two organizations. The offer was politely declined, partly because the Central Office of the CFTC did not feel authorized to speak for the entire organization under conditions of illegality, and, more important, because the Catholic unionists would not forego the right of free association, which to them meant the right to organize in their own trade unions.[27] Thus complete unity of the labor movement could not be achieved, but an 'Interconfederal Committee of Unity' assured continuous unity in action.

The absolute and relative strength of the Catholic trade-union movement on the eve of liberation is impossible to gauge from available reports. It is sometimes maintained that the numerical relationship between the CGT and the CFTC had not changed, but there are also claims to the effect that in some regions and professions the Catholic unions reached almost equal strength with the CGT. In any case there can be no doubt that the Catholic unions, like those of the CGT, acquired new vitality from the straightforwardness with which their leaders engaged in the struggle against every form of totalitarianism.

IV

A program launched by the CGT at the end of 1943 offered a comprehensive catalogue of the immediate objectives of the trade-union movement. The CGT declared that its aim was to strive, 'without waiting for the liberation of the country'—ultimate goal of the entire resistance movement—'for the increase of wages, for improvement of the food situation, against the deportation of workers, for the return of those already deported, for the unconditional liberation of the prisoners of war, against overtime work and compulsory labor service, against war production benefiting the enemy, against the Labor Charter.' [28]

The trade-union movement was well aware that political conditions would not permit the Vichy or the German authorities to make major concessions in regard to any of these requests. But this did not prevent the legal and illegal organizations of both CGT and CFTC from actively putting forward their claims on every occasion, thereby increasing the difficulties of the government and of the employers who had chosen to collaborate with the invader. Moreover, in many cases the workers did win limited victories, and this enhanced their determination to persevere in the course set forth by their organizations.

By the end of 1943 a general wage increase of 50 per cent was requested, in order to make up for the rise in living costs. Increases were actually obtained wherever the needs for production were so pressing that an interruption of the work was deemed intolerable. Worker delegates were sent to management with remonstrances about the insufficiency of the slight increases decreed by the government. Sometimes the employers yielded to the demands, not infrequently as an open protest against the official wage policy; sometimes they sought excuse in the rules imposed upon them by the Germans. Union meetings in the plants decided upon further action where this was considered necessary. Public demonstrations, however short, tried successfully to enlist the support of public opinion.[29]

A general slowdown of work was often found an excellent because unobtrusive means of wresting concessions from the employers and at the same time impeding war production for the enemy. The trade unions claimed that in some cases production was whittled down by as much as 70 per cent, and often such results led to a speedy granting of at least part of the workers' requests. Sabotage was committed wherever possible, and in many cases with a high degree of ingenuity.[30]

The ultimate weapon, the strike, though outlawed by the Vichy legislation, was frequently resorted to, especially toward the end of the period of occupation. Some of these strike movements lasted no longer than one hour; others extended to one or two weeks. The most successful strikes were conducted in the mining and the metal industries. The underground press claimed that at a given moment 50,000 workers were on strike in the mines of northern France alone, in defiance of the occupation authorities. Even if such figures were exaggerated, the movement was impressive enough to exact certain wage concessions.

The same means that the workers used to obtain increases in wages were often successfully employed to force a reduction of the work week to 48 hours, or the suspension of Sunday work. At first the Vichy regime had reduced the average number of working hours, in order to prevent the spread of unemployment. Later the 48-hour week was gradually reintroduced, and in many cases Sunday work and overtime up to 60 hours was ordered, with the sole aim of setting free a greater number of workers for work in Germany.[31] Hence the resistance to such measures was intended also to impede the official collaboration with the Nazis.

Many of these movements originated spontaneously from the bitterness of the workers, who were fully aware of their own strength, precisely because of the services rendered by French industry to the German war machine. In other cases the illegal directing bodies of the trade unions co-ordinated or prepared the strikes; this was especially the case after the CGT had achieved unity of action and organization. A new emphasis was given to the strike weapon. The requests for an improvement of living conditions were not conceived solely as 'class action' directed against the employer, but were regarded as dictated partly by concern for the health of the French race and the safekeeping of the working population. 'Under present conditions,' the CGT declared in its directives for the year 1944, 'the strike becomes a social and patriotic action.'[32]

The betterment of labor conditions was by no means the unique concern of workers' resistance. The complete opposition to a regime that had forsworn republican institutions was shown by demonstrations against official orders and persons. Often when a Vichy Minister of Labor visited one of the bigger factories, he found himself greeted by the howling of sirens and the indifference or even the abuse of the workers. When the government tried to turn the First of May into a holiday honoring labor, the trade unions decided not to participate in any official demonstrations. Instead the CGT made Armistice Day, commemorating the victory over the Germans in 1918, a national manifestation of 'struggle and hope.'

The struggle of the workers reached its greatest force in the resistance to the deportation measures ordered by the Germans and executed by Laval. By the end of March 1942 between 140,000 and 150,000 skilled and unskilled workers had been recruited, mainly in the Paris region. Three months later 350,000 more workers were requested. In February of the following year 250,000 others were called, and approximately the same number was due in June 1943.[33] The deportation of hundreds of thousands could not be prevented, but the quotas were less and less completely filled, as a result of the determined attitude of all labor organizations.

The trade unions not only exhorted the workers to evade individually the call to work in Germany, but also tried, often successfully, to back the evaders by collective action. In factories in which the management informed groups of workers of their imminent departure for the Reich, strikes were organized, sometimes even with occupation of the premises. When such determined action led to the arrest of patriotic workers and their subsequent conviction to the death penalty, widespread movements of solidarity constituted such a threat to production that sometimes the execution or even the deportation measures had to be stayed by the authorities. In similar fashion some of the hostages apprehended by the Nazis, in reprisal for the successful resistance to deportation that was offered by entire localities, were saved by their comrades. The railroad workers, whose services were particularly valuable, achieved spectacular success by preventing the execution of seven of their colleagues who had been condemned to die.

When the Maquis, composed to a large extent of workers who had eluded the mobilization, had to fight off the concentrated attacks of Vichy police and military formations, the CGT called upon all workers' organizations, including the Catholic unions, to come to the resisters' assistance. The intensification of sabotage, the spreading of strikes, and the organization of popular demonstrations were requested in order to increase the difficulties which beset the Vichy regime from all sides.

In its New Year's appeal of 1944 the CGT invited the workers, engineers, technicians, teachers, and civil servants to form in the plants, towns, and cities groups of patriotic militia, to serve as backbone of the popular army of liberation. Thus the trade-union movement and its adherents became an indivisible part of the general resistance movement.[34]

The widespread illegal activities in which the labor movement engaged could not be carried out without a heavy toll in victims of brutalities by Gestapo and Vichy police. It was customary to see in different underground papers a small column in which biographical data about the few 'felonious' trade-union leaders were juxtaposed with long lists of men who had been tortured in prisons and concentration camps or killed for having organized workers' resistance. The communists had to endure the most from the official terror, but no one active in the reconstruction of a genuine labor movement was spared.

It was anticipated that the strivings of labor would culminate in a general strike to be launched at the moment of the Allied landings.[35] Like some of the other strikes, this demonstration was conceived not as the economic weapon of labor against capital but as the contribution of the workers to the national uprising.

The course of military events made it impracticable to call the projected general strike as early as had been planned. Orders given by the Allied Commander-in-Chief on D-day explicitly warned the French people against exposing themselves and their resistance organizations to wholesale slaughter. But when the Allied armies converged on Paris and the free labor movement of the capital was able to shake off the restrictions of illegality, both the CGT and the CFTC called upon their followers to launch a 'general strike for liberation.' This was the first time in their history that the Catholic labor unions had supported a general strike. 'Under the banner of liberation,' exhorted the strike call, 'let us unite, brothers in the plants and in the fields, ever more closely connected with the entire nation, let us reconquer our freedom.' The plea concluded by hailing the provisional government under Charles de Gaulle, the resistance movement of France as the land of liberty and social progress, and the United Nations.[36]

Ever since the inception of the French labor movement the general strike had carried a mythical importance in the philosophy of the trade unions, but when such a demonstration was called, it usually deepened the cleavage of the nation into antagonistic classes. Not quite realistically, the general strike had been considered an instrument of the workers for overthrowing their own government in case of war and substituting social revolution for national defense. In 1944, however, the general strike was looked upon, quite to the contrary, as a means of national emancipation and an emblem of national unity.

The three general strikes launched by the trade unions during the period covered in this study may be said to symbolize the history of those years. The strike of 1934 incarnated the will of the French working class to resist attacks on its cherished liberties, and initiated the upswing of republican feeling in the country. That of 1938 typified the division of the nation against itself and became a prelude to national disaster. That of 1944 betokened the final struggle against the foreign oppressor and the internal enemies of the republic.

V

The stress and the difficulties of the period of illegality did not prevent the French labor movement from supplementing its day-to-day activities by a discussion of general aims and philosophies and by drawing plans for the future. During the first two years, before the reorganization of the CGT and its affiliates was accomplished, a wide variety of proposals was brought forward, ranging from a monolithic socialism to a revival of economic federalism.[37] By the end of 1943, however, the illegal CGT had arrived at the formulation of a fairly unified program, comprising measures for the immediate post-liberation period and also long-range proposals.[38]

Immediate and drastic punishment was to be meted out to all who had collaborated with the enemy, had taken an undignified attitude, or made illicit profits. Though special popular courts were to be created, the punishment was to be inflicted under due process of law, and a definite period was set after which no exceptional measures would be tolerated. The labor movement ridiculed from the outset the objection that the liquidation of too many public servants would cause a paralysis of administration and of economic life. It was asserted that it would always be possible to find a few hundred men who would make excellent prefects, to unearth enough able labor inspectors, police chiefs, judges, and the like.[39] The amnesty and liberation of all political prisoners held for acts of resistance to the enemy or to the Vichy government was considered a matter of course.

The first concern of social policy was to be an immediate increase of wages, by a specified percentage to be fixed with reference to the price level. The adaptation of wages to prices and the supervision of prices were to be undertaken by the government in continuous consultation with the trade unions. A sliding wage-scale, which had previously been turned down by the Senate of the Third Republic, was once more requested. An increase of rations, and at the same time a gradual and cautious abolition of rationing measures, combined with strict measures against the black market, were next on the list of CGT demands.

The rehabilitation of worker prisoners and deportees was to be effected by their return to their former jobs, with all the privileges that would have accrued to them had they remained in France. Where this would not be possible a comprehensive program of public works was to absorb workers threatened by unemployment; here again the CGT reverted to its earlier proposals. The concrete problems of reconstruction and retooling were not developed by the program, probably because when it was laid down the amount of devastation and deterioration was not yet known.

The re-establishment of a free labor movement was to be assured by a repeal of Vichy's anti-trade-union legislation, in particular the Labor Charter, and by an immediate and full recognition of the principle of the freedom of association, including its reference to public employees. Not only the CGT was to retrieve its funds confiscated by Vichy, but also the labor organizations dissolved in 1939 by the Daladier government as communistic. An outward modernization of the trade-union movement was sought by a request that the authorities grant more suitable accommodations for offices and meeting halls. Formerly the French unions had clung with a certain pride to archaic forms of organization and to modest headquarters in the Bourses du Travail, most of them half a century old. In its postwar program the CGT acknowledged the importance of more progressive business methods.

The trade-union movement drew also other lessons from its previous experience, especially from the Popular Front period. At that time the CGT organizations had seen their suddenly acquired membership vanish as soon as the unions lost their control over jobs. Thus the demands for the enactment of a modern labor law, which the National Council of the CGT had formulated in 1937, were reiterated.

On the question how job control was to be assured, the communist members of the illegal CGT directorate were in significant disagreement with the majority. The communist delegates wanted to see the shop stewards elected by all the workers in the plant and endowed with the greatest possible powers, especially in matters of hiring and firing. The majority of the delegates, however, wanted the unions to elect the shop stewards, thereby eliminating the possibility of a dualism between shop stewards and trade unions. In their proposal hiring was to be exclusively in the hands of public employment offices, in whose administration the trade unions would take a decisive part. Each dismissal was to be approved by the labor inspector, who would consult the trade unions. The difference between the two proposals is obvious, and neither side regarded any compromise solution as possible.

The French trade-union movement was unanimous in the belief that a transformation of capitalist economy was necessary. In spite of labor's efforts toward national unity among all Frenchmen with the exclusion of collaborators, and its unconditional adherence to the cause of the United Nations, anti-capitalist propaganda was not absent from the underground press. It was stated that any alliance of French banking and industry with the City of London or Wall Street would be regarded with hardly more favor than would collaboration with Berlin. There were again polemics against the Comité des Forges, which had survived under a different guise after its formal dissolution by law. American discussion on the subjects of free enterprise, the rule of monopolies, and economic planning was followed with keen interest and definite partisanship in favor of an unrepentant New Deal.[40]

The case for economic planning was considered by French trade unionists as strong as it ever was,[41] although a good number of its advocates within the CGT had been all too prone to join the collaborationists. This very development led to a new realization that economic planning must be planning for freedom, lest it lead to dangerous precipices. As for the organs of such planning, here, too, differences of opinion existed between the communists and the majority of the CGT leadership. The communists demanded the complete and immediate abolition of the Organization Committees, which formed the backbone of Vichy's economic organization. The majority of the CGT directorate proposed to use these bodies at least provisionally, after their thorough reorganization, as instruments of economic planning. The representatives of the trusts, it was said, would have to give way on the committees to representatives of all categories of producers, nominated by the trade unions. The committees were to be headed by public servants.

In regard to the question of nationalization, which had been so controversial in prewar times between communist and non-communist trade unionists, the programmatic differences seemed somewhat smaller. The communists no longer refused to envisage a transformation of the economic system, but they still resorted to generalities that were quite the opposite of their former Marxist creed. In a new France, where the trusts would be completely eliminated, human exploitation would cease, but private property, far from disappearing, would actually expand and become stabilized. Such an economic order, the communists hoped, would make possible the realization of French unity. In the France of their dreams there would no longer be a class struggle, for classes would no longer exist. The three communist members of the CGT directorate voted in favor of confiscating the fortunes and the wealth of all businessmen who had engaged in economic collaboration for the sake of personal profits.

On the last point the non-communist leaders of the CGT, and all underground labor publications, fully agreed with the communists. But the majority sought, as in prewar times, to give a concrete content to demands for a transformation of the economy, by calling for an extensive program of nationalization. Banking, insurance, production and distribution of power, water supply, mining, the metal and chemical industries, transport by land, sea, and air, importation and distribution of liquid fuels, publishing houses, and advertising agencies were to be run as public corporations. Such corporations would be administered by an executive organ appointed by the state, composed of representatives of the several branches of industry and of the trade-union organizations of the workers employed therein.

It was stressed that the CGT did not envisage such a system for those branches of production in which the process of concentration was not far advanced and there was still room for competition. In such branches the state was to confine itself to a controlling function, exercised through a rigorously enforced price and production policy. A sector left to free enterprise, such as small-scale handicraft industry and trade, would give full scope to individual initiative. In general this postwar program of the labor underground corresponded very closely to earlier proposals of the CGT.

There were relatively few references to the international outlook of the trade-union movement, as the ejection of the invader from the country prevailed over all other political considerations. It is evident, however, that in this field, too, the CGT maintained most of the principles it had adhered to previously. *La Vie ouvrière* confined itself to praise of the Red Army and of Soviet Russia's foreign policy. The non-communist trade-union leaders asserted that as soon as the war criminals in Germany and in Europe as a whole were punished, it would be possible, indeed necessary, to revive the hopes for an establishment of a United States of Europe. It was suggested that at first certain customs barriers should be maintained, but that this would not preclude the promotion of a federation comprising all European countries. Economic planning on an international scale was frankly advocated. One of the underground papers, founded by active members of the CGT, ran as its motto: 'For the international unity of the workers. . . For a peaceful world. . . For the liberation of all oppressed peoples in a reorganized and socialist Europe.' [42]

In regard to the German problem it was pointed out by spokesmen of the CGT that trade unionists who hoped to build a powerful international movement could not desire the destruction of Germany, but statesmen entrusted with the shaping of the peace were enjoined to find the means of preventing a recurrence of aggressive German imperialism. 'The German worker is a slave of the military machine of Hitlerism; the French worker who goes to Germany is at the same time a slave and a hostage,' declared a paper of the illegal trade-union movement.[43]

The unions' demands for an effective control of the monopolistic groups by the political power received a considerable amount of popular support, particularly because of the attitude of big business during the period of German occupation. This is evident in the fact that the Charter of the National Council of Resistance, drawn up in March 1944, incorporated many of the economic requests that had formerly been made only by the CGT and the socialist party. Thus the Charter called for the nationalization of mines, electric power, big banks, and insurance companies, and the abolition of trusts in fields left to private enterprise. Also it advocated planned economy by the state, the development of co-operation, and the participation of labor unions in the management of industry.

VI

The forces united in the National Council of Resistance represented an alliance of organized labor, the intelligentsia, and the urban and rural middle classes. The success of their joint hopes for the future of France depends fundamentally on whether it will be possible to preserve their alliance—attempted once before under the Popular Front and subsequently broken by the misfortunes of that experiment—and on the continued strength, unity, and independence of the labor movement itself.

On the eve of liberation French labor leaders expected to see the future membership of the CGT grow to seven or eight million, thus exceeding by two or three million the peak reached for a short period during the Popular Front. The development of the trade unions during the period of illegality and the record membership figures which the labor movement in North Africa achieved after 1943 make it likely that at least during the immediate postwar period the French working class will feel a stronger urge toward organization than ever before. The trade unions stand a good chance of rallying the masses of former prisoners of war and deported workers. The industrial rehabilitation of the country outranks in magnitude the tasks that awaited France after 1918. The material devastations of war have to be repaired, and industrial retooling of the country must be undertaken, a necessity even before the war and now rendered still more urgent, since the attempts to adapt French production to the needs of the German war machine. All this will increase the role in society of the industrial working classes, and enhance the importance of their organizations.

There are also better chances now than there were before for the labor movement to manifest a reasonable degree of unity, and thus to overcome the notorious reluctance of the French workers to join organizations that are competing with one another or torn by internal strife. As was suggested above, it is not likely that the CGT and the CFTC will achieve complete fusion, but the affiliates of the two confederations appear to have achieved enough similarity of views and activities to prevent jurisdictional disputes and enervating polemics.

To what extent the newly achieved unity of communists and non-communists within the CGT will survive, now that the enemy has been expelled from the country, depends on general political developments. It is unlikely that the communists will forego the opportunities afforded them by the democratic organization of the CGT to strive for an increase of their influence within the unions. But this does not necessarily mean conflict. As long as the former Allies maintain their unity, at least in regard to French affairs, it is not to be expected that French communists will take a position fundamentally different from that of other trade unionists. Also, the French labor movement has far greater opportunities than in 1936 to be instrumental in founding an international organization which would include the trade unions of the Soviet Union.

Labor's attitude during the occupation period toward schemes of totalitarian control makes it appear unlikely that trade-union independence will be sacrificed to state domination. To be sure, in its postwar program for wider and more firmly established social legislation, organized labor has acknowledged the unavoidable role of the state in industrial relations. The weakness of the CGT before the war was due partly to its inability to adapt its philosophy to the changing character of industrial society and the increasing necessity for state intervention; that labor's spokesmen occasionally lapsed into mere sentimentalism was only an outward symptom of this insufficient adjustment to reality. The mere fact that trade-union leaders now no longer consider it improper to be represented in both the legislative and the executive branches of the government reveals their awareness not only of the state's role in industrial relations but also of the political role incumbent upon labor. French trade unionists have made an almost complete about-face since the anarcho-syndicalist founders of the CGT sang their proud boast, 'We are the perennial rebels, men truly without God, or ruler, or homeland.' But despite this willingness to re-examine their old beliefs, the trade unionists of France have not wavered in their conviction, essential if democracy is to be maintained, that the functions of labor organizations must not be merged with those of the state.

It cannot be doubted that many exacting tests face organized labor in the France of today, now able to examine her problems of regeneration in the heady and dissonant atmosphere of freedom. But the difficulties are no greater than the rewards of success. Never before has the fate of democratic institutions in France been so closely dependent on the influence of a strong labor movement, bold in its aspirations and realistic in its procedures.

APPENDIX I

*Preamble to the Statutes of the CGT Adopted by the Congress of
Unification in Toulouse, March 1936* *

The trade-union movement, at all levels of organization, administers itself and decides on its activities in complete independence of employers, governments, political parties, philosophical sects, or other groups outside the labor movement.

It reserves the right to reply favorably or negatively to appeals that may be addressed to it by other groups regarding a specific action. It also reserves the right to bring about such temporary collaboration by its own initiative, in view of the fact that despite its neutrality regarding political parties it cannot be indifferent about dangers that may threaten public liberties and social gains already acquired or to be acquired.

Only the statutory conventions and congresses of the trade unions are qualified to make decisions.

The democratic principle of the trade-union movement gives to every union member the guarantee that he can, within the union, freely defend his point of view on all questions of interest to the life and development of the organization.

Since the unions organize wage earners of all opinions, their adherents are perfectly free to express their opinions outside the trade-union organization.

The freedom of opinion and the rules of democracy provided for and fixed in the fundamental principles of trade unionism neither justify nor tolerate the constitution of organisms agitating within the trade unions as factions intended to influence and falsify the normal application of democratic rule.

The trade unions, since because of their very nature and composition they assemble workers of various opinions, will always show the greatest magnanimity in their efforts to maintain unity.

Their statutes must provide means of maintaining cohesion and respect for the principles and charters adhered to by the two delegations.†

They must ensure the maintenance of the unions in their constant role of defending the interests of the workers.

* From *La Voix du peuple*, vol. 18 (1936), p. 176.
† The reformist CGT and the communist CGTU (author's note).

APPENDIX II

The Matignon Agreement *

The delegates of the General Confederation of French Production [CGPF] and of the General Confederation of Labor [CGT] have met under the chairmanship of the Président de Conseil [Prime Minister Léon Blum] and in the presence of the Minister of the Interior, and have concluded, after arbitration by the Président de Conseil, the following agreement.

Article 1: The delegates of the employers agree to the immediate conclusion of collective bargaining agreements.

Article 2: These agreements must contain especially the following Articles 3-5.

Article 3: Since all citizens are obliged to abide by the law the employers recognize the freedom of opinion of the workers and their right to join freely and belong to a trade union established in accordance with Part III of the Labor Code.

The employers declare their willingness not to take into consideration the fact whether a worker belongs or does not belong to a union in making their decisions concerning hiring, or the organization or distribution of work, or measures of discipline or of firing.

If one of the parties to this agreement contends that the firing of a worker took place in violation of the above-mentioned right to organize freely in trade unions, both parties will help to clarify the true facts of the case and to find an equitable solution for all controversial cases. This does not interfere with the right of the parties to claim damages before the courts for any prejudice to their interests.

The exercise of the right to organize in trade unions must not lead to acts that are contrary to existing laws.

Article 4: The wages paid to all workers on the date of 25 May 1936 will be readjusted, beginning with the day on which work starts again. This readjustment will take place according to a diminishing scale, starting with an increase of 15 per cent for the lowest wages and arriving at an increase of 7 per cent for the highest wages. The total wages paid out by any firm must in no case be increased by more than 12 per cent. The wage

* From *Le Populaire*, 8 June 1936.

increases already granted since the afore-mentioned date will be counted against the readjustments defined above, but the amount of any such increase that is in excess of these readjustments will remain in the possession of the beneficiaries.

The negotiations for the conclusion of collective agreements determining minimum wages according to regions and professions will deal particularly with the necessary readjustments of abnormally low wages.

The delegates of the employers declare their willingness to undertake any readjustments that are necessary in order to maintain a normal relationship between the earnings of the wage earners and of the salary earners.

Article 5: Except in special cases provided for by law, every plant employing more than 10 workers, after agreement with the trade unions or with the interested parties, will have two (titular) or several (titular and deputy) shop stewards, according to the size of the plant. These shop stewards are entitled to present to the employer those individual grievances which have not been satisfied directly and which concern the application of laws, decrees, or regulations of the Labor Code, wage scales, and measures of hygiene and security.

All workers over 18 years of age will be entitled to vote, provided they have been employed for more than three months in the plant at the time of the election, and have not been deprived of their civil rights.

All those entitled to vote can be eligible for election, provided they are French citizens over 25 years of age who have worked in the plant without interruption for at least one year. This time must be shortened if otherwise the number of candidates is reduced to less than five.

Workers who themselves or whose wives keep a retail store cannot be elected.

Article 6: The delegates of the employers pledge that no sanctions against strike actions will be taken.

Article 7: The trade-union delegates will ask striking workers to resume work as soon as the directors of the plants have accepted the general agreement concluded herewith, and as soon as the negotiations concerning its application have started between the directors and the personnel of the plants.

Paris, 7 June 1936

APPENDIX III

Increase in Membership, 1936 to 1937, of the Federations Affiliated with the CGT *

	1 March 1936	1 March 1937	Ratio of 1937 to 1936 figures
Agriculture	12,000	156,000	13 times
Food industries	15,000	300,000	20
Designers and technicians	500	79,100	158+
Paper and paper-box industry	1,500	72,500	48+
Construction and wood	65,000	540,000	8+
Jewelry	2,000	12,000	6
Ceramics	3,000	36,000	12
Hatters	3,000	10,000	3+
Railroads	165,000	320,000	2−
Public enterprises	40,000	75,000	2−
Hairdressers	3,000	22,000	7+
Leather and skins	10,000	88,000	9−
Light and gas	35,500	80,000	2+
White-collar workers	15,000	285,000	19
Civil servants			
General administration	14,000	23,000	2−
Air force, army, navy	14,000	16,000	1+
Teachers	90,000	101,000	1+
Finance	46,000	55,000	1+
Garment workers	6,000	110,000	18+
Chemical industries	4,000	190,000	48−
Printing	25,000	60,000	2+
Maritime unions	13,000	38,000	3−
Metal industries	50,000	775,000	16−
Pharmacy and drugs	2,500	47,500	19
Ports and docks	20,000	92,000	5−
Postal workers	75,000	119,000	2−
Public services	70,000 ⎫	180,000	2−
Public-health service	25,000 ⎭		
Miners	75,000	270,000	4−
Theaters	8,000	14,000	2−
Tobacco workers	11,000 ⎫	14,500	1+
Match industry	1,000 ⎭		
Textiles	47,000	360,000	8−
Barrelmakers	1,000	18,000	18
Transportation workers	53,000	150,000	3−
Glassmakers	3,000	30,000	10
TOTAL	1,024,000	4,738,600	4.6

* From Georges Lefranc, *Histoire du mouvement syndical français* (Paris, 1937), p. 471.

NOTES

CHAPTER I

1. *Le Peuple*, 8 March 1936.
2. D. W. Brogan, *France under the Republic. The Development of Modern France* (1870-1939) (London, 1940), p. 722.
3. *La Voix du peuple*, vol. 18 (1936), pp. 172-3.
4. Robert Lacoste, in a report to the civil servants federation, *La Tribune des fonctionnaires*, 25 February 1939.
5. The basic data for the following survey are taken, unless otherwise stated, from the invaluable symposium, 'De la France d'avant-guerre à la France d'aujourd'hui,' *Revue d'économie politique*, vol. 53 (1939), pp. 1-593, or from the *Résultats statistiques du recensement général de la population en 1931* (Paris, 1933), vol. 1.
6. See Louis Franck, *French Price Control* (Washington, 1942), pp. 1-3; also Georges Gurvitch, 'Social Structure of Pre-War France,' *American Journal of Sociology*, vol. 48 (1943), pp. 535 ff.
7. Pierre Frédérix, *Etat des forces en France* (Paris, 1935), p. 36. This work may be consulted for information on the various abortive attempts to organize rural pressure groups.
8. Confédération Générale du Travail, Congrès Confédéral 1925, *Compte rendu des débats du XXIVᵉ Congrès National Corporatif (XVIIIᵉ de la CGT)* (Paris, 1925), pp. 174-6; André Delmas (secretary of the teachers federation), *Le Rôle social de l'instituteur* (Paris, 1937).
9. Frédérix, op. cit. (n. 1-7), p. 92. For the history of the CGPF between 1919 and 1935 see Robert Brady, *Business as a System of Power* (New York, 1943), pp. 120-39, and René P. Duchemin, *Organisation syndicale patronale en France* (Paris, 1940).
10. Revealing figures have been made public for the textile industry. There only 10 per cent of the enterprises were grouped in employer organizations, but 80 per cent of all the personnel employed in the textile industry worked in these enterprises. See Conseil National Economique, *Les Conventions Collectives du Travail, Journal officiel*, Annexe, 3 January 1935, p. (12).
11. For incisive remarks on the breakdown of law enforcement in this respect see Alfred Sauvy, 'Mécanisme et niveau des prix,' in 'De la France d'avant-guerre . . .' (n. 1-5), pp. 299-300. For the point of view of the trade-union movement see *La Voix du peuple*, vol. 21 (1939), p. 360.
12. See, for example, Raymond Bouyer (assistant secretary of the CGT), *Le Capitalisme contemporain, fiction et réalité* (Paris, 1937); Jules Moch (a leading figure in the French socialist party), *Arguments et documents contre capitalisme, crise, déflation* (Paris, 1936). For a penetrating and very popular criticism of the Bank of France see Francis Delaisi (then the most distinguished economist assisting the CGT in the formulation of its programs), *La Banque de France aux mains des 200 familles* (Paris, 1936).
13. Brogan, op. cit. (n. 1-2), p. 680.
14. Louis Franck, 'The Forces of Collaboration,' *Foreign Affairs*, vol. 21

(1942-3), p. 45, remarks that 'the high civil bureaucracy had really become a caste, somewhat similar to the Prussian Junkers.'

15. *Statistical Year-Book of the League of Nations*, 1938-9, p. 181.

16. *Bulletin du Ministère du Travail*, vol. 43 (1936), pp. 3, 11. The figure for total unemployment given in the text is arrived at by multiplying the number of assisted unemployed by 1.7. Because of the lack of general unemployment insurance the number of assisted unemployed is not identical with the total number of unemployed. The figure of 1.7 is derived by comparing the unemployment figures of the 1936 census with the figures on assisted unemployed in the same period. Indications for other periods suggest that this coefficient is approximately accurate.

17. *Statistical Year-Book of the League of Nations*, 1938-9, p. 70.

18. *Bulletin du Ministère du Travail*, vol. 43 (1936), p. 12.

19. See ibid. vol. 42 (1935), pp. 1-12, 188-9; vol. 43 (1936), pp. 37-45, 101-7.

20. See *Le Peuple*, 9 February 1934; *La Tribune des fonctionnaires*, 24 February 1934.

21. Evidence that a fascist coup was favored in certain business circles before the Stavisky scandal became known is offered by Georges Michon, *Les Puissances d'argent et l'émeute du 6 février* (Paris, 1934), pp. 6-12.

22. For a detailed account see Edouard Dolléans, *L'Histoire du mouvement ouvrier*, vol. 2 (Paris, 1937), p. 383, and *Le Peuple*, 13 and 14 February 1934.

CHAPTER II

1. For the history of the trade-union movement during this period see David Saposs, *The Labor Movement in Post-War France* (New York, 1931); Roger Picard, *Le Mouvement syndical durant la guerre* (Paris and New York, 1927); and Georges Lefranc, *Histoire du mouvement syndical français* (Paris, 1937). An excellent study of the genesis of the conflict during the war is provided by Alfred Rosmer, *Le Mouvement ouvrier pendant la guerre; de l'union sacrée à Zimmerwald* (Paris, 1936).

2. There is extreme confusion regarding the numerical strength of the French trade-union movement at different periods. In the absence of any reliable indication by the movement itself, writers on the subject give widely varying figures; it may be noted here that Saposs, in his otherwise excellent book, op. cit. (n. II-1), provides figures that are altogether too high. There was a tendency to inflate the membership figures, especially during the split between the CGT and the CGTU, an attempt that was facilitated by the fact that the statistics were avowedly not based on payment of dues. Thus the figures communicated by the organizations to the Ministry of Labor and published in the *Bulletin du Ministère du Travail* are almost worthless. Throughout the present study the figures given have been arrived at by a comparison of contradictory statements and, wherever possible, by a critical appraisal on the basis of privately obtained data. Nevertheless, the official figures could not be challenged in every instance, and it is likely that the membership figures given in the text are too high rather than too low.

3. Léon Jouhaux, *La CGT, ce qu'elle est, ce qu'elle veut* (Paris, 1937), p. 81.

4. Translation by Saposs, op. cit. (n. II-1), pp. 489-90.

5. René Garmy, *Histoire du mouvement syndical en France*, vol. 2 (Paris, 1934), p. 160.

6. For details see André Philip in H. A. Marquand and others, *Organized Labour in Four Continents* (London and New York, 1939), p. 25. For a concise and interesting history of the civil servants federation by its long-time secretary-general, on the occasion of the thirtieth anniversary of the organization, see *La Tribune des fonctionnaires*, 10, 17, 24 June; 1, 8, 22 July; 12 August 1939. See also, by the same writer, Charles Laurent, *Le Syndicalisme des fonctionnaires* (Paris, 1938).

7. See Georges Dumoulin, *La CGT et le parti socialiste* (Paris, 1935), p. 21.

8. The figures of 775,024 for the CGT and 231,222 for the CGTU were officially communicated by the two confederations as of October 1935; see *La Voix du peuple*, vol. 18 (1936), p. 83. The figures provided by Lefranc, *Histoire . . .* (n. II-1), p. 412, for the reunited movement as of 1 March 1936, correspond almost exactly. See also Appendix III of the present study.

9. *La Tribune des fonctionnaires*, 30 January 1937.

10. See Philip in Marquand, op. cit. (n. II-6), p. 15.

11. See *Bulletin du Ministère du Travail*, vols. 38-43 (1931-6), passim.

12. See Pierre Laroque, *Les Rapports entre patrons et ouvriers, leur évolution en France* (Paris, 1938), p. 344.

13. Incorporated as Articles 31 and 32 in the French Labor Code, Book I, Chapter II.

14. For the discussion contained in this and the following paragraph see the report of the Conseil National Economique, op. cit. (n. I-10), p. (18) and passim; also the concise historical survey in Alexander Lorch, *Trends in European Social Legislation Between the Two World Wars* (New York, 1943), pp. 56-63.

15. Léon Jouhaux, *Le Syndicalisme et la CGT* (Paris, 1920), pp. 227 ff.

16. For a complete account of the movement toward the reconstitution of trade-union unity see Confédération Générale du Travail, Congrès Confédéral de Paris 1935, *Rapports moral et financier, Compte rendu sténographique des débats* (Paris, 1935), pp. 11-19.

17. For a valuable analysis of the various changes in communist policy see Franz Borkenau, *The Communist International* (London, 1938), especially pp. 413-30.

18. See *L'Humanité*, 5-10 February 1934; J. Berlioz, 'The French Workers United Against Fascism,' *International Press Correspondence*, 16 February 1934.

19. See Berlioz, ibid.; also his 'The Chautemps Ministry Sinking into the Morass,' *International Press Correspondence*, 2 February 1934.

20. J. Berlioz, 'The Face of France Has Changed' and 'The Reformist CGT of France—The Best Tool of Fascism,' *International Press Correspondence*, 23 March and 20 April 1934.

21. *Le Populaire*, 25 February 1935.

22. For the communist view of the negotiations see J. Berlioz, 'A Year of Effort for Trade-Union Unity in France' and 'Trade-Union Unity Established in France' and 'The United CGT in the Making,' *International*

Press Correspondence, 13 July, 5 October, 21 December 1935. For the views of the CGT see the report on its Congrès Confédéral de Paris (n. II-16).

23. On the debates and votes at Toulouse see *Le Peuple*, 3-6 March 1936; on the new statutes of the CGT see *La Voix du peuple*, vol. 18 (1936), pp. 176-81.

CHAPTER III

1. For the interesting correspondence between the CGT and the socialist party see *La Voix du peuple*, vol. 18 (1936), pp. 344-6.

2. For a criticism of the alleged antinomy between trade unionism and political action see André Philip, *Trade unionisme et syndicalisme* (Paris, 1936), especially the conclusions on pp. 327-41, and Adolf Sturmthal, *The Tragedy of European Labor*, 1918-1939 (New York, 1943), pp. 3-15 and passim.

3. Jouhaux, *Le Syndicalisme et la CGT* (n. II-15), p. 41. See also Maurice Harmel, editor of *Le Peuple*, in Bibliothèque de Philosophie Moderne, *Proudhon et notre temps* (Paris, 1920), pp. 33-51; Gaetan Pirou, *Proudhonisme et syndicalisme révolutionnaire* (Paris, 1910); and the lengthy chapter devoted to Proudhon in Lefranc's official history of the trade-union movement, *Histoire . . .* (n. II-1), pp. 103-13.

4. See Jouhaux in *La Tribune des fonctionnaires*, 9 May 1936, and the 18 May resolution of the National Council in *La Voix du peuple*, vol. 18 (1936), pp. 345-6.

5. The following account is largely based on the excellent and richly documented article by Salomon Schwarz, 'Les Occupations d'usines en France de mai et juin 1936,' *International Review for Social History*, vol. 2 (1937), pp. 50-104. See also Henri Prouteau, *Les Occupations d'usines en Italie et en France*, 1920-1936 (Paris, 1937), pp. 91-242. For a legal discussion see Georges Salomon, *Les Occupations d'usines devant la loi et les tribunaux* (Paris, 1937).

6. *Bulletin du Ministère du Travail*, vol. 43 (1936), pp. 354-7. No reliable figures exist for May 1936.

7. It is surprising that such a close observer as Pierre Cot, in his *Triumph of Treason* (Chicago and New York, 1944), p. 96, attempts to convey the impression that the Trotskyites had a noticeable influence on the strike movement.

8. See *La Voix du peuple*, vol. 18 (1936), pp. 362 ff. The situation of real helplessness into which the union organizers were driven, even those in relatively well-organized regions, is clearly described by Georges Dumoulin, *Carnets de route* (Lille, 1938), pp. 298-303.

9. See *L'Humanité*, 12 and 14 June 1936; J. Berlioz in *International Press Correspondence*, 20 June 1936; André Ulman, 'Syndicalisme et politique,' *Esprit*, vol. 4 (1935-6), p. 517.

10. The atmosphere prevailing during the night of 7 June at the Matignon Palace is interestingly suggested by René P. Duchemin, 'L'Accord Matignon, Ce que j'ai vu et entendu,' *Revue de Paris*, vol. 44 (February 1937), pp. 584-94. In 1936 Duchemin was president of the CGPF, and in that capacity he was head of the delegation of management during the negotiations. It is true that his article was partly a defense against the

accusation that he had given in too easily to labor's demands; thus he stressed that he and his colleagues were strongly influenced by the fact that at Matignon they heard for the first time about the low wage rates that prevailed in certain industries.

11. See Débats Parlementaires, Chambre des Députés, Session of 6 June 1936, *Journal officiel* (1936), p. 1319.

12. For an interesting though controversial comment on the Matignon Agreement see François de Menthon in *Le Droit social*, vol. 1 (1938), pp. 33-5.

13. Law of 20 June, *Journal officiel*, 26 June 1936, p. 6698, and decree of 1 August, *J.o.*, 3-4 August 1936, p. 8255 (paid vacations); law of 21 June, *J.o.*, 26 June 1936, p. 6699 (40-hour week); law of 24 June, *J.o.*, 26 June 1936, p. 6698 (collective bargaining).

14. See the Lefas judgment, 14 April 1938, in re Syndicat des Employés du Commerce et de l'Industrie c. Société des Etablissements Pigier, *Le Droit social*, vol. 1 (1938), pp. 205-6.

15. See Léon Duguit, *Traité de droit constitutionnel*, vol. 5 (Paris, 1925), pp. 176-7. In 1925 Duguit did not consider the trade-union movement sufficiently influential to assure a smoothly functioning system of collective bargaining.

16. For the circular of the Minister of Labor see *Journal officiel*, 3 September 1936, p. 9392; for the decision of the Hague Court see *Le Droit social*, vol. 1 (1938), pp. 41-5, with commentary by Charles Blondel.

17. Award by Charles Blondel on 12 October 1937, *Le Droit social*, vol. 1 (1938), pp. 31-2, ruling explicitly that the Union des Syndicats Professionels Français, an 'autonomous' trade union, could not be considered entitled under the law to participate in the signing of collective agreements.

18. *Bulletin du Ministère du Travail*, vol. 43 (1936), pp. 505 ff., and vol. 46 (1939), p. 342. For the text of a collective agreement which served as pattern for many others see ibid. vol. 43 (1936), pp. 224-33.

19. Lorch, op. cit. (n. 11-14), p. 71.

20. See, for example, the law of 18 July, *Journal officiel*, 20 July 1937, p. 8164, and that of 11 January, *J.o.*, 13 January 1938, p. 586.

21. A good defense of the sliding scale by a spokesman for the CGT is to be found in Albert Gazier, *L'Echelle mobile des salaires* (Paris, 1937).

22. Law of 1 October, Article 15, *Journal officiel*, 2 October 1936, p. 10,403. For an excellent account of the role which the Senate played during the period of the Popular Front see Lindsay Rogers, 'Mr. Blum and the French Senate,' *Political Science Quarterly*, vol. 52 (1937), pp. 321 ff.

23. For the documents concerning the negotiations, including the letter by which Gignoux notified Prime Minister Blum of the unwillingness of the employers to continue negotiations, see *La Voix du peuple*, vol. 18 (1936), pp. 651-5.

24. Law of 31 December 1936, *Journal officiel*, 1 January 1937, p. 127. For the subsequent legislative texts on arbitration see decree of 16 January, *J.o.*, 17 January 1937, p. 706; decree of 18 September, *J.o.*, 19 September 1937, p. 10,748; law of 4 March, *J.o.*, 5 March 1938, p. 2570; decree law of 12 November, *J.o.*, 13 November 1938, p. 12,866. An exhaustive survey of the development of industrial arbitration is presented in the richly documented studies of William Oualid, 'L'Arbitrage obligatoire en France,'

Revue d'économie politique, vol. 53 (1939), pp. 665-711; of Ludwig Hamburger, *Les Procédures de conciliation et d'arbitrage en France* (Geneva, 1938); and of Paul Pic, 'La Double Assise juridique du statut moderne du travail,' *Revue politique et parlementaire*, vol. 175 (1938), pp. 428-52. For a good legal discussion see Rudolf Sobernheim and V. Henry Rothschild, 'Labor Unions and Labor Disputes in France,' *Michigan Law Review*, vol. 37 (1939), pp. 1025-77. See also the interesting analysis by Lorch, op. cit. (n. II-14), pp. 95-109. The practice and the pitfalls of arbitration are described by Maisondieu, 'La Grande Pitié des sur-arbitres,' *La République*, 12-14 August 1937, and by 'xxx,' 'L'Application des procédures d'arbitrage,' *Le Droit social*, vol. 2 (1939), pp. 44-5 (remarkably well informed). The complaints of the workers' organizations are summarized in *La Voix du peuple*, vol. 20 (1938), p. 534.

25. See the memorandum of the Minister of Justice of 11 October 1937, *Le Droit social*, vol. 1 (1938), pp. 46-7, and the general legal comment on matters of industrial arbitration by Savatier, ibid. pp. 22-5; also Philip in Marquand, op. cit. (n. II-6), pp. 50-51.

26. On this point see the important study by Paul Vignaux, 'Some Ideas on Property in the French Labor Movement,' *Journal of Legal and Political Sociology*, vol. 1 (1942-3), p. 146.

27. The figures are provided by Oualid, op. cit. (n. III-24), pp. 706-7, on the basis of information from the Ministry of Labor.

28. For example, the German Betriebsrategesetz of 1920, *Reichsgesetzblatt*, 4 February 1920, p. 147.

29. Well-informed studies on the actual role played by the shop stewards are those of Roger Brial, 'Les Délégués d'atelier,' *Esprit*, vol. 7 (1938-9), pp. 823-30, and Pierre Sauvage, 'Où en est le problème des délégués,' *Nouveaux Cahiers*, vol. 4 (May 1940), pp. 11-12. On the rapidly shrinking influence of the shop stewards, even in a district where industrial relations were somewhat better than the average, see André Braun, 'L'Ouvrier alsacien et l'expérience du front populaire,' *L'Activité économique*, vol. 4 (1938-9), pp. 97-100. For a legal discussion see Pierre André, *Les Délégués ouvriers* (Paris, 1937), and the interesting arbitration award of 14 November 1937 in re Société Baffrey-Hennebique c. Syndicat des Cimentiers et Maçons d'Art, *Le Droit social*, vol. 1 (1938), pp. 29-31.

30. See, for example, a speech of General Fleming, *The New York Times*, 11 September 1940; an editorial, ibid. 13 September 1940; and an open letter by Secretary of Labor Perkins, ibid. 9 October 1940.

31. International Labour Office, *Yearbook*, 1938-9, p. 409. This figure, the highest reported by the CGT, is as of 1 January 1938, but there is some doubt on how long it was actually maintained. Jules Zirnheld, *Cinquante Années de syndicalisme chrétien* (Paris, 1937), p. 240, calculates on the basis of elections to certain tripartite boards that even in May 1937 the membership of the CGT amounted to no more than 3 million. This figure is certainly too low. On the general subject of membership figures see above, n. II-2.

32. These estimates have been obtained by comparing the figures on union membership as shown in Appendix III of this study with those on the total number of gainfully employed according to the census of 1931, *Résultats statistiques . . .* (n. I-5), vol. 1, part 3, p. 75. The comparison is

necessarily rough, and not only because of the discrepancy in time, but it does permit an approximate evaluation of union strength in 1936-7.

33. See Jouhaux's plea in *La Voix du peuple*, vol. 18 (1936), p. 372.

34. A detailed description of the work of the Institute is given by its director, Georges Lefranc, 'The CGT and Workers Education in France,' *International Labour Review*, vol. 37 (1938), pp. 618-43. See also *La Voix du peuple*, vol. 20 (1938), pp. 573-5, and, for a critical appraisal of the educational work of the Institute, Dumoulin, *Carnets de route* (n. III-8), p. 272.

35. For a comprehensive discussion of the changes see Brady, op. cit. (n. 1-9), pp. 139-49. Important details and documents are provided by Duchemin, *Organisation syndicale* . . . (n. 1-9).

36. Claude Joseph Gignoux, *Patrons, soyez des patrons* (Paris, 1937), p. 45.

37. See the important speech by Gignoux before the General Council of the CGPF on 9 October 1936, published in *Revue générale des industries radio-électriques* (1936) and reprinted in *La Tribune des fonctionnaires*, 28 November 1936. On the structure of the CGPF at the outbreak of the war in 1939 see *Confédération Générale du patronat français, Annuaire* (Paris, 1939).

38. *L'Elan social* (Paris), the weekly publication of the organization, is of remarkable interest for the social history of France between 1937 and the outbreak of the war. See also the pamphlet, *Aux Patrons français* (Paris, 1939), published by this committee, and J. Duret in *La Tribune des fonctionnaires*, 23 January 1937.

39. *La Voix du peuple*, vol. 19 (1937), p. 271.

40. See Gerard Tehove, *Le Contrôle ouvrier en France* (Paris, 1937).

41. *La Voix du peuple*, vol. 19 (1937), pp. 540-51, including the reply of the government and a letter by Gignoux in the name of the CGPF.

42. For a development of the employers' thesis see Philippe Fargeaud, *Le Problème de l'embauchage et du licenciement de la main d'œuvre* (Paris, 1939). On the side of labor, nearly all conventions held by the federations in 1936 complained about the 'mass dismissal of union members'; see *La Voix du peuple*, vol. 20 (1938), pp. 448-9.

43. See Claude Joseph Gignoux, 'Le Statut moderne du travail,' *Revue politique et parlementaire*, vol. 174 (1938), pp. 201-14.

44. On this situation see the study by Otto Kirchheimer, 'Decree Powers and Constitutional Law in France under the Third Republic,' *American Political Science Review*, vol. 34 (1940), pp. 1104-23.

45. Decree law of 12 November, *Journal officiel*, 13 November 1938, p. 12,867. For a legal comment on the labor legislation of the Reynaud decree laws see Paul Pic, 'Le Nouveau Statut du travail et le redressement national,' *Revue politique et parlementaire*, vol. 178 (1939), pp. 24-42.

46. Franz Neumann, *European Trade-Unionism and Politics* (New York, 1936), p. 27.

47. Jouhaux, *La CGT* . . . (n. II-3).

48. On the communists see Croisat in *L'Humanité*, 1 December 1936. On the generally friendly attitude of the CGT toward arbitration in the pre-1936 period see Saposs, op. cit. (n. II-1), pp. 220-23.

49. Quoted from Philip in Marquand, op. cit. (n. ii-6), p. 53.
50. See *La Tribune des fonctionnaires*, 19 June 1937 and 25 February 1939.

CHAPTER IV

1. There does not exist as yet an adequate and complete treatment of these problems. Cot's work, op. cit. (n. iii-7), is admittedly a sample of special pleading, though it does provide much inside information. Stimu-' lating studies have been published by Albert Guérard, *The France of To-morrow* (Cambridge Mass., 1942), pp. 182-204, and by Sturmthal, op. cit. (n. iii-2), pp. 144-66. Melvin M. Fagen, 'The Lesson of France,' *New Republic*, vol. 103 (1940), pp. 296-9, 341-3, and Henry W. Ehrmann, 'The Blum Experiment and the Downfall of France,' *Foreign Affairs*, vol. 20 (1941-2), pp. 152-65, attempt to investigate the controversial question whether the French republic perished because the experiment was tried or because the experiment was not allowed to succeed. Among earlier writings the most interesting are still Louis Rosenstock-Franck, *Démocraties en crise, Roosevelt, Van Zeeland, Blum* (Paris, 1937), and M. Kalecki, 'The Lesson of the Blum Experiment,' *Economic Journal*, vol. 48 (1938), pp. 26-41. Much material is to be found in René Théry, *Un An d'audaces et de contradictions, juin 1936-1937* (Paris, 1937), and in Fernand Maurette, 'A Year of Experiment in France,' *International Labour Review*, vol. 36 (1937), pp. 1-25, 149-66.
2. The gist of Henri de Man's theories is to be found in his *Au delà du Marxisme* (Brussels, 1929). For a generally friendly comment on his planism see Sturmthal, op. cit. (n. iii-2), pp. 224-30. Sturmthal regards de Man's failure and his final capitulation to Nazism as explainable mainly by his personal instability and his appeasement tendencies. But the fact that many of his French followers took the same path suggests that the dangers of the planist movement are to be found elsewhere than in mere personal accidents.
3. See, for example, Lefranc, *Histoire* . . . (n. ii-1), pp. 364-79.
4. For more details see Saposs, op. cit. (n. ii-1), pp. 80-91.
5. A detailed account of the plan and a discussion of its history, its merits, and its weaknesses is given by Raymond Veillard, *Le Plan de la CGT* (Lyons-Annecy, 1938).
6. See Lefranc, *Histoire* . . . (n. ii-1), p. 389, and, for a communist denunciation of the plan, Berlioz, 'The Reformist CGT . . . (n. ii-20).
7. For an English translation of the Popular Front program see Cot, op. cit. (n. iii-7), pp. 397-9; this work, pp. 89-90, contains also a very favorable appraisal of the program.
8. Débats Parlementaires, Chambre des Députés, Session of 6 June 1936, *Journal officiel* (1936), p. 1316, and Léon Blum, *L'Exercice du pouvoir* (Paris, 1937), p. 246; an elaboration of these ideas is presented in the latter, pp. 52-5.
9. For very pertinent remarks on this subject see Gaetan Pirou, *Essais sur le corporatisme* (Paris, 1938), pp. 152-3. An interesting account of the extent of state control in France at that period is provided by an article in the London *Economist*, vol. 124 (1936), pp. 382-3. For a general survey of the role of the state in French economy see Shepard B. Clough, *France,*

A History of National Economics (New York, 1939), pp. 333-7 and 339-42.

10. See Achille Dauphin-Meunier, *La Banque de France* (Paris, 1937) p. 199, and *L'Humanité*, 16 July 1936.

11. For a good statement of the attitude of the CGT toward the devaluation of the franc see a speech by Jouhaux, *La Voix du peuple*, vol. 19 (1937), p. 264, and Robert Lacoste in *La Tribune des fonctionnaires*, 3 October 1936. For communist criticism see Jean Duclos, 'Le Parti communiste devant la dévaluation,' *Les Cahiers du bolchevisme*, vol. 13 (1936), pp. 1007-09.

12. For a stringent criticism of this move see Jouhaux in *Vendredi*, 12 March 1937.

13. See *La Voix du peuple*, vol. 19 (1937), pp. 75, 454-6, and *La Tribune des fonctionnaires*, 20 February and 6 March 1937.

14. For a lucid discussion of this question see Robert Lacoste in *La Tribune des fonctionnaires*, 1 May 1937.

15. See J. Berlioz, 'The Programme of the People's Front,' *International Press Correspondence*, 18 January 1936, and, for the change of the communist attitude, *La Voix du peuple*, vol. 19 (1937), p. 269.

16. One of the few trade-union leaders who had a clear insight into the interrelation between France's national interests and the need for structural reforms was Charles Laurent, of the civil servants federation. See his article in *La Tribune des fonctionnaires*, 15 January 1938.

17. *La Voix du peuple*, vol. 20 (1938), pp. 493-4.

18. See ibid. p. 841, and, for the proposal of the teachers federation, *La Tribune des fonctionnaires*, 25 February 1939, which presents also, through Lacoste, the reasoning of those who in spite of a thorough criticism of the Popular Front did not favor the desertion of the CGT.

19. See Léo Dugé de Bernonville, 'Les Revenues privés et les consommations,' *Revue d'économie politique*, vol. 53 (1939), p. 950; also ibid. p. 326.

20. The same conclusion, derived from detailed figures and calculations, is reached in *L'Activité économique*, vol. 4 (1938-9), pp. 12-13.

21. For the reasons see Franck, *French Price Control* (n. 1-6), pp. 13-22.

22. *Bulletin du Ministère du Travail*, vols. 43-5 (1936-8), passim.

23. *Statistical Year-Book of the League of Nations*, 1938-9, p. 181.

24. *La Voix du peuple*, vol. 19 (1937), pp. 260-61.

25. For a good account of this strike, and of the public reaction, see Roger Picard, 'Le Marché du travail et le mouvement syndical,' *Revue d'économie politique*, vol. 52 (1938), pp. 962-3.

26. *Ce Soir*, 13 April 1938; see also *L'Humanité*, 13 April 1938. For a strong, though not too outspoken, criticism of the strike movement by Vincent Auriol, one of the socialist ministers of the Blum cabinet, see *Le Populaire*, 17 April 1938. Equally critical was one of the organizers of the non-communist postal workers federation, as reported in *L'Humanité*, 12 May 1938.

27. The calculations, by statisticians of the General Statistical Service of France, are quoted in *L'Activité économique*, vol. 4 (1938-9), p. 15. See also the very interesting study, 'Dividendes des valeurs françaises côtées à la bourse officielle,' *Bulletin de la statistique générale de la France*, vol. 28 (1938-9), pp. 439 ff.

CHAPTER V

1. Léon Jouhaux, *Le Syndicalisme français* (Paris, 1913), p. 37.
2. For a vivid, detailed, and documented description of the attitude of the CGT during the days of July and August 1914, by a leader of the revolutionary opposition, see Rosmer, op. cit. (n. II-1), pp. 105 ff. For the *post hoc* explanation given by Jouhaux see Confédération Générale du Travail, Congrès Confédéral 1919, *Compte rendu des débats du XXᵉ Congrès National Corporatif (XIVᵉ de la CGT)* (Paris, 1920), pp. 228-9 and passim. For the explanation offered by Georges Dumoulin see his *Les Syndicalistes et la guerre* (Paris, 1921), p. 13; also his *Carnets de route* (n. III-8), pp. 64-70.
3. On the history of French labor during the war see Rosmer, op. cit. (n. II-1); Saposs, op. cit. (n. II-1), pp. 25-42; Picard, *Le Mouvement syndical* . . . (n. II-1); and Lucien March, *Mouvement des prix et des salaires pendant la guerre* (New York and Paris, 1925).
4. See Documents Parlementaires, Chambre des Députés, *Journal officiel*, Annexe, 10 January 1924, pp. (85-99). For the parliamentary history of the bill see the report of Jean Fabry, in Débats Parlementaires, Chambre des Députés, Session of 3 March 1927, *Journal officiel* (1927), pp. 596-8.
5. For the highly interesting debates and votes see ibid. Session of 3 March 1927, pp. 598-604, 607-19; Session of 4 March 1927, pp. 635-45; 648-64; Session of 5 March 1927, pp. 675-88; Session of 7 March 1927, pp. 701-24.
6. *L'Humanité*, 12 March 1927, and the article by Monmousseau, ibid. 17 March 1927.
7. Jean Jaurès, *L'Armée nouvelle* (Paris, 1911).
8. *Le Peuple*, 29 April 1927.
9. See Léon Blum in *Le Populaire*, 1 April 1927, and 'Déclaration,' *Europe*, vol. 13 (1927), pp. 433-6.
10. For details see Pertinax, *The Gravediggers of France* (New York, 1944), pp. 22 ff.
11. Decree of 6 June, *Journal officiel*, 7 June 1936, p. 6075, in connection with the law of 21 January, *J.o.*, 24 January 1935, p. 746, the law of 23 July, *J.o.*, 25 July 1911, p. 6202, and the law of 3 July, *J.o.*, 6 July 1877, p. 5053. For a good legal discussion of the entire legislation concerning requisitioning see Maurice Kulbert Wise, *Requisition in France and Italy, The Treatment of National Property and Services* (New York, 1944), pp. 9-86.
12. Law of 11 August, *Journal officiel*, 12 August 1936, p. 8674; decree of 14 August, *J.o.*, 15 August 1936, p. 8834. For a comprehensive treatment of the question of nationalization see A. Bigant, *La Loi de nationalisation des usines de guerre* (Paris, 1938).
13. Cot, op. cit. (n. III-7), pp. 320-29, provides an able defense of the nationalization which took place in the aviation industry.
14. Decrees of 15 December, *Journal officiel*, 22 December 1936, pp. 13,174 and 13,176; 16 January, *J.o.*, 17 January 1937, pp. 722, 723, and 19 January 1937, p. 771; 26 January, *J.o.*, 27 January 1937, p. 1117, and 28 January 1937, pp. 1153, 1154; 13 February, *J.o.*, 16 February 1937, p.

2039; 18 February, *J.o.*, 20 February 1937, p. 2332; 2 March, *J.o.*, 4 March 1937, p. 2694, and 7 March 1937, p. 2829; 11 March, *J.o.*, 13 March 1937, p. 3060; 13 March, *J.o.*, 16 March 1937, p. 3158, and 20 March 1937, pp. 3364-5; 31 March, *J.o.*, 11 May 1937, p. 5154.

15. Law of 11 July, *Journal officiel*, 13 July 1938, p. 8330. For the discussions of the bill in the Chamber see Débats Parlementaires, Chambre des Députés, Sessions of 22-4 March 1938, *J.o.* (1938), pp. 868 and passim; in the Senate, Débats Parlementaires, Sénat, Sessions of 16-17 June 1938, *J.o.* (1938), pp. 651 and passim.

16. *Journal officiel*, 13 November 1938, pp. 12,855-930.

17. It is very doubtful whether such a plan actually existed; in the reports introducing the decrees the constant reference to a 'three-year plan' may well have been merely a verbal concession to the fashion of conceiving the economic development of a country in terms of a 'plan.'

18. For a detailed analysis of the system adopted, and also of the previous wage-hour legislation, see United States Department of Labor, *Maximum Hour Legislation in France, 1936-1940* (Washington, 1941), pp. 44 ff.

19. The question of the 40-hour week cannot be discussed here in full. For more details see Ehrmann, op. cit. (n. iv-1), especially pp. 158-62.

20. *Bulletin du Ministère du Travail*, vol. 43 (1936), p. 276, and vol. 45 (1938), p. 242.

21. *Journal officiel*, 16 December 1937, pp. 13,738 ff.

22. For the basic statute see ibid. 26 June 1936, p. 6699; for examples of decrees concerning its application see ibid. 28 October 1936, p. 11,229; 18 November 1936, p. 11,598; 14 February 1937, p. 1936. For Blum's admission see the report accompanying the Reynaud decree laws, ibid. 13 November 1938, p. 12,858, and a dispatch by P. J. Philip, *The New York Times*, 29 August 1937.

23. International Labour Office, *Year-Book of Labour Statistics, 1939*, p. 62.

24. See *Le Peuple*, 14 April 1937, and René Belin, *La Semaine de 40 heures et la réduction du temps du travail* (Paris, 1937), especially p. 27.

25. *Le Temps*, 23 August 1938.

26. See Débats Parlementaires, Sénat, Session of 18 June 1936, *Journal officiel* (1936), pp. 560-61.

27. See *L'Activité économique*, vol. 3 (1937-8), p. 215.

28. The only reliable figures concerning average productivity are those for the mining industry. They show a marked decline, which by the end of 1937 reached 8.5 per cent and afterward became even sharper. See *Bulletin du Ministère du Travail*, vols. 43 and 45 (1936 and 1938), passim. In other branches of industry the decline was equally marked. *L'Activité économique*, vol. 3 (1937-8), p. 120, stated that in comparison with the problem of declining labor productivity the question of the 40-hour week almost lost its importance. The assertion by Pertinax, op. cit. (n. v-10), p. 369, that average productivity declined by 10 per cent is not based on precise data but may well be close to reality.

29. Alfred Sauvy (a statistician of the official Statistique Générale), *Bulletin du centre polytechnique d'études économiques* (May 1939), quoted

from Philippe Schwob, 'Jugements sur la conjoncture française,' *Revue d'économie politique*, vol. 53 (1939), p. 860.
30. International Labour Office, *Year-Book of Labour Statistics*, 1939, p. 62.
31. *Le Peuple*, 25 August and 1 September 1938.
32. Decree of 30 August, *Journal officiel*, 31 August 1938, p. 10,312.
33. *La Voix du peuple*, vol. 20 (1938), pp. 661-2; see also *L'Humanité*, 10 August 1938.
34. See, for example, Jean Mistler, chairman of the Foreign Affairs Committee of the Chamber of Deputies, in *L'Ere nouvelle*, 4 and 12 October 1938.
35. See Confédération Générale du Travail, Congrès Confédéral de Nantes 1938, *Rapports moral et financier, Compte rendu sténographique des débats* (Paris, 1939).
36. *La Voix du peuple*, vol. 20 (1938), pp. 825 ff.
37. *La Vie ouvrière*, 29 November 1938.

CHAPTER VI

1. A typical expression of the new orientation was the speech of the French delegate, André Marty, to the 7th World Congress of the Communist International, held in Moscow in August 1935; see *International Press Correspondence*, 11 January 1936.
2. Blum, *L'Exercice du pouvoir* (n. IV-8), p. 127. For a similar attitude taken in 1936 by one of the secretaries of the civil servants federation, which later took a definite stand for resistance to fascist aggression, see a speech by Neumeyer, *La Tribune des fonctionnaires*, 26 December 1936.
3. Florimond Bonte, 'Unité d'action, Front Populaire, Union de la nation française,' *Les Cahiers du bolchevisme*, vol. 14 (1937), pp. 28-37. For the first open declaration of this communist line see *L'Humanité*, 22 March 1936.
4. See Louis Lévy, *The Truth about France* (London, 1941), p. 127.
5. See, for example, *Le Peuple*, 4 and 20 August 1936.
6. For more details see Sturmthal, op. cit. (n. III-2), pp. 282 ff., and Brogan, op. cit., p. 714.
7. See *La Voix du peuple*, vol. 18 (1936), pp. 744-7.
8. Ibid. vol. 20 (1938), p. 221.
9. For an able description of the attitude of the French right see Charles Micaud, *The French Right and Nazi Germany* (1933-1939), *A Study of Public Opinion* (Durham, 1943).
10. See *Le Populaire*, 7 June 1938, which, however, gives a rather moderate account of the pacifist utterances of Zoretti and Lefranc; actually they were much more outspoken.
11. On the attitude of the French press during this period, including *Syndicats*, see Alexander Werth, *France and Munich: Before and After the Surrender* (New York, 1939), especially p. 123.
12. The arguments of both sides were fully developed even in 1937, at a meeting of the National Council of the CGT; see *La Voix du peuple*, vol. 19 (1937), pp. 518-40. For a well-documented though highly partisan report on the growing disunity within the CGT see Jacques Leblanc,

'La CGT depuis la reconstitution de l'unité syndicale,' *Revue de Paris*, vol. 46 (July 1939), pp. 414-34.

13. For examples see *Syndicats*, 14 and 28 December 1938; 10 May 1939.
14. *Le Peuple*, 16 September 1938.
15. *La Voix du peuple*, vol. 20 (1938), p. 730.
16. André Delmas in *L'Ecole libératrice*, 8 October 1938.
17. *La Voix du peuple*, vol. 20 (1938), pp. 781 ff.
18. For the complete text of the appeal and the list of projected speeches see *Le Libertaire*, 15 September 1938.
19. *L'Ecole libératrice*, 8 October 1938.
20. *Le Libertaire*, 29 September 1938.
21. *La Lumière*, 30 September 1938, quoting from *Le Petit Normand*.
22. See *L'Ecole libératrice*, 1 October 1938; *La Voix du peuple*, vol. 20 (1938), p. 862; and *La Tribune des fonctionnaires*, 1 April 1939. For the self-defense of Delmas, who was probably the most active advocate of capitulation among the trade unionists, see André Delmas, *Combats pour la paix* (Paris, 1939).
23. See *La Voix du peuple*, vol. 20 (1938), pp. 727-8.
24. The best and most objective account of these days and of the popular reactions to mobilization is given by Werth, *France and Munich* . . . (n. VI-11), especially pp. 273 ff.
25. See Hagnauer in *La Tribune des fonctionnaires*, 4 March 1939. This illusion was particularly widespread among French intellectuals of the left. See, for example, Edouard Dolléans, 'Fatalité de guerre ou volonté des hommes,' *L'Ecole libératrice*, 8 October 1938, and Jean Giono, *Précisions* (Paris, 1939), p. 23.
26. The controversies summarized hereafter found expression, unless noted otherwise, in the discussions of the Administrative Committee in October 1938 and of the Congress of Nantes in November 1938. See *La Voix du peuple*, vol. 20 (1938), pp. 776 ff., 834 ff.
27. Ibid. vol. 21 (1939), pp. 212 and 321-2.
28. See *L'Œuvre*, 19 February 1939, and *Syndicats*, 1 March 1939.
29. Raymond Froideval in *Syndicats*, 10 May 1939; André Delmas in *L'Ecole émancipatrice*, 6 May 1939; Pierre Vigne in *Syndicats*, 12 and 26 July 1939.
30. See *Le Peuple*, 18 November 1938. The resolution for strict trade-union independence obtained 7221 votes, the isolationist resolution 6419. An additional 76 votes were cast for a more violent resolution of the revolutionary pacifists, who on the question of trade-union independence sustained the *Syndicats* group. The majority resolutions obtained 16,582 and 16,784 votes respectively.
31. For figures see the votes at a convention of the federation, *La Tribune des fonctionnaires*, 25 March 1939.
32. See *La Voix du peuple*, vol. 18 (1936), pp. 221 and 214.
33. Ibid. vol. 20 (1938), p. 221.
34. See, for example, the various resolutions voted in October 1938, ibid. vol. 20 (1938), p. 805, and Jouhaux's explanation at the Congress of Nantes, ibid. vol. 20 (1938), p. 875; also ibid. vol. 21 (1939), p. 51.
35. Ibid. vol. 20 (1938), p. 682.
36. Ibid. vol. 20 (1938), pp. 790-99.

37. See Robert Lacoste in *La Tribune des fonctionnaires*, 1 May 1937.
38. Ibid. 15 and 22 January 1938.
39. Ibid. 8 October 1938.
40. *La Voix du peuple*, vol. 20 (1938), p. 874.
41. Jouhaux, *La CGT* . . . (n. II-3), p. 109.
42. *La Voix du peuple*, vol. 20 (1938), pp. 906 ff.
43. See, for example, the criticism voiced by M. Chambelland, a spokesman for the revolutionary syndicalists, in 'Après le mercredi noir,' *La Révolution proletarienne*, vol. 15 (1939), pp. 25-6.
44. *La Voix du peuple*, vol. 20 (1938), p. 826.
45. See the report by Robert Lacoste in *La Tribune des fonctionnaires*, 25 February 1939.
46. See *Le Peuple*, 29 November 1938, and *Les Cahiers des droits de l'homme*, vol. 39 (1939), pp. 28 ff.
47. *Nouvel Age*, 29 November 1938.
48. See decree of 28 November, *Journal officiel*, 29 November 1938, pp. 13,423-9, for general provisions making application of the National Service law; decrees of 24 and 25 November, *J.o.*, 25 November 1938, p. 13,304, and 27 November 1938, p. 13,391 (railroads); decrees of 25 and 28 November, *J.o.*, 26 November 1938, p. 13,358, and 29 November 1938, p. 13,433 (mines); decree of 28 November, *J.o.*, 30 November 1938, p. 13,457 (potash mines); decree of 28 November, *J.o.*, 29 November 1938, p. 13,434 (maritime transport); decree of 28 November, *J.o.*, 29 November 1938, p. 13,422 (public services).
49. *La Voix du peuple*, vol. 20 (1938), pp. 972 ff. A more realistic picture is provided by Roger Picard, 'Le Marché du travail et le mouvement syndical,' *Revue d'économie politique*, vol. 53 (1939), pp. 1360 ff., and by André Philip, 'The Shifting Status of French Labor,' *Foreign Affairs*, vol. 17 (1938-9), p. 751.
50. Decree of 30 August, *Journal officiel*, 7 September 1938, p. 10,558.
51. For an attempt at legal justification see Reuter, 'Le Droit de réquisition et les conflits du travail,' *Le Droit social*, vol. 2 (1939), pp. 90-93.
52. Decrees of 7 December, *Journal officiel*, 8 December 1938, pp. 13,732-3; 10 December, *J.o.*, 13 December 1938, p. 13,964; 10 December, *J.o.*, 14 December 1938, p. 14,010.
53. On these developments see *La Voix du peuple*, vol. 20 (1938), pp. 980-83, 1002-3.
54. *Syndicats*, 21 December 1938.
55. *La Tribune des fonctionnaires*, 3 December 1938.
56. See A. Lambert-Ribot, 'Les Enseignements d'une grève politique,' *U.I.M.M.*, vol. 226 (1938), p. 394.
57. See, for example, *La Voix du peuple*, vol. 20 (1938), p. 995.
58. Débats Parlementaires, Chambre des Députés, Session of 7 February 1939, *Journal officiel* (1939), p. 423.
59. For this reason the quarterly strike statistics of the Ministry of Labor were discontinued. See *Bulletin du Ministère du Travail*, vol. 46 (1939), nos. 4-9, and *Le Temps*, 24 March 1939.
60. *La Voix du peuple*, vol. 21 (1939), p. 216.
61. See ibid. vol. 21 (1939), pp. 114-16, 124, 323, 388, and Georges Lefranc, 'Le Comité National Confédéral de la CGT,' *L'Europe nouvelle*,

vol. 23 (1940), pp. 63-4. For a general picture of trade-union development during this period see also Philip, 'The Shifting Status . . .' (n. VI-49), pp. 740-52.

62. Georges Lefranc, 'Le Redressement syndical,' *L'Europe nouvelle*, vol. 22 (1939), pp. 1386-7, and a confidential document released by the French Ministry of Information; its author was probably Lefranc.

63. *Le Temps*, 27 and 28 February 1939.

64. *Le Peuple*, 18 November 1938.

65. International Labour Office, *Yearbook*, 1939-40, p. 324.

66. This figure is in accordance with estimates made by trade-union officials in the summer of 1939. Similarly Ludovic Frossard, in *Justice sociale*, 26 January 1939, estimated the membership at the end of 1938 (after the general strike) at 2.5 million.

67. For an interesting history of the different trade unions of professionals and technicians see Henri Chateau, *Le Syndicalisme des techniciens en France* (Paris, 1938).

68. For a brilliant discussion by a Catholic writer see Jacques Madaule, 'Préfascisme français,' *Esprit*, vol. 7 (1938-9), pp. 327 ff. See also Julien Benda, 'Les Démocracies bourgeoises devant l'Allemagne,' *Nouvelle Revue française*, vol. 51 (1938), pp. 761 ff.

CHAPTER VII

1. For the point of view of the CGT see *La Voix du peuple*, vol. 18 (1936), p. 368; for that of the CFTC see Zirnheld, op. cit. (n. III-31), p. 235. Zirnheld was for decades the secretary-general of the CFTC, his functions corresponding to those of Jouhaux in the CGT.

2. The expressions were used by Zirnheld, ibid. p. 239, and by Paul Vignaux, 'La Confédération Française des Travailleurs Chrétiens,' *Revue de Paris*, vol. 44 (August 1937), p. 929.

3. See Paul Vignaux, *Traditionalisme et syndicalisme, Essai d'histoire sociale* (1884-1914) (New York, 1943), pp. 43-4.

4. The history of these movements after 1936 is traced by Jean Brethe de la Gressaye, 'Le Mouvement syndical depuis 1936,' *Le Droit social*, vol. 1 (1938), pp. 227-30. These unions are not dealt with in the present study because neither the courts nor the confederations (the CGT and the CFTC) regarded them as part of the genuine French labor movement. For an arbitration award denying a union of this kind the character of a 'representative organization,' even when it met the requirements of numerical importance, see Philip in Marquand, op. cit. (n. II-6), p. 40.

5. On the Social Catholic movement see Parker T. Moon, *The Labor Problem and the Social Catholic Movement in France* (New York, 1921), especially pp. 80-120, and Vignaux, *Traditionalisme . . .* (n. VII-3), pp. 31 ff.

6. Thoughtful reflections on the relationship between the clergy and the Catholic trade-union movement are presented in Paul Vignaux, 'Introduction à l'étude historique du mouvement syndical chrétien,' *International Review for Social History*, vol. 2 (1937), pp. 28 ff., especially p. 30. A vivid picture of the actual relationship between the high church digni-

taries, including the pope, and the officials of the movement is provided by Zirnheld, op. cit. (n. III-31), passim.

7. See Zirnheld, ibid. p. 199. For a comparison of the Charter of Amiens and the doctrine of the Catholic trade unions see Pierre Ramond, 'Le Problème du syndicalisme chrétien,' *Esprit*, vol. 4 (1935-6), p. 505.

8. Philip, *Trade unionisme* . . . (n. III-2), p. 305.

9. For the text of the CFTC plan see Zirnheld, op. cit. (n. III-31), pp. 261-75. For a good analysis of the plan see Vignaux, 'Some Ideas on Property . . .' (n. III-26), pp. 141 ff. For a valid criticism of the plan by a CGT official see Albert Gazier, *Le Syndicalisme chrétien* (Paris, 1937).

10. See Zirnheld, op. cit. (n. III-31), pp. 95 and 226. Saposs, op. cit. (n. II-1), p. 107, quotes a passage from the newspaper of the most prominent Catholic union which shows that the 1926 general strike of the British trade unions was condemned with equal vehemence.

11. For detailed figures see the report of the Conseil National Economique, op. cit. (n. I-10), p. (13).

12. See Vignaux, 'La CFTC' (n. VII-2), p. 920, and Zirnheld, op. cit. (n. III-31), p. 95; the latter declares that the Catholic trade unions gave to all strikes in which they participated a character of 'special calm and dignity.'

13. See Zirnheld, ibid. p. 200.

14. For more details on this point see Vignaux, 'Introduction . . .' (n. VII-6), p. 36.

15. International Labour Office, *Yearbook*, 1937-8, p. 616; see also Zirnheld, op. cit. (n. III-31), p. 211.

16. See Vignaux, 'La CFTC' (n. VII-2), p. 921.

17. For details concerning the relations between the JOC and the unions affiliated with the CFTC see Vignaux, *Traditionalisme* . . . (n. VII-3), pp. 54 ff.

18. See ibid. pp. 60-61.

19. See Zirnheld, op. cit. (n. III-31), p. 230.

20. Quoted by Vignaux, *Traditionalisme* . . . (n. VII-3), p. 72.

21. On this development see ibid. pp. 64-5, and Fargeaud, op. cit. (n. III-42), p. 18; also 'Congress of French Christian Trade Unions,' International Labour Office, *Industrial and Labour Information*, vol. 71 (1939), pp. 74-5. For an expression of hostility as late as 1939, by an official publication of the CGT, see *La Voix du peuple*, vol. 21 (1939), p. 124, where the Catholic trade unions are referred to as the 'furiously attacking Christian obstructionists of labor unity.'

22. See Philip, *Trade unionisme* . . . (n. III-2), pp. 310-11.

23. See Zirnheld, op. cit. (n. III-31), p. 249, and Vignaux, 'La CFTC' (n. VII-2), p. 929.

24. See Vignaux, *Traditionalisme* . . . (n. VII-3), pp. 101-2.

25. See Zirnheld, op. cit. (n. III-31), p. 212.

26. See, for example, a declaration published in *Le Temps*, 27 March 1938.

27. 'Congress of French Christian Trade Unions,' op. cit. (n. VII-21), p. 75.

28. Ibid. p. 75

CHAPTER VIII

1. *Le Peuple*, 25 August 1939.
2. Ibid. 1 September 1939.
3. Ibid. 25 August, 2 and 5 September 1939.
4. *L'Humanité*, 25 August 1939.
5. *La Vie ouvrière*, 17 August 1939.
6. See Anatole de Monzie, *Ci-devant* (Paris, 1941), quoted from the Italian translation published under the title *La Pace, la guerra e la sconfitta* (Verona, 1941), pp. 145-7. These memoirs of the ofttimes minister of the French republic and zealous henchman of the Vichy regime are not to be regarded as having the value of an historical document. Nevertheless, the existence of the Sadoul memorandum, which de Monzie reprints at length, was common knowledge during the first months of the war.
7. *La Vie ouvrière*, 31 August; 7, 14, 21 September 1939.
8. *Le Temps*, 5, 15, 19 September 1939.
9. See *Le Peuple*, 5 October 1939.
10. Ibid. 5 October 1939.
11. Ibid. 18 January 1940.
12. *Le Journal*, 29 September 1939. The *Bulletin quotidien*, 29 September 1939, p. A4, commenting on Belin's declaration, rightly remarked that 'actually the operation is much more complicated.'
13. *Le Peuple*, 18 January 1940.
14. See ibid. 5, 12, 19, 26 October 1939; *Le Temps*, 6, 19 October 1939. The buildings of the Bourses du Travail were the property of the municipalities, but were open to all organizations of the working class, without distinction as to opinion. During the earlier split between the CGT and the CGTU both organizations were allowed to have offices in the Bourses du Travail. See Garmy, op. cit. (n. 11-5), vol. 2, p. 137.
15. See *Le Peuple*, 26 October 1939, 18 January 1940; this position is elaborated most comprehensively in *Les Informations hebdomadaires*, 1 December 1939.
16. On this controversy see *Le Peuple*, 9 November 1939.
17. Decree of 26 September, *Journal officiel*, 27 September 1939, p. 11,770.
18. See *Le Temps*, 20 October 1939.
19. See ibid. 11 November 1939; 4, 7, 8 April 1940; Georges Lefranc, 'Inquiétudes ouvrières,' *Nouveaux Cahiers*, vol. 4 (May 1940), p. 3.
20. See decree of 18 November, *Journal officiel*, 19 November 1939, p. 13,218. For an account of the arbitrary actions that often occurred see the speech by René Nicot, *Débats Parlementaires, Chambre des Députés*, Session of 14 December 1939, *Journal officiel* (1939), p. 2300.
21. See decree law of 20 January, *Journal officiel*, 21 January 1940, p. 602, and *La Tribune des fonctionnaires*, 20 February and 15 March 1940.
22. *Le Peuple*, 23 November 1939.
23. Ibid. 28 March 1940.
24. For the texts of various communist publications see ibid. 9 November 1939; 15 February 1940; and *Le Temps*, 4 November 1939.

25. See, for example, *Les Informations hebdomadaires*, 22, 29 December 1939; 5 January 1940.
26. See Robert Bothereau, *Histoire du syndicalisme français* (Paris, 1945), p. 94.
27. On the polemics between the civil servants federation and the *Syndicats* group see *Le Peuple*, 3 November 1939; *Syndicats*, 9 November 1939; *Bulletin quotidien*, 10 November 1939; *Le Populaire*, 28 November 1939; Robert Lacoste, 'Politique démocratique, politique sociale hardie,' *La Lumière*, 26 January 1940; *La Tribune des fonctionnaires*, 20 April 1940.
28. De Monzie, op. cit. (n. VIII-6).
29. For a brilliant study of the communist propaganda during this and the subsequent period see Paule Berault, 'The Party Line in France,' *Commonweal*, vol. 39 (1944), pp. 318-22.
30. Through the anti-appeasement campaign led by the paper *Nouvel Age* some details became known, in spite of strict censorship regulations, concerning the intrigues which as early as November 1939 were connected with the name of Pétain. See *Nouvel Age*, 1, 15 November; 1, 15 December 1939.
31. For the CGT point of view on the Russian-Finnish war see *Les Informations hebdomadaires*, 8 December 1939; 22 March 1940.
32. See *Le Peuple*, 7 March 1940.
33. See *Le Populaire*, 23 May 1940.

CHAPTER IX

1. See, for example, *Le Populaire*, 18 April 1940.
2. In the autumn of 1939 confidential comments relating to this strange affair were communicated to a narrow circle by Léon Blum. Paul Faure, when some of his friends hesitated to enter into a plot with Laval, encouraged them with the remark, 'To save peace I would not hesitate to plunge into garbage cans.' After the armistice Laval had the continuous collaboration of Paul Faure, Zoretti, and their friends.
3. See *Le Temps*, 14 October 1939, and *Nouvel Age*, 26 September and 2 October 1939.
4. Quoted by Alexander Werth, *The Twilight of France* (London, 1942), p. 375, from *Le Pays socialiste*.
5. *Le Peuple*, 25 January 1940.
6. Raymond Froideval in *Syndicats*, 18 April 1940.
7. Ibid. 25 April 1940.
8. Ibid. 1 February 1940.
9. *Le Peuple*, 6 June 1940.
10. It was believed among some of the trade unionists of the center group that *Syndicats* was being financed by the secret funds of the Quai d'Orsay, and that *Le Pays socialiste* was supporting *Syndicats* in creating disunity within the union movement.
11. Lefranc, 'Le Comité . . .' (n. VI-61).
12. *Le Peuple*, 18 January 1940.
13. *Bulletin des informations ouvrières* (the government-sponsored information bulletin), 1 March 1940; *Le Populaire*, 17 January 1940.
14. *La Tribune des fonctionnaires*, 15 March 1940.

15. See, for example, *Le Peuple*, 6 and 12 September 1939.

16. Ibid. 23 May 1940. There are assertions to the effect that the communists also made a last-minute appeal through underground channels, changing once more from *défaitisme* to patriotism. While this is not impossible, since Soviet Russia was probably surprised by the rapidity of the German victory in the west, the fact cannot be definitely ascertained.

17. *La Tribune des fonctionnaires*, 18 May 1940.

18. The Minister of Interior mentioned in Parliament that he had dissolved 620 unions: Débats Parlementaires, Sénat, Session of 19 March 1940, *Journal officiel* (1940), p. 265. This figure, however, affords no estimate of the actual strength of the communists in the union movement at the outbreak of the war, for it is only an indication of the number of cases in which the communists openly resisted expulsion from leading positions.

19. See, for example, the article by Raymond Froideval in *Syndicats*, 23 November 1939.

20. International Labour Office, *Yearbook*, 1939-40, p. 324. Paul Ramadier, 'La Collaboration, antidote de l'extrémisme se heurte cependant à la résistance patronale,' *La Lumière*, 3 May 1940, estimated the membership at between 700,000 and 800,000, evidently on the basis of information given by Jouhaux.

21. *La Tribune des fonctionnaires*, 18 February 1939.

22. See a report for the Parisian area in *Le Peuple*, 9 May 1940.

23. See the remarks by the assistant secretary Georges Buisson and by Jouhaux, ibid. 7 December 1939 and 4 January 1940.

24. See Vignaux, *Traditionalisme* . . . (n. VII-3), p. 108.

25. *Le Droit social*, vol. 3 (1940), p. 134.

26. See Vignaux, *Traditionalisme* . . . (n. VII-3), p. 111. Chapter 3 of that book contains an excellent and concise account of the history of the CFTC between 1939 and 1941. See also the same author's 'Le Syndicalisme libre, force d'avenir,' *Nouveaux Cahiers*, vol. 4 (May 1940), pp. 4-5.

27. Gaston Tessier, 'Vers un ordre nouveau,' *Bulletin des informations ouvrières*, 1 March 1940, p. 11.

28. See *Le Droit social*, vol. 3 (1940), p. 31.

29. Vignaux, 'Le Syndicalisme libre . . .' (n. IX-26).

30. Georges Dumoulin at the meeting of the National Council of the CGT, *Le Peuple*, 18 January 1940.

CHAPTER X

1. *International Labour Review*, vol. 40 (1939), pp. 611 ff. For an account of labor-government collaboration during World War I see Picard, *Le Mouvement syndical* . . . (n. II-1), and Saposs, op. cit. (n. II-1), pp. 24-42.

2. For a general survey of French wartime labor legislation see Paul Pic, 'La Législation ouvrière et la guerre,' *Revue politique et parlementaire*, vol. 182 (1940), pp. 141-61.

3. See Aurèle Gilbert, 'La Mobilisation de la main d'œuvre,' *Revue des questions de défense nationale*, vol. 3 (1940), pp. 379-400. This very detailed article by a high official of the Ministry of Labor indulges in an over-optimistic evaluation of the beneficial effect of the measures taken.

4. Law of 11 July, *Journal officiel*, 13 July 1938, p. 8330; administrative

order of 28 November, *J.o.*, 29 November 1938, p. 13,423; order of 2 May, *J.o.*, 7 May 1939, p. 5814; order of 24 August, *J.o.*, 25 August, 1939, p. 10,691; decree of 19 October, *J.o.*, 30 October 1939, p. 12,745. See Odette René-Bloch, 'Revenons aux requis civils,' *Le Peuple*, 4 April 1940.

5. See a communique by the Minister of Labor, *Le Temps*, 29 October 1939, describing in detail conditions of employment of requisitioned personnel.

6. See Georges Scelle, *Précis élémentaire de législation industrielle* (Paris, 1927), pp. 192, 266.

7. See decree of 1 September, *Journal officiel*, 6 September 1939, pp. 11,161-2. For examples of convictions, chosen at random, see *Le Temps*, 20 January and 9 April 1940.

8. According to information communicated to the Chamber by Raoul Dautry, Minister of Armament; see Débats Parlementaires, Chambre des Députés, Session of 1 March 1940, *Journal officiel* (1940), pp. 420-21.

9. According to Charles Pomaret, Minister of Labor; see *Le Temps*, 7 March 1940.

10. See decree of 4 October, *Journal officiel*, 13-14 October 1930, p. 11,681; decree of 15 May, *J.o.*, 31 May 1939, p. 6859; decree of 20 May, *J.o.*, 22 May 1940, p. 3806. See also Odette René-Bloch, 'Physionomie de l'affecté spécial,' *Le Peuple*, 25 January 1940.

11. For details see the speeches of the deputies Max Hymans and Pierre Mathé, Débats Parlementaires, Chambre des Députés, Session of 8 December 1939, *Journal officiel* (1939), p. 2143, and Session of 1 March 1940, *J.o.* (1940), p. 363, and the reform proposals of the socialist group in the Chamber, published in *Le Populaire*, 22 April 1940. See also Lefranc, 'Inquiétudes ouvrières' (n. VIII-19), p. 3, and *Le Peuple*, 11 April and 2 May 1940.

12. After April 1940 these companies were transformed into companies of military workers, but the conditions of work and pay remained substantially unchanged. For details see the speech of the deputy Emile Brachard, Débats Parlementaires, Chambre des Députés, Session of 8 December 1939, *Journal officiel* (1939), p. 2136, the speech of Minister of Armament Raoul Dautry on 1 March 1940 (n. x-8), and the written answer of the Minister of Defense (Question No. 11,258), Débats Parlementaires, Chambre des Députés, Session of 3 April 1940, *J.o.* (1940), p. 634. See also Odette René-Bloch, 'Les Compagnies de renforcement,' *Le Peuple*, 18 April and 9 May 1940.

13. Speech of Max Hymans (n. x-11). For other similar pessimistic statements see the other speeches cited in the two foregoing footnotes.

14. Speech of Emile Brachard (n. x-12).

15. See the article by August Savoie, *Le Peuple*, 18 April 1940, and *La Tribune des fonctionnaires*, 20 April 1940.

16. Decree of 16 September, *Journal officiel*, 17 September 1939, p. 11,540, and 21 September 1939, p. 11,624; decree of 26 September, *J.o.*, 27 September 1939, p. 11,788. The latter decree declared that both the National Labor Supply Council and the Superior Labor Council were superseded by a newly created Committee for the Study of Social Questions. Actually all the functions of the National Labor Supply Council were taken over by the Labor Co-ordination Committee mentioned in the text.

17. See Ernest F. Penrose, 'Economic Organization for Total War,' *International Labour Review*, vol. 42 (1940), p. 182; also Douglas Brown and Helen Baker, *Optimum Hours of Work in War Production* (Princeton, 1942).

18. Decree of 1 September, *Journal officiel*, 6 September 1939, pp. 11,158-9; order of 2 September, *J.o.*, 3 September 1939, p. 11,048. A similar decree, fixing the maximum hours for miners at 52½ a week, was issued on 10 September, *J.o.*, 13 September 1939, p. 11,362.

19. See Horst Mendershausen, *The Economics of War* (New York, 1943), p. 187, and Brown and Baker, op. cit. (n. x-17), p. 5.

20. Order of 2 September, *Journal officiel*, 3 September 1939, p. 11,048; circular of the Minister of Labor, 5 December 1939, quoted in International Labour Office, *Industrial and Labour Information*, vol. 74 (1940), pp. 4-5; order of 2 April, *J.o.*, 3 April 1940, p. 2413; and decree of 13 April, *J.o.*, 14 April 1940, p. 2730.

21. See decree of 27 October, *Journal officiel*, 31 October 1930, p. 12,755, and the statement in the Chamber by Charles Pomaret, the Minister of Labor, Débats Parlementaires, Chambre des Députés, Session of 8 December 1939, *J.o.* (1939), p. 2145. See also *Le Populaire*, 3 April 1940.

22. See *Le Peuple*, 3 November 1939 and 11 April 1940 (the latter a speech by Jouhaux on 4 April).

23. Decree of 1 September, *Journal officiel*, 6 September 1939, pp. 11,158-9.

24. Decree of 9 September, *Journal officiel*, 16 September 1939, pp. 11,486-7. For a detailed study of price control in France see Franck, *French Price Control* (n. 1-6), especially pp. 22-34.

25. See *Bulletin de la Statistique Générale de la France*, vol. 25 (1935-6), p. 497, and vol. 28 (1938-9), p. 537.

26. Decree of 9 April, *Journal officiel*, 10 April 1940, pp. 2624-5; see *Le Temps hebdomadaire*, 30 April 1940.

27. For wholesale commodity prices see Librairie Technique et Economique, *Economie française*, Supplément (April 1940); for an estimate of the rise in living costs see the London *Economist*, vol. 138 (1940), p. 466. See also Jouhaux in *Le Peuple*, 14 March 1940.

28. The wartime wage legislation is embodied in the decrees of 1 September, *Journal officiel*, 6 September 1939, p. 11,158; 26 September, *J.o.*, 4 October 1939, p. 11,986; 27 October, *J.o.*, 31 October 1939, p. 12,755; 5 December 1939, *J.o.*, 7 January 1940, p. 211; and 20 May, *J.o.*, 23 May 1940, p. 3838.

29. For an example concerning the construction trade in the region of the Nord see *Le Temps*, 19 March 1940.

30. Decree of 10 November, *Journal officiel*, 17 November 1939, pp. 13,162-4.

31. See *Le Peuple*, 3 November 1939.

32. On the development of wages and prices during World War I see March, op. cit. (n. v-3). On the wage policy pursued by the government see William Oualid and Charles Picquenard, *Salaires et tarifs, Conventions collectives et grèves* (Paris and New Haven, 1928), which also contains (p. 87) the full text of Thomas's letter.

33. Decree of 1 September, *Journal officiel*, 6 September 1939, pp.

11,158-9. For a comment on the abolition of arbitration procedures see *Le Droit social*, vol. 2 (1939), p. 339. Even pending arbitration procedures were discontinued; see a reply to a deputy, made by the Minister of Labor (Réponse No. 10,294), Débats Parlementaires, Chambre des Députés, Session of 9 January 1940, *J.o.* (1940) pp. 6-7.

34. Decree of 10 November, *Journal officiel*, 16 November 1939, p. 13,144. See also the subsequent decree of 18 December, *J.o.*, 24 December 1939, p. 14,165, and the administrative order of 8 February, *J.o.*, 10 February 1940, pp. 1067-8.

35. For example, on the clothing industry of Paris and adjoining districts, see the orders of 8 February, *Journal officiel*, 10 February 1940, p. 1068, and 12 March, *J.o.*, 13 March 1940, p. 1875. See also *Le Temps*, 11 March 1940, for a communiqué of the Minister of Labor.

36. See his statement of 8 December 1939 (n. x-21), p. 2145, and *Le Droit social*, vol. 2 (1939), p. 372.

37. This is manifest also in the few published decisions of the Higher Committee; see *Le Droit social*, vol. 3 (1940), pp. 56-8, 68, 129-30.

38. See decree of 29 November, *Journal officiel*, 2 December 1939, p. 13,572, and Pomaret's statement of 8 December 1939 (n. x-21), pp. 2144-5.

39. *Le Peuple*, 17 May 1940.

40. Ibid. 18 January 1940.

41. *Syndicats*, 28 September 1939.

42. Charles Laurent in *La Tribune des fonctionnaires*, 20 February and 20 April 1940. The criticism by Belin in *Syndicats*, 25 January 1940, was less general in scope, but stressed equally the necessity of thoroughgoing reforms of the wartime social legislation.

43. *Le Peuple*, 11 April 1940.

44. See, for example, his statement of 8 December 1939 (n. x-21), pp. 2144-5.

45. *La Lumière*, 8 March 1940.

46. Decree of 16 October, *Journal officiel*, 2 November 1939, p. 12,819.

47. See *Le Temps*, 4 November 1939.

48. Decree of 26 September, *Journal officiel*, 27 September 1939, p. 11,788.

49. In his statement of 8 December 1939 (n. x-21), pp. 2144-5; see also *Le Temps*, 3 October 1939.

50. See decrees of 3 November, *Journal officiel*, 7 November 1939, p. 12,917; 29 November, *J.o.*, 2 December 1939, p. 13,575; 13 February, *J.o.*, 14 February 1940, pp. 1145-6.

51. Decree of 16 September, *Journal officiel*, 17 September 1939, p. 11,540.

52. Decree of 13 April, *Journal officiel*, 14 April 1940, p. 2730.

53. International Labour Office, *Wartime Development in Government-Employer-Worker Collaboration* (Geneva, 1941), p. vii, and *Methods of Collaboration between the Public Authorities, Workers' Organizations and Employers' Organizations* (Geneva, 1940), especially pp. 310-32.

54. The governmental decrees not only froze wages but also substantially curtailed all profits arising out of war production, though this aspect

of French wartime legislation cannot be discussed here. That the export industries were less heavily taxed than defense production was yet another factor in preventing the increase of France's war potential.

CHAPTER XI

1. See Raoul Dautry, *Métier d'homme* (Paris, 1937). For Dautry's business connections see *Annuaire-Chaix* (Paris), 1937, 1938.

2. *Le Temps*, 11 October 1939.

3. Paul Ramadier, 'Collaboration de guerre et collaboration sociale sont deux choses,' *La Lumière*, 8 March 1940.

4. Speeches in St. Nazaire and in Nantes; see *Le Temps*, 15 and 16 April 1940.

5. See, for example, *Le Peuple*, 19 October 1939, and 18 January, 21 and 28 March 1940; *Syndicats*, 7 December 1939.

6. Most notable among them were *La Bataille, Syndicalisme* 40, *L'Elan social.* The fact that these labor papers suffered as little as *Syndicats* from the general curtailment of newsprint led to the suspicion that because of their pacifism they, too, enjoyed the special favors of certain government circles.

7. *Le Peuple*, 6 March 1936.

8. On the Pontigny Affair see *Le Temps*, 26 and 27 June 1938; *Le Peuple*, 28 June 1938; *L'Œuvre*, 30 June 1938; Nouvel Age, 1 and 5 July 1938; also Georges Lefranc, 'Le Régime du travail pendant la guerre,' *L'Europe nouvelle*, vol. 23 (1940), p. 47, and Vignaux, 'Some Ideas on Property . . .' (n. III-26), pp. 142-3.

9. See Robert Lacoste, 'La Lutte des classes, est-elle supprimée ou prend-elle un nouvel aspect?,' *La Lumière*, 16 February 1940; Jean Zyromski in *Le Populaire*, 13 February and 24 April 1940.

10. See Jouhaux in *Le Peuple*, 25 January and 1 February 1940; *Le Populaire*, 31 January and 25, 28 April 1940.

11. On this point see, for example, Franz Neumann, *Behemoth* (New York, 1942), p. 11. For a criticism of the pluralist doctrine see William Y. Elliott, *The Pragmatic Revolt in Politics: Syndicalism, Fascism and the Constitutional State* (New York, 1928).

12. See *Le Peuple*, 18 January 1940; Pierre-Aimé Touchard, 'Evolution du syndicalisme,' *Esprit*, vol. 8 (1939-40), pp. 299-301; Belin in *Syndicats*, 15 February 1940; Jean Mersch, 'Réflexions sur la lutte des classes,' *Syndicats*, 30 November 1939. (Mersch had formerly been a full-fledged Marxist.)

13. Lefranc, 'Inquiétudes ouvrières' (n. VIII-19), p. 2. On the following see especially the discussions at the National Council of the CGT, *Le Peuple*, 18 January 1940, and Touchard, op. cit. (n. XI-12), pp. 299-301.

14. *Syndicats*, 18 April 1940.

15. See Belin in *Syndicats*, 30 November and 7, 14, 28 December 1939; Chaussin, ibid. 26 October 1939; Mersch, ibid. 30 November 1939; Lefranc, 'Le Régime du travail . . .' (n. XI-8), p. 47.

16. *Syndicats*, 25 April 1940. The article was unsigned, but its style and presentation suggest strongly that it was written by Belin.

17. See René de La Tour du Pin, Marquis de la Charce, *Aphorismes de politique sociale* (Paris, 1909).

18. On the French discussion of corporativism see Pirou, *Essais sur le corporatisme* (n. IV-9), a collection of essays written between 1933 and 1938. An excellent critical exposition of the differences between trade unionism and corporativism is provided by Roger Bonnard, 'Syndicalisme, corporatisme et état corporatif,' *Revue du droit public et de la science politique*, vol. 54 (1937), pp. 58-128 and 177-253. For a defense of the corporative theories see Jean Brethe de la Gressaye, 'La représentation professionnelle et corporative,' *Archives de philosophie du droit et de sociologie juridique*, vol. 4 (1934), pp. 58 ff., and the same author's *Le Syndicalisme, l'organisation professionnelle et l'état* (Paris, 1930); also François Perroux, *Capitalisme et communauté de travail* (Paris, 1938), and Henri Denis, *La Corporation* (1941; published in German-occupied Paris). For a partly critical appraisal of the last two works see Paul Vignaux, 'Corporativism in Europe,' *Review of Politics*, vol. 4 (1942), pp. 194-205, 303-14.

19. Typical of the 'escapist' and largely sentimental appeal of the corporativists is the description of the corporative state by Perroux, op. cit. (n. XI-18), quoted by Vignaux, 'Corporativism in Europe' (n. XI-18), p. 197: 'A hyperconscious state in which my being is sacrificed, to reappear in the plural *we*, a communion above the concepts of the individualistic debit and credit, a transforming knowledge of self and others based upon mutual presence.'

20. *La République*, 19 June 1934.

21. Débats Parlementaires, Chambre des Députés, Session of 27 June 1934, *Journal officiel* (1934), pp. 1825-6.

22. See Pirou, *Essais sur le corporatisme* (n. IV-9), p. 23, and Emil Lederer, 'National Economic Councils,' *Encyclopaedia of the Social Sciences*, vol. 11 (New York, 1933), pp. 192 ff.

23. *L'Homme réel*, no. 15-16 (1934), p. 5. It is justifiable here to translate the French word *syndicalisme* as trade unionism.

24. On the opposition of the prewar CGT to corporative ideas see the debates of the Congress of Toulouse, *Le Peuple*, 5 March 1936; also Lefranc, *Histoire* . . . (n. II-1), pp. 449-50, and *La Voix du peuple*, vol. 19 (1937), p. 207, and vol. 21 (1939), p. 146.

25. In an interview given to the reactionary Croix de Feu paper, *Le Petit Journal*, quoted in *La Lumière*, 19 January 1940.

26. See Vignaux, 'Some Ideas on Property . . .' (n. III-26), p. 141.

27. See, for example, Proudhon's *L'Idée générale de la révolution* (Paris, 1851), p. 284. On his hostility to any 'class warfare' waged by organized labor see his *De la Capacité politique des classes ouvrières* (ed. of Paris, 1924), pp. 372-400.

28. René Belin, 'Le Comité syndical franco-britannique,' *Le Droit social*, vol. 3 (1940), pp. 65-6. See also Georges Lefranc, 'Le Comité syndical franco-britannique,' *L'Europe nouvelle*, vol. 23 (1940), pp. 159-60.

29. *Le Peuple*, 25 April 1940.

30. See Vignaux, *Traditionalisme* . . . (n. VII-3), pp. 43 ff.; Ramond, op. cit. (n. VII-7), pp. 505 ff.

31. *La Croix*, 22 September 1939, and Vignaux in *Temps présents* (May 1940).

32. See F. Gay in *L'Aube*, 9 January 1940, and Vignaux in *Temps présents* (May 1940). For an exposition of the modern federalist principle as conceived in France see Jean Paul-Boncour, *Le Fédéralisme économique, Etude sur les rapports de l'individu et des groupements professionnels* (Paris, 1900).

33. Guérin in *Le Petit Démocrate* (February 1940), quoted from *Nouvel Age*, 6 February 1940.

34. 'Déclaration du Parti Démocrate Populaire,' *Le Droit social*, vol. 3 (1940), pp. 96-7.

35. On the formula of 'communion of labor' see Perroux, op. cit. (n. XI-18), especially pp. 35 and 207-10; for a criticism of it see Vignaux, 'Corporativism in Europe' (n. XI-18), p. 308.

36. For a detailed analysis of this development see Vignaux, *Traditionalisme . . .* (n. VII-3), especially pp. 23-7, 50 ff., 88 ff.

37. See especially 'Semaines sociales de France,' *L'Organisation corporative*, reports of 27th congress (Rouen, 1935). Vignaux, in *Traditionalisme . . .* (n. VII-3), admitted (p. 51) that the conclusions reached at the debates in Angers were at best 'uncertain'; as to the formula of the 'free union in an organized profession,' he declared (p. 46) that like many others it raised as many problems as it solved.

38. See Denis, op. cit. (n. XI-18), p. 117, and Vignaux, 'Some Ideas on Property . . .' (n. III-26), p. 145.

39. See Paul Vignaux, 'Les Travailleurs chrétiens devant les problems actuels de l'organisation professionnelle,' *La Vie intellectuelle*, vol. 11 (1939), pp. 361-82.

40. Vignaux, 'Le Syndicalisme libre . . .' (n. IX-26), p. 5.

41. *Bulletin quotidien*, 11 October 1939, p. A9.

42. On the various attitudes of business leaders to corporative schemes see Pirou, *Essais sur le corporatisme* (n. IV-9), pp. 65, 97 ff.

43. *Syndicats*, 18 April 1940, and Belin, ibid. 9 May 1940. Olivier's proposals were politely but firmly declined by Zyromski; see *Le Populaire*, 24 April 1940.

44. See Georges Gurvitch, *L'Expérience juridique et la philosophie pluraliste du droit* (Paris, 1935), pp. 282 ff., and Vignaux, 'Some Ideas on Property . . .' (n. III-26).

45. Marcel Tardy and E. Bonnefous, *Le Corporatisme* (Paris, 1935), published by the Société d'Etudes et d'Informations Economiques as a supplement to the *Bulletin quotidien*.

46. See *Le Temps hebdomadaire*, especially 4 May 1940.

47. See *Le Temps*, 31 October 1939, 23 January and 1 February 1940; *Le Peuple*, 25 January and 1 February 1940; *Le Populaire*, 31 January and 25 April 1940.

48. *Bulletin quotidien*, 5 April 1940, p. A14.

CHAPTER XII

1. See Lefranc, 'Inquiétudes ouvrières' (n. VIII-19).

2. *Le Peuple*, 18 January 1940.

3. See 'La Politique sociale du temps de guerre,' *Le Droit social*, vol. 2 (1939), pp. 381-2; *Le Populaire*, 14, 16 February and 19 April 1940; *Le Temps*, 16 and 25 November 1939.

4. In his statement of 8 December 1939 (n. x-21), p. 2145.

5. Letter of 1 January 1940, published in *Le Droit social*, vol. 3 (1940), p. 96.

6. See his statement of 8 December 1939 (n. x-21), p. 2145.

7. See *Le Peuple*, 19 October 1939.

8. Decree of 10 November, *Journal officiel*, 16 November 1939, pp. 13,143-6; circular letter to the labor inspectors of 14 December, *J.o.*, 16 December 1939, pp. 13,972-3. For a critical appraisal of the new legislation see Pic, 'La Législation ouvrière . . .' (n. x-2), pp. 141-61. For a good account of the activities and the role of worker delegates during the last war see Oualid and Picquenard, op. cit. (n. x-32), pp. 420-40.

9. Decree of 29 November, *Journal officiel*, 2 December 1939, pp. 13,574-5.

10. Maurice Chevalme, at the meeting of the National Council of the CGT; see *Le Peuple*, 18 January 1940.

11. René Belin, 'A-propos des Délégués d'atelier,' *Le Peuple*, 30 November 1939; see also Lefranc, 'Le Régime du travail . . .' (n. xi-8).

12. Compare *Le Temps*, 24 November 1939, and 10 February and 9 March 1917, quoted by Oualid and Picquenard, op. cit. (n. x-32), p. 448.

13. See, for example, *Journal des débats*, 28 November 1939.

14. Ayme Bernard, in a meeting on 15 March; see *Bulletin quotidien*, 5 April 1940, p. 12. See also *Le Temps*, 19 December 1939, discussing the circular letter by the Minister of Labor.

15. *Le Peuple*, 1 February 1940.

16. *Le Droit social*, vol. 3 (1940), pp. 96-7.

17. *Le Populaire*, 5 May 1940, and *Le Peuple*, 17 May 1940; see also *Le Droit social*, vol. 3 (1940), p. 104.

18. See *Le Peuple*, 18 April 1940; Sauvage, op. cit. (n. iii-29), pp. 11-12.

19. An objective account of labor's grievances is given by Lefranc, 'Inquiétudes ouvrières' (n. viii-19). Lefranc was an extremely moderate observer, and he was writing for a review that was run by industrialists. His factual statements have been corroborated by the oral statements of many others. On the various points mentioned in the text see also the article by Albert Cané, one of the secretaries of the regional union of Paris, in *Le Peuple*, 11 April 1940, and Roger Paul, ibid. 17 May 1940.

20. See *Le Droit social*, vol. 3 (1940), pp. 165-6.

21. Ramadier, 'La Collaboration . . .' (n. ix-20). Albert Perrot, secretary of the postmen's federation and after the outbreak of the war secretary-general of the regional union of Paris, expressed himself in a similar vein in *Le Peuple*, 18 April 1940.

22. *Le Peuple*, 9 May 1940.

23. *Syndicats*, 4 April 1940.

24. *Le Peuple*, 18 April 1940. Other unions voiced the strongest warnings against this kind of state intervention. See, for example, Charles Pineau, 'Entre Patrons et ouvriers,' *Nouveaux Cahiers*, vol. 4 (May 1940), p. 7.

25. Vignaux, 'Corporativism in Europe' (n. xi-18), especially p. 314. Vignaux, however, still believed that a modified corporative system could achieve a 'humanized economy.'

26. *Le Peuple*, 6 June 1940.

CHAPTER XIII

1. For developments in the summer of 1940 see Vignaux, *Traditionalisme* . . . (n. vii-3), pp. 112 ff.

2. Quoted from Bothereau, op. cit. (n. viii-26), p. 98.

3. Probably fairly accurate details about the 'synarchy,' a group of French industrialists and financiers to which Belin belonged, were published by the French underground newspaper *Le Franc Tireur* and reprinted in *France Speaks*, vol. 1, no. 33 (1942), pp. 6-7.

4. Similarly the deputy Marcel Déat, who became an ardent advocate of collaboration in Paris, was known to cherish a deep enmity for Léon Blum, the leader of the socialist party to which Déat had once belonged. Such animosities not only reflect a difference of personalities but also reveal the difficulties that arise with the bureaucratization of labor organizations. A characterization of Belin was published in the underground newspaper *La Résistance ouvrière*, no. 1 (1943).

5. Law of 16 August, *Journal officiel*, 18 August 1940, pp. 4731-3.

6. For a discussion of the composition and activities of the Organization Committees see Dyno Lowenstein and David H. Popper, 'Vichy's Economic Policies,' *Foreign Policy Reports*, vol. 18 (1942), pp. 131-3; Pierre Tissier, *The Government of Vichy* (London, 1942), pp. 244-7; Brady, op. cit. (n. 1-9), pp. 120-49; Shepard B. Clough, 'The House that Pétain Built,' *Political Science Quarterly*, vol. 59 (1944), pp. 30 ff.

7. Decree of 9 November, *Journal officiel*, 12 November 1940, p. 5653.

8. Law of 15 October, ibid. 5 November 1940, p. 5567.

9. See *L'Effort* (a paper published by former members of the socialist party who had belonged to the appeasement faction and later accepted collaboration with Vichy), 4, 18, 24 August 1940, and 'The Position of Employers' and Workers' Organisations in France,' *International Labour Review*, vol. 43 (1941), pp. 418-20.

10. See, for example, *Les Nouveaux Temps*, 2-3 May 1943, which declared that Proudhon's teachings, in comparison with those of Marx, 'conform infinitely more to the French mentality.' For a new evaluation of Proudhon see J. Salwyn Schapiro, 'Pierre-Joseph Proudhon, Harbinger of Fascism,' *American Historical Review*, vol. 50 (1945), pp. 714-37.

11. Law of 14 October, *Journal officiel*, 26 October 1941, p. 4650. For an excellent analysis of the Labor Charter by a group of French trade unionists writing under conditions of semi-illegality, see Comité d'Etudes Economiques et Syndicales, *La Future Charte du travail*, Etude no. 9, 10 September 1941, and *La Charte du 4ᵉ octobre*, Etude no. 10, 11 November 1941. For a critical analysis see also *France and Britain*, no. 8 (1942), p. 6, and no. 9 (1942), pp. 4-7; Vignaux, *Traditionalisme* . . . (n. vii-3), pp. 163 ff.; Bothereau, op. cit. (n. viii-26), pp. 123-6.

12. *Pariser Zeitung*, 31 October 1941, quoted by Vignaux, *Traditionalisme* . . . (n. vii-3), p. 177.

13. See the speech of Hubert Lagardelle, then Minister of Labor, *Le Petit Parisien,* 19 April 1943.

14. See Franz Neumann, 'Labor Mobilization in the National Socialist New Order,' *Law and Contemporary Problems,* vol. 9 (1942), p. 554.

15. Decrees of 28 August, *Journal officiel,* 7-8 September 1942, p. 3070.

16. See, for example, *L'Emancipation nationale* (Paris), 3 July 1943; *L'Effort* and *La Dépêche de Royan,* both of 23 November 1943.

17. See *La Future Charte du travail* (n. xiii-11).

18. See, for example, *Au Travail,* 27 June and 25 July 1942.

19. Dumoulin's autobiography, *Carnets de route* (n. iii-8), written before the war, offers interesting material both on the social history of the period and on the mentality of a labor leader turned renegade. A short biographical sketch of Dumoulin, with quotations from his writings, was presented by *La Résistance ouvrière,* no. 2 (1943).

20. See, for example, *L'Atelier,* 8 February 1941.

21. See ibid. 18 July, 31 October, 14 and 21 November, 12 December 1942; the articles signed G. Dharnes were written by Dumoulin.

22. See Bothereau, op. cit. (n. viii-26), p. 100.

23. See the law of 30 November, *Journal officiel,* 24 December 1941, p. 5518; order of 19 June, *J.o.,* 25 June 1943, p. 1739; order of 21 June, *J.o.,* 25 June 1943, p. 1740; order of 21 June, *J.o.,* 25 June 1943, p. 1743.

24. See a well-reasoned study published by the Comité d'Études Economiques et Syndicales, *Revalorisation des salaires et traitements considérés en juillet 1942,* 10 July 1942. Also *La Vie ouvrière,* 7 July 1943; *Les Cahiers français,* no. 55 (May 1944), p. 29; 'Labor Conditions in France,' *Monthly Labor Review,* vol. 59 (1944), pp. 716-18.

25. See, for example, *Au Travail,* 27 June, 25 July, 28 November, and 12 December 1942.

26. No trustworthy and complete data on the extent of this collaboration are as yet available. For the earlier period a good survey is provided by Thomas Kernan, *France on Berlin Time* (Philadelphia and New York, 1941), especially pp. 76-108, and by Lowenstein and Popper, op. cit. (n. xiii-6), pp. 131-6. See also *France Speaks,* vol. 1, no. 27 (1942), p. 6, and vol. 1, no. 35 (1942), p. 8.

27. See *France Speaks,* vol. 1, no. 47 (1943), p. 1.

28. For the complete text see *France and Britain,* no. 5-6 (1941), pp. 7-10.

29. See *France Speaks,* vol. 1, no. 9 (1941), p. 2.

30. See, for example, an untitled sheet, published by the Comité d'Etudes Economique et Syndicales (No. Hors Série), 1 August 1941, and *France Speaks,* vol. 1, no. 44 (1942), pp. 5-6.

31. *France Speaks,* vol. 1, no. 17 (1941), p. 4; see also *La Vie ouvrière,* November 1941. For later reports on the effective resistance of the workers and their organizations to the Labor Charter see, for example, *Le Mouvement ouvrier français,* no. 3 (August 1943), and *La Résistance ouvrière,* no. 6 (1944).

32. See, for example, the significant study (untitled) by the Comité d'Etudes Economiques et Syndicales (No. Hors Série), 15 March 1942, and *France Speaks,* vol. 1, no. 44 (1942), pp. 3-4.

33. See Vignaux, 'Some Ideas on Property . . .' (n. III-26), pp. 147-8. Vignaux viewed this development with some concern.

34. First-of-May appeal of the Comité Ouvrier Français, *France Speaks*, vol. I, no. 40 (1942), p. 2.

35. Ibid. vol. I, no. 6 (1941), p. 5

36. Ibid. vol. I, no. 18 (1941), pp. 4-6.

CHAPTER XIV

1. For a short description of the scheme of organization see Bothereau, op. cit. (n. VIII-26), p. 102.

2. For examples see *La Vie ouvrière*, 3 November and 7 December 1943.

3. See Charles Laurent, 'The French Trade Union Movement Today,' *International Transport Workers' Journal* (1943), p. 55; *France Speaks*, vol. I, no. 33 (1942), p. 2

4. *France Speaks*, vol. I, no. 1 (1941), p. 6.

5. *La Résistance ouvrière*, no. 5, 15 January 1944.

6. For examples see *La Vie ouvrière*, 7 June 1943.

7. See ibid. 3 November and 7 December 1943, and *Les Cahiers français*, no. 55 (May 1944), p. 25.

8. Quoted from Bothereau, op. cit. (n. VIII-26), pp. 104-5.

9. On the French labor movement between 1852 and 1864 see Albert Thomas, 'Le Second Empire,' in *Histoire socialiste 1789-1900*, ed. by Jean Jaurès (Paris, n.d.), pp. 161-245, and Paul Bernard (pseudonym of the present writer), 'Le Mouvement ouvrier en France pendant les années 1852-1864 d'après les rapports politiques des procureurs généraux, Documents inédits,' *International Review for Social History*, vol. 4 (1939), pp. 231-80.

10. See *France Speaks*, vol. I, no. 40 (1942), p. 14.

11. For more details see a reprint from the underground newspaper *Libération*, ibid. vol. I, no. 27 (1942), p. 5.

12. *Les Cahiers français*, no. 55 (May 1944), p. 28.

13. The quotations in this paragraph are from Berault, op. cit. (n. VIII-29).

14. See 'L'Entrée des communistes dans le CFLN,' *Les Cahiers français*, no. 55 (May 1944), p. 8.

15. For details see ibid. no. 55 (May 1944), pp. 7 ff

16. For the communist position see especially the articles by Benoît Frachon and Julien Racamond in *La Vie ouvrière*, 7 June and 7 July 1943; also ibid. 4 May and 1 October 1943.

17. Quoted from Bothereau, op. cit. (n. VIII-26), p. 103.

18. *La Résistance ouvrière*, no. 5, 15 January 1944; see also *Le Peuple syndicaliste*, no. 13 (1944), and *La Vie ouvrière*, 4 May 1943.

19. The hope to the contrary expressed by André Philip, 'French Unionism and the Fighting French,' *Free World*, vol. 6 (1943), p. 9, was based on the author's experience in the underground struggle at an earlier period, when the communists were still concerned mainly with political and military resistance.

20. For the general attitude of French Catholics, conformists and resisters alike, see the richly documented article by Georgette Vignaux,

'The Catholics in France since the Armistice,' *Review of Politics*, vol. 5 (1943), pp. 194-215.

21. For details see Vignaux, *Traditionalisme* . . . (n. VII-3), pp. 118 ff. For a general survey see also Herbert Morris, 'Catholic Labor and Vichy,' *Commonweal*, vol. 36 (1942), pp. 547-9.

22. See *France Speaks*, vol. 1, no. 13 (1941), pp. 8, 9.

23. Ibid. vol. 1, no. 5 (1941), p. 3.

24. This point is stressed by Maritain in his preface to Vignaux, *Traditionalisme* . . . (n. VII-3), pp. 8 and 10.

25. See *France Speaks*, vol. 1, no. 6 (1941), p. 8, and Georgette Vignaux, op. cit. (n. XIV-20), p. 208.

26. See, for example, Philip, 'French Unionism . . .' (n. XIV-19).

27. See Bothereau, op. cit. (n. VIII-26), p. 121.

28. *Les Cahiers français*, no. 55 (May 1944), p. 25.

29. For a report on numerous movements for higher wages see ibid. no. 55 (May 1944), pp. 31-2; see also *La Vie ouvrière*, 7 December 1943.

30. See *France Speaks*, vol. 1, no. 23 (1942), p. 8.

31. See 'Labor Conditions in France' (n. XIII-24), pp. 719-20.

32. *Les Cahiers français*, no. 55 (May 1944), p. 27. For an impressive narrative of strikes of all kinds see *Libération*, November 1943, and Guigui, 'Trade Unionist Organization and Action in France,' *Labour Press Service* (London), International Supplement, 9 February 1944.

33. A very full account of the mobilization of French workers for Germany at different periods is presented in 'The Recruitment of French Labour for Germany,' *International Labour Review*, vol. 47 (1943), pp. 312-43, and in 'The Mobilisation of French Workers for Germany,' ibid. vol. 49 (1944), pp. 38-51.

34. See *Les Cahiers français*, no. 55 (May 1944), pp. 28-9, and *Action*, no. 2 (December 1943).

35. This course was advocated, for example, in a speech by a resistance delegate over the Brazzaville radio on 18 February 1944. The communist trade-union press was sometimes more cautious and realistic about a general strike at the moment of the invasion. See, for example, *L'Humanité*, 1 September 1943, and *La Vie ouvrière*, 6 March 1944.

36. For the complete text see *L'Humanité*, 21 August 1944.

37. For a brief survey see Vignaux, 'Some Ideas on Property . . .' (n. III-26), pp. 148-51.

38. Unless otherwise stated the following analysis is based on the Postwar Action Program of the CGT, published in *Les Cahiers français*, no. 55 (May 1944), pp. 29-31. See also *International Labour Review*, vol. 50 (1944), p. 543.

39. *Le Mouvement ouvrier français*, no. 3 (August 1943).

40. See ibid. no. 2 (July 1943); *La Vie ouvrière*, 6 March 1944; *Les Informations sociales*, no. 1 (June-July 1943).

41. See Laurent, 'The French Trade Union Movement Today' (n. XIV-3), p. 56.

42. *Le Peuple syndicaliste*, no. 13 (1944).

43. *Le Mouvement ouvrier français*, no. 3 (August 1943).

INDEX

317

DATE DUE

GAYLORD			PRINTED IN U.S.A.